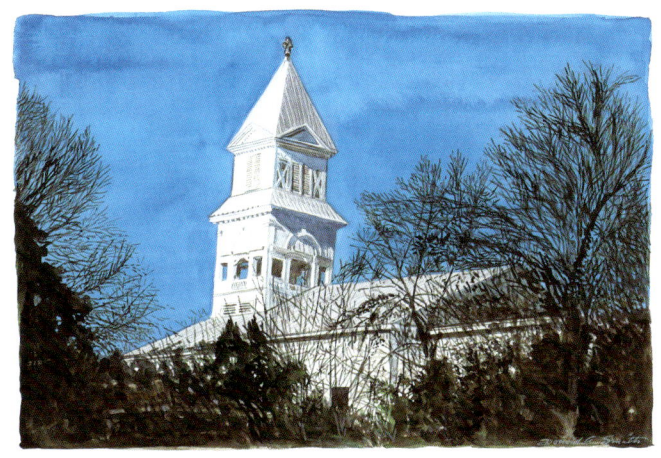

CHURCHES

PHOTOGRAPHS & WATERCOLORS

Watercolors by
Donald A. Smith

■ ■ ■

Photographs by
Dr. Roy Ward

Mercer University Press | 2005

MUP/H641

ISBN 0-86554-932-X

Copyright 2005
MERCER UNIVERSITY PRESS
1400 Coleman Avenue | Macon, Georgia 31207
All rights reserved

FIRST EDITION

The paper used in this publication meets the minimum
requirements of American National Standard for Information Sciences
Permanence of Paper for Printed Library Materials, ANSI Z39.48-1992.

Layout design by Burt and Burt Studio

Library of Congress Cataloging-in-Publication Data

Smith, Donald A., 1934–
Churches: photographs and watercolors
watercolors by Donald A. Smith; photographs by Roy Ward.–1st ed.
p. cm.
(hardcover : alk. paper)

1. Smith, Donald A., 1934–Themes, motives. 2. Ward, Roy, M.D.–Themes, motives.
3. Church buildings–Georgia. 4. Church buildings in art. 5. Church buildings–Pictorial works.

I. Ward, Roy, M.D. II. Title.
ND1839.S554A4 2005
726.5'09758–dc22

2005008875

Printed in Canada

Preface

A romantic paleontologist believed that the ribs of giant whales sometimes provided the arching framework for shelters of ancient men. Living as some of them did on the virtually treeless shores of northern seas which lacked the easy fruits of Biblical Eden, plucking and snaring dependable food from cold water, the notion of covering stripped and bleached rib cages with animal skins is not as unlikely an idea as you might at first think. There must have been lots of them at the edges of the sea.

In timbered lands like Europe, as the retreat of glaciers allowed humans to move farther and farther into them, people lived in caves and burned wood. They learned to pen animals, chiefly reindeer, and to keep dogs. A wolf fed from puppyhood started the line of helpful hunters. The proximity of confined animals provided warmth as well. The origins of larger rooms grew from these early barns. The enclosures saw the births of animals and the births of people, and as a matter of fact, the most northerly of our own ancestors, the Scots, preserve the word or sound "bairn" as a synonym both for the building and for the newborn babe.

For the building of enclosures where living and dying timber spread in primeval abundance, entire limbs were used, having grown already into the desired shapes. I think of the pair of redbirds constructing a nest in my studio garden. Each broke off a brittle twig from an azalea bush, and with only its beak for hands, threaded it into its chosen place. It was more a matter of choosing than it was of changing. Primitive man must have chosen from millennia of dead things. The arching forms of enormous ribs, like the bent limbs of fallen trees, may easily – if romantically – be seen as the progenitors of the framework of large barns leading eventually to vaulted cathedrals, even though it took a long time. Between shelters and the vaulted roofs there came the arch upside down, forming the hulls of ships.

In the simple sanctuary spaces of these churches the people of the community met as a necessary expression of community. It was, in most Southern communities, the Town House, where kin and non-kin made their union manifest. Here, with two races, those races met separately as an expression of individual community. So far as buildings were concerned, a church for whites might become a church of blacks after the white congregation built a bigger place. There was a little-noted but oft-occurring visiting back and forth, most particularly when black servants or employees of whites accompanied those whites to church. A white child cared for by a black nurse might go with her to her black church. This was a common and unselfconscious occurrence as late as the 1930's, decades before legal integration.

Where the early churches stood there might be no schoolhouse, and children came to Sunday School before they were old enough to enter even the earliest level of public school. After a brief program of perhaps a prayer and a song, the barn-like sanctuary would be symbolically divided up, each class taking a corner for itself with one or more adult classes clustering on the more central benches, or retiring to the pastor's study if the building held such a room. In each group the drone of its teacher would go on as if there were no other speakers within earshot. In my church, we sat on tiny oak chairs and a bedsheet was drawn across the corner, but in others there might not be even a visual division. After the lesson, everyone returned to the sanctuary benches and each class recited a brief Bible verse and made its report which would include the collection, always meager. A brief break between the school and the preaching service enabled some to leave and others, including adults who had not brought children, to come in.

When more than one denomination graced the town, as in ours, full church service would be held in each one individually and regularly on some Sundays. All denominations combined in a single church on other Sundays, and the site went in rotation. On that Sunday only one steeple bell would ring, a reminder and guide to all.

In Sunday School a child would hear the story of a man and a whale without realizing that thousands of years earlier, in the misty distance of time, someone on some distant beach could have come upon the skeleton of a whale with the skeleton of a man inside it as if it had been swallowed. The possible relationship of cultural anthropology with this fragment of our Bible would not have been suspected; and if it had been, it would have impressed no one in our churches when the buildings in this book were erected and Faith ruled in them.

About the Paintings

In his paintings of churches, Don Smith has concentrated on the simpler and earlier buildings of Georgia, places he can visit in a single day's drive from his home in Athens. He is a literal painter who takes liberties. He will, for example, reproduce precisely the rusty tin of a roof, just as he finds it; but he may leave off the recent disability ramp as well as the annex which the more affluent congregations have added in recent years. He prefers the wood siding, whether unpainted or white, of the early buildings, to brick veneers. The oldest and simplest structures now stand in the poorer communities, or , in fact, as lonely remnants of a community long vanished. It is this tenacity of purpose which has made Smith's beautiful record such an important historical document. In his illustrations he recovers the truth of our cultural past in a convincing way, supporting any memory or history that might be written about it. His record is astonishing in quality and quantity.

His hand and eye, long skilled, were accustomed to the portrayal of many things, from portraits to automobiles, before he began the churches. With them he has evoked more history and spirituality than perhaps even he himself foresaw!

Roy Ward

I can't remember when I didn't draw. As a child, my older brother drew, so it never occurred to me that there was an option. I drew, too. He showed me how to observe detail. He provided subject matter with his interests in animals, cowboys, and later, musicians. I grew up knowing the names of Bill Mauldin, Arthur Szyk, Norman Rockwell, Al Parker, George Herriman and Al Hershfeld, better than I did any sports celebrity.

I studied under R. Nicky Brumbaugh at Coker College while I was in high school and under Lamar Dodd at the University of Georgia, but credentials don't really mean anything. You either like the paintings or you don't. Some will like them because they are "realistic" and others won't like them for the same reason.

Like many others, as I grow older I feel an increased fondness for things of the past. The simpler world I inhabited as a child. So, also like many others, I have found pleasure in painting that disappearing world. Some evidences of it still exist, but they are being swept away with alarming speed. In a drive through North Georgia in the early nineties I found numerous subjects to paint in that rural setting. Ten years later I made the trip again and was shocked to find that the few remaining barns, old stores, and country churches had become anachronisms, sprinkled sparsely among expensive housing developments, shopping centers and expanding communities. I saw with alarm that America's population explosion had reached the agrarian Southland, stripping it of its simplicity and charm. After that second trip I felt a compulsion to record these remaining treasures before they all disappeared.

Since then, my primary subjects have been those scenes that represent the simple Southland that I associate with my growing up...the decaying cotton gins, the farmhouses and barns, the aging and abandoned country stores and filling stations and the simple country churches. Many of those old churches, still in use today, have been modified with Sunday School wings and handicapped ramps that are undoubtedly essential to their needs, but which are architectural aberrations. Consequently, I have omitted such additions in my paintings.

I have travelled down miles of country roads following signs that promised a church nearby, only to find time and again, a simple old church gussied up with a shiny new plastic steeple. I've also seen that almost any enclosure will serve as a church, from a mobile home to a tent.

Some of the churches included in this book are already gone, a few have been encased in brick or otherwise remodeled and dressed up by a more affluent congregation, some are now used for other purposes (a playhouse in Monroe, a community center in Watkinsville), and some have simply been abandoned.

As for commenting on the paintings themselves, I will leave that to others. I can't recall what clever person observed that talking about painting is like dancing about architecture, but I agree. I make no claims that my paintings are art. I don't even know what art is anymore. The administrator of the Chicago Art Institute said that, "everything is art." In that case nothing is art – the term is meaningless.

I hope you enjoy this trip through Georgia, with examples of its churches selected from St. Simons to Blairsville. I certainly haven't discovered or painted them all, but perhaps your favorite is among them. You'll see a couple of churches from South Carolina that have a special meaning for me. I was married in Pisgah Methodist outside Florence and my uncle, Paul D. Patrick served as minister of the First Presbyterian Church in Latta early in his ministry.

It's a real treat to be able to share this book with my friend and fellow artist, Dr. Roy Ward. I have been an admirer of his watercolors for years and it was he, more than anyone else, who encouraged me to record many of these country churches. I hope you agree that his black and white photos make an interesting contrast to my paintings as well as providing a provocatively different point of view. Whether in his paintings or with a camera, Dr. Ward has an incomparable eye for composition.

Donald A. Smith

About the Photographs

Roy Ward, besides practicing medicine as a general practitioner in Watkinsville, Georgia for many years, is an artist. "I have never had a lesson in painting," he says. "I drew from early age, and at the University of Georgia I associated with the staff and the students in the Art Department, and exhibited with them, winning prizes. I had several exhibits in the southeast and won some more prizes. But my time spent in painting was almost always very short, due to the demands of school, and it was only during a brief summer vacation in 1947 that I achieved real competence. For the next ten or fifteen years I hardly painted at all, and when I returned to it part-time in the 1960's it took a while to regain real expertise.

"My grandmother, Florine Langford Meadors, employed me as a dishwasher at the old Camp Wilkins dormitory on the Agricultural campus of the University of Georgia in the late 1930's. With my first pay, I bought a camera, a Kodak Junior 620 with f 6.3 lens and 1/100 shutter. It seemed to me both elegant and high tech. I used it intermittently for many years."

In an earlier book devoted to Dr. Ward's watercolors, Francis Ruzicka, former head of the University of Georgia Art Department, said that Roy Ward's "vision of the Southern landscape, particularly the rural scene, has resulted in a vast treasure-trove of perceptions of these rapidly vanishing aspects of our environment." Though writing about Dr. Ward's watercolors, this is equally true of his photographic record.

Roy Ward's watercolors are painted on the spot. As he travels around the countryside he also often carries his camera. The country churches he finds along these Georgia back roads have become one of his primary interests. Many of those he painted in the sixties and seventies are now gone. His photos in this book pre-date my paintings, so we often find images of the same church as it appears in different decades and different times of the year. More interesting, however, is the manner in which two artists have approached the same subject as well as the dramatic contrast between Ward's black and white photos and my paintings.

Roy Ward's photos are never simply visual recordings of a building. Each picture embodies a statement, whether it's a paean to the symmetry of the church's architecture (such as the cover photo), or a eulogium to the drama of light and shadow (the night shot of Ashford Methodist in Watkinsville) or a social commentary (the Lincolnton church half hidden by the fast food chicken restaurant). Every image is a hymn of praise—perhaps to God, but certainly to the simple, hardscrabble land in which Roy has lived and dedicated his life.

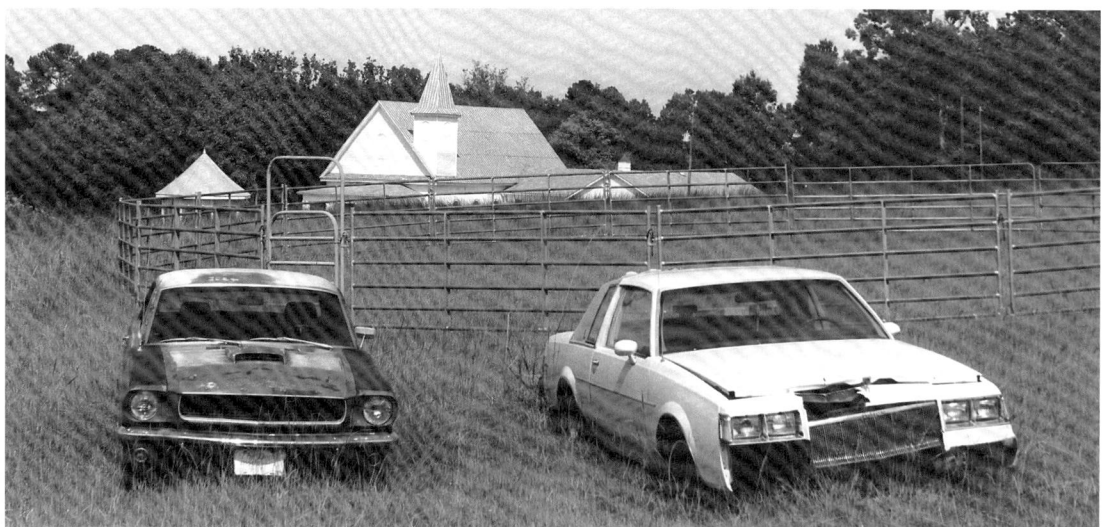

The noted photographer William Bake said that before he saw Roy Ward's work he believed that "Local people see their surroundings so often that they don't see them at all—that's what I thought. But I was wrong. You don't need to be from somewhere else to feel the spirit of the land and people. Roy Ward proves that through his photographs and paintings." The long, melancholy return of the landscape is lovingly portrayed here. These are photographs of return. They give us hope, both for land and people –hope in an age of pessimism. For that alone they are to be treasured.

I have learned what to look for in landscape art. It is an ineffable combination of human qualities, such as emotion and understanding, and technical skills, like proper use of the camera and good printing. When someone has that combination I can recognize it just as you will see it in these pages. These are wonderful photographs. They are the kind of images to be savored. The more you come back to them, the more they reveal, not only about the subject matter, but also about the artist.

CHURCHES

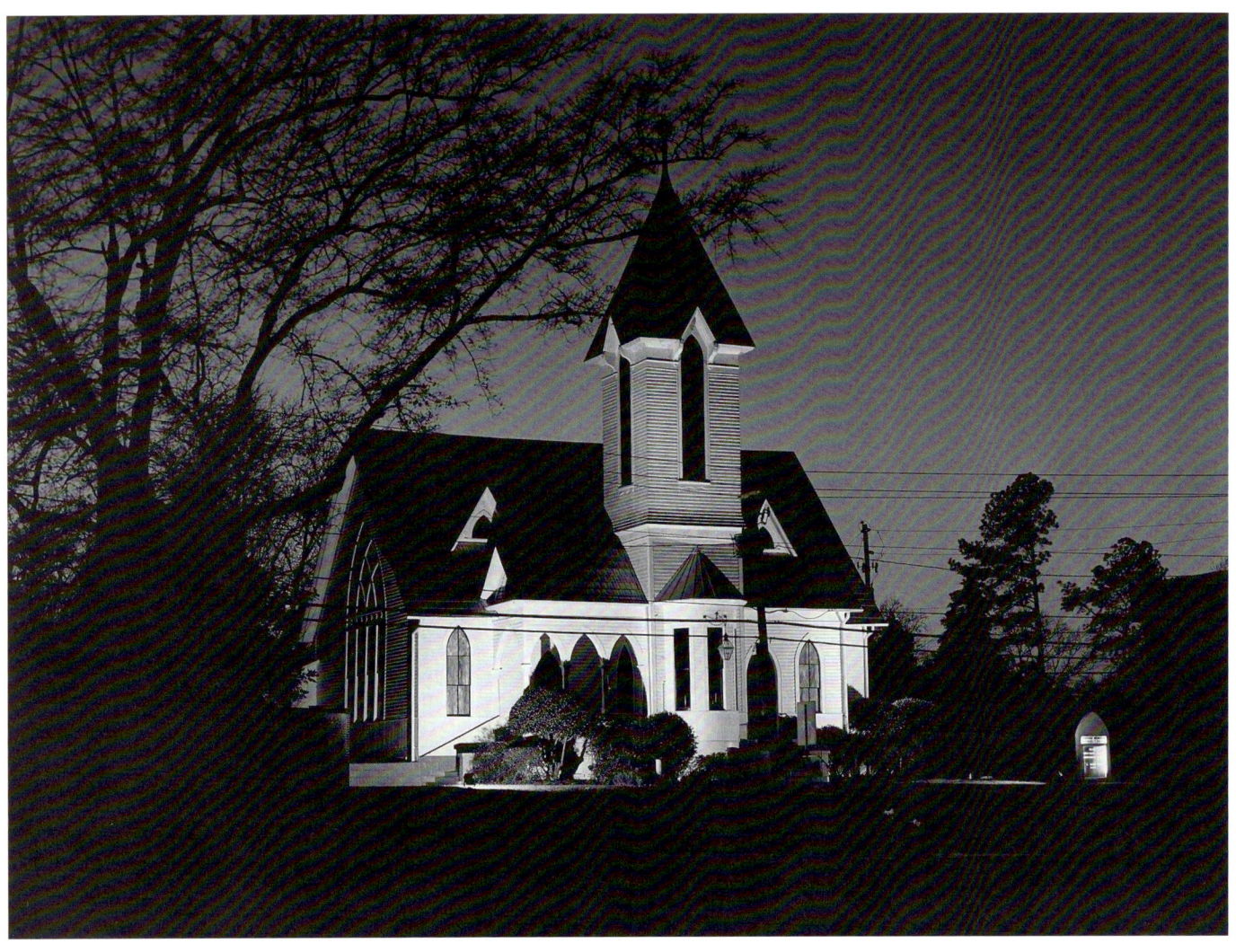

Watkinsville

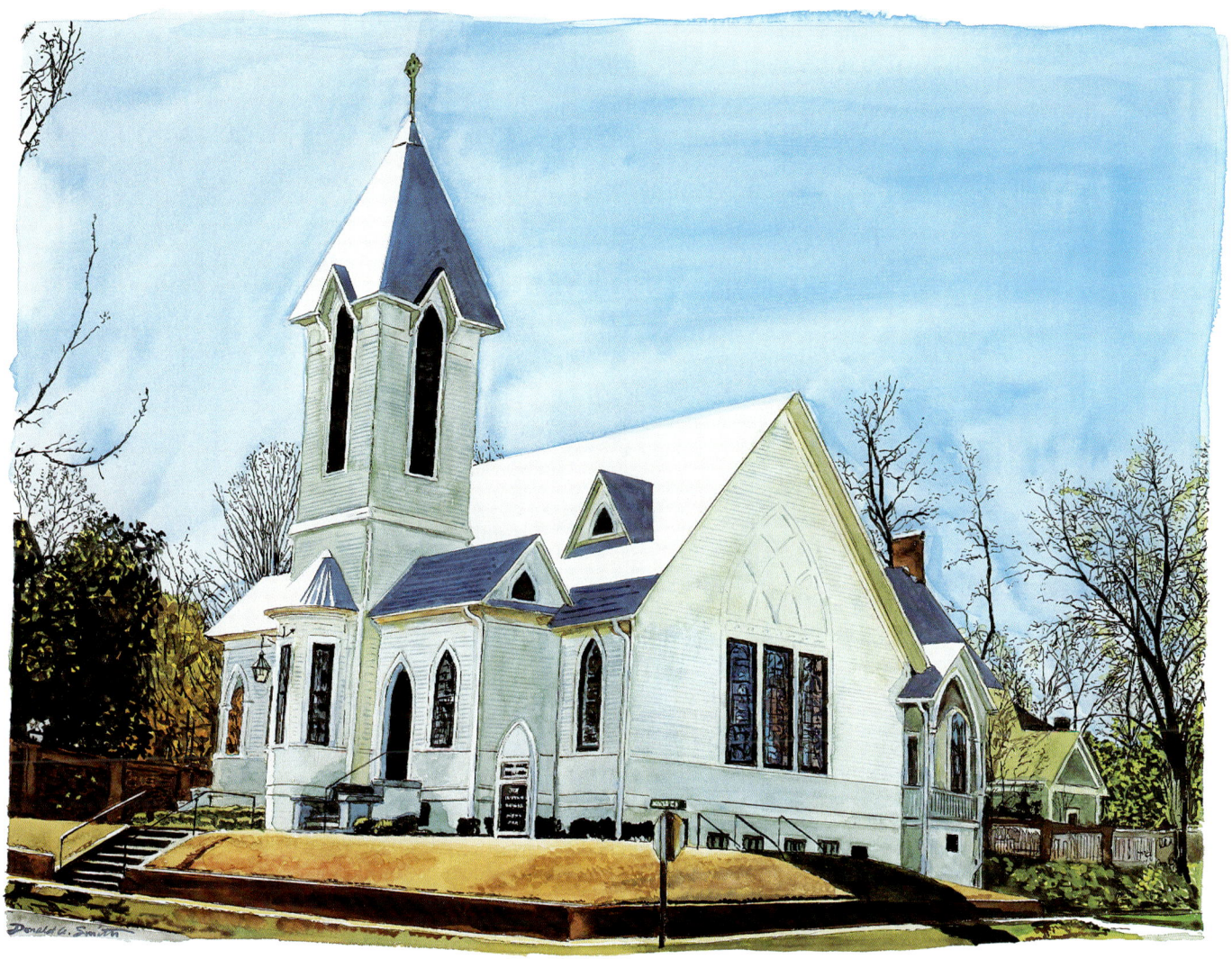

Watkinsville

CHURCHES

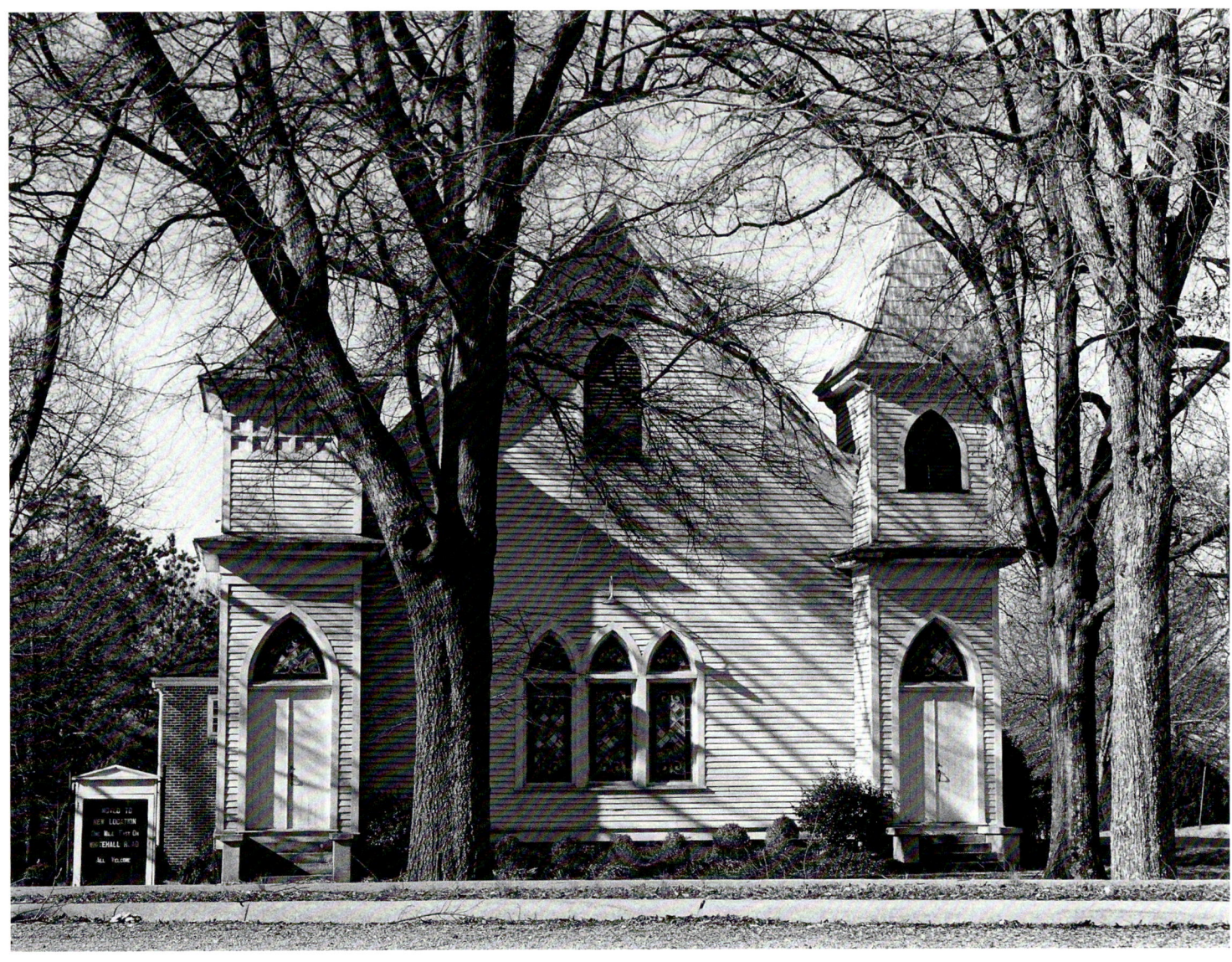

Watkinsville

CHURCHES

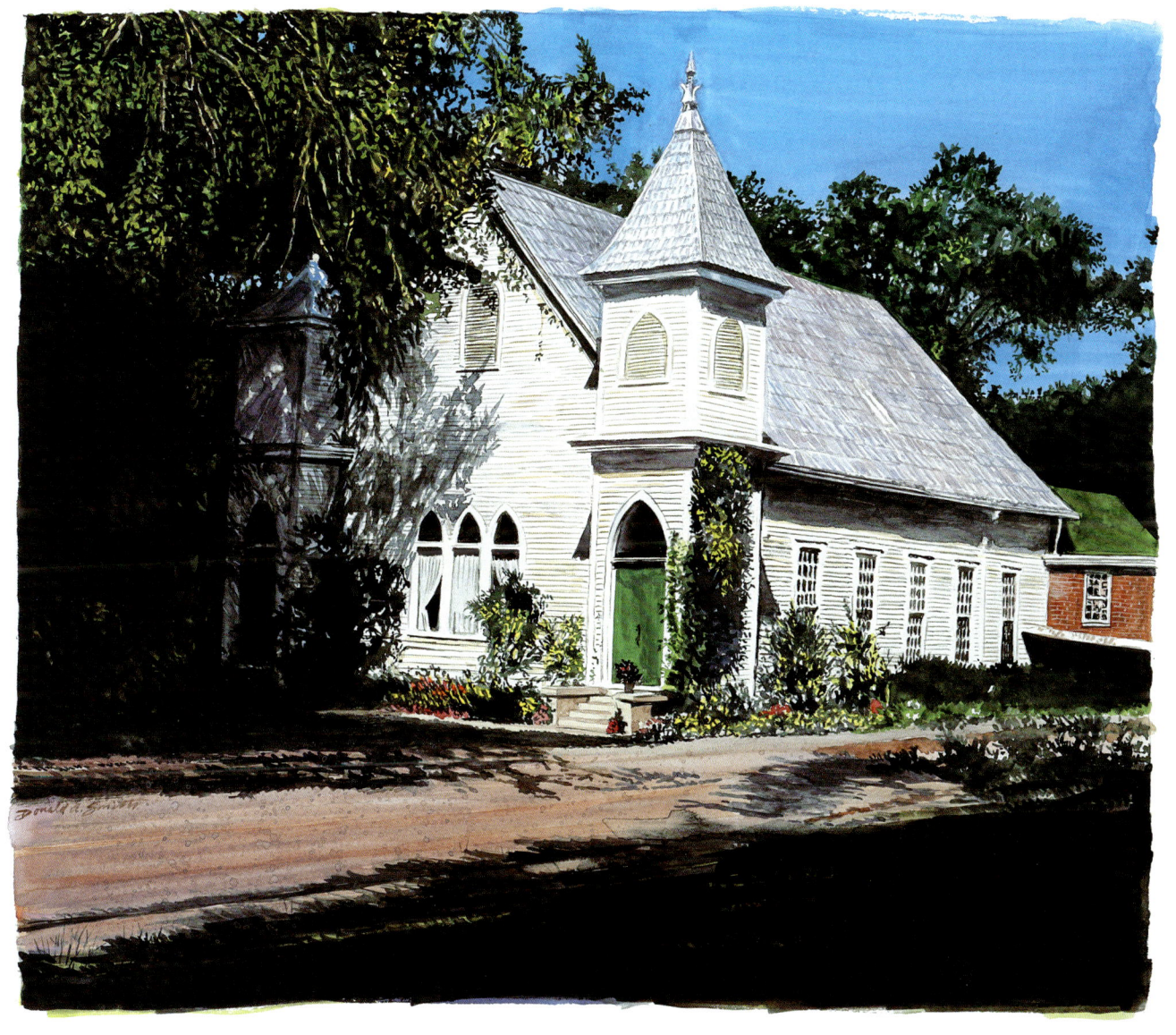

Watkinsville

CHURCHES

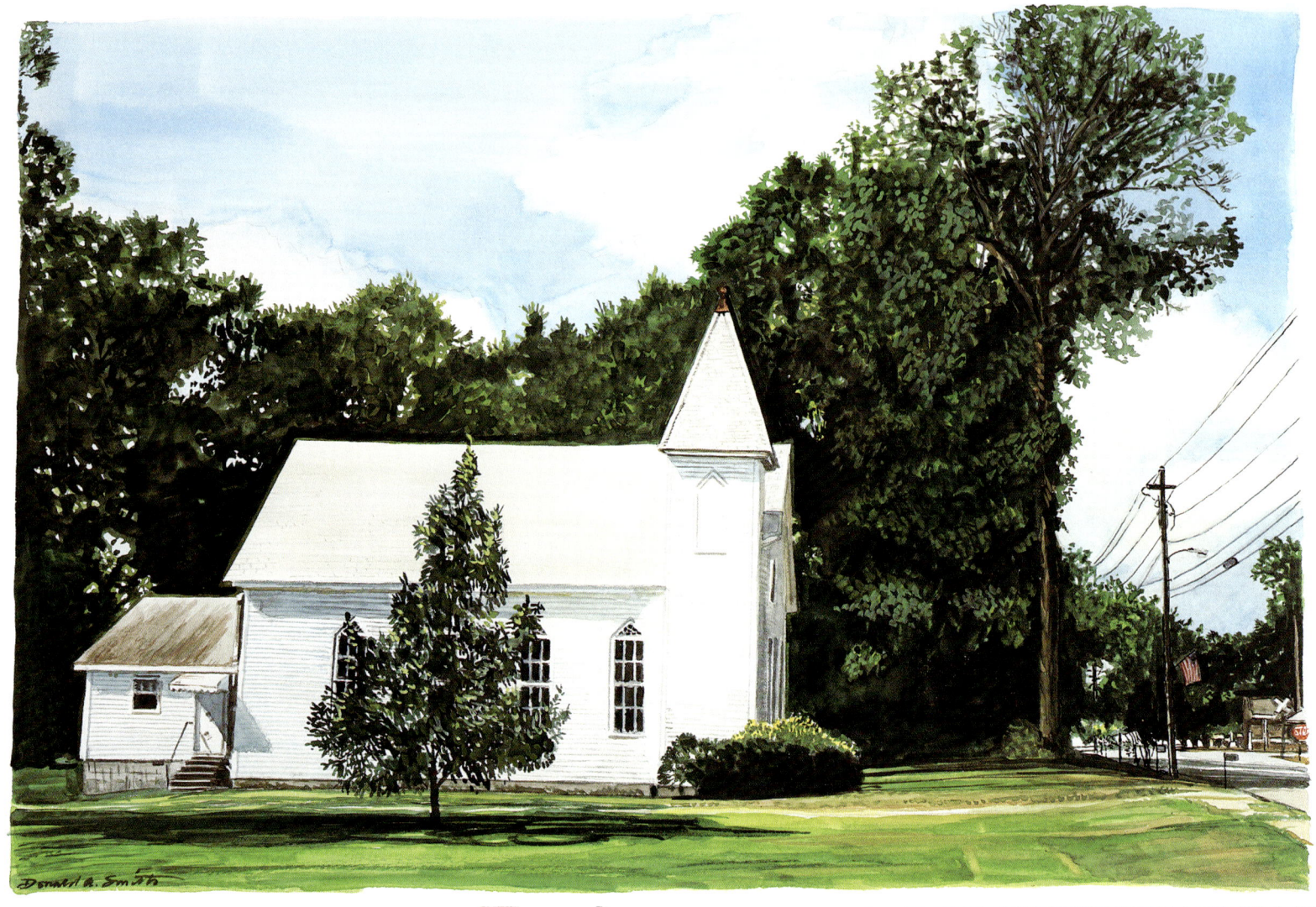

Bishop

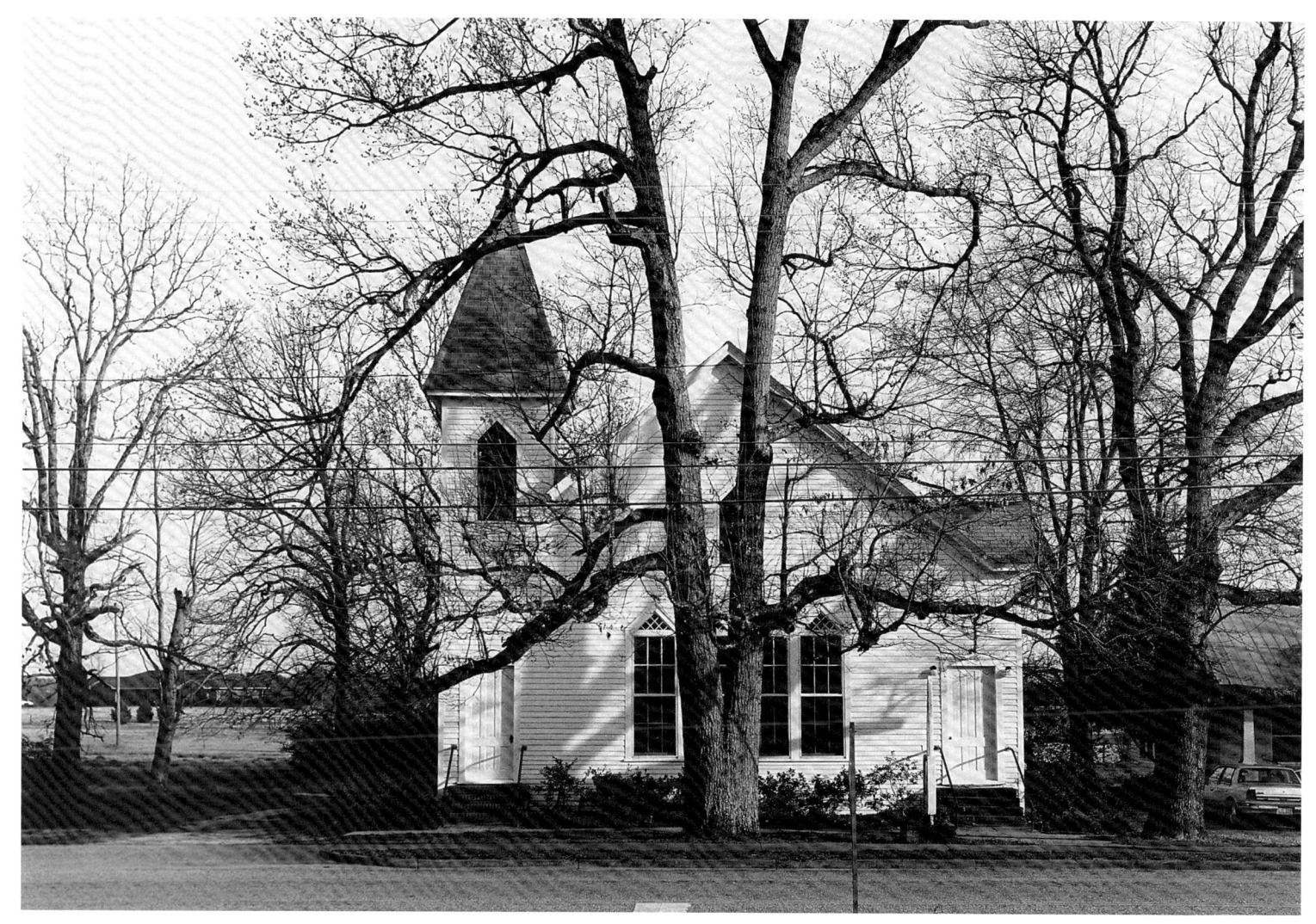

Bishop

CHURCHES

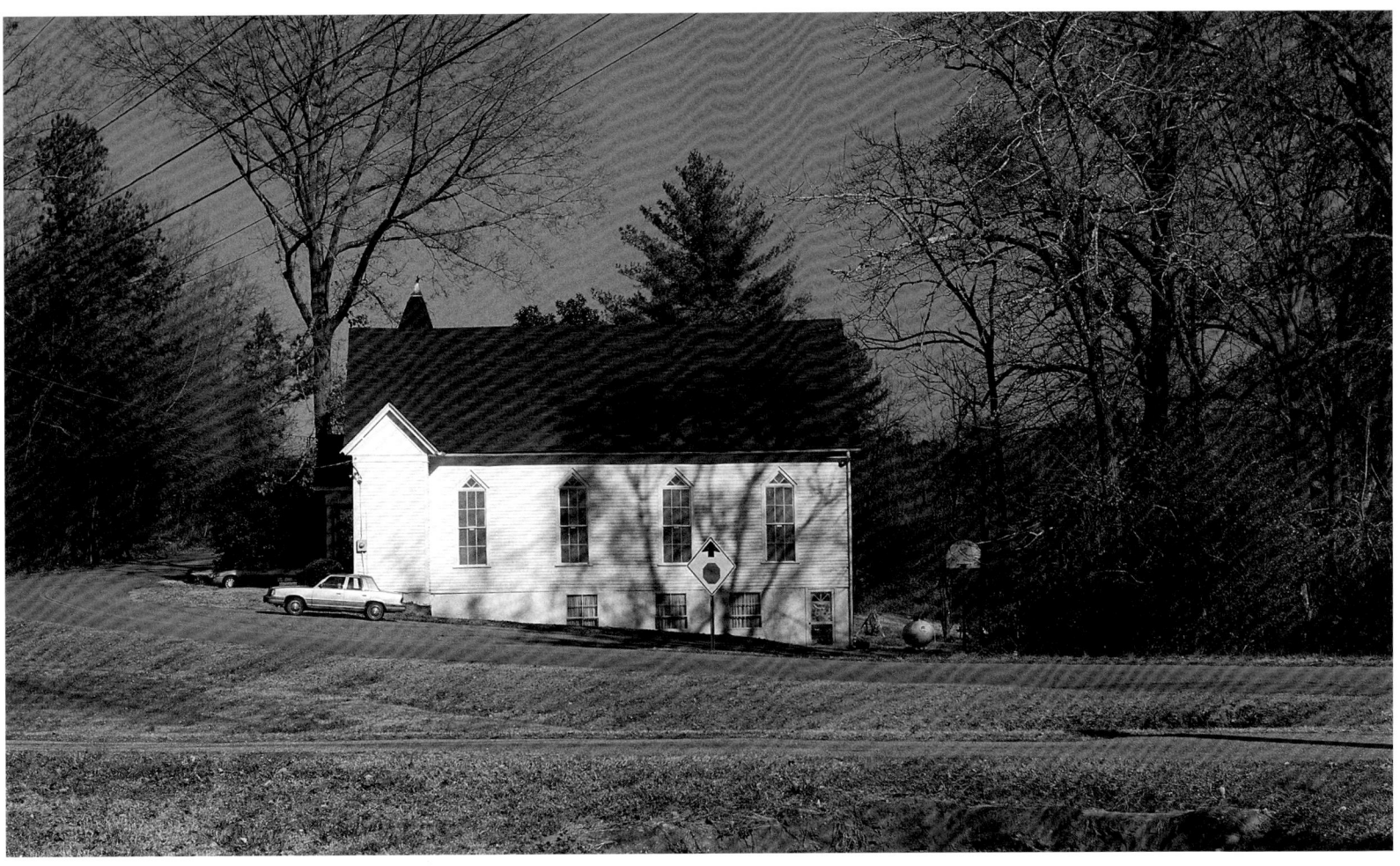

High Shoals

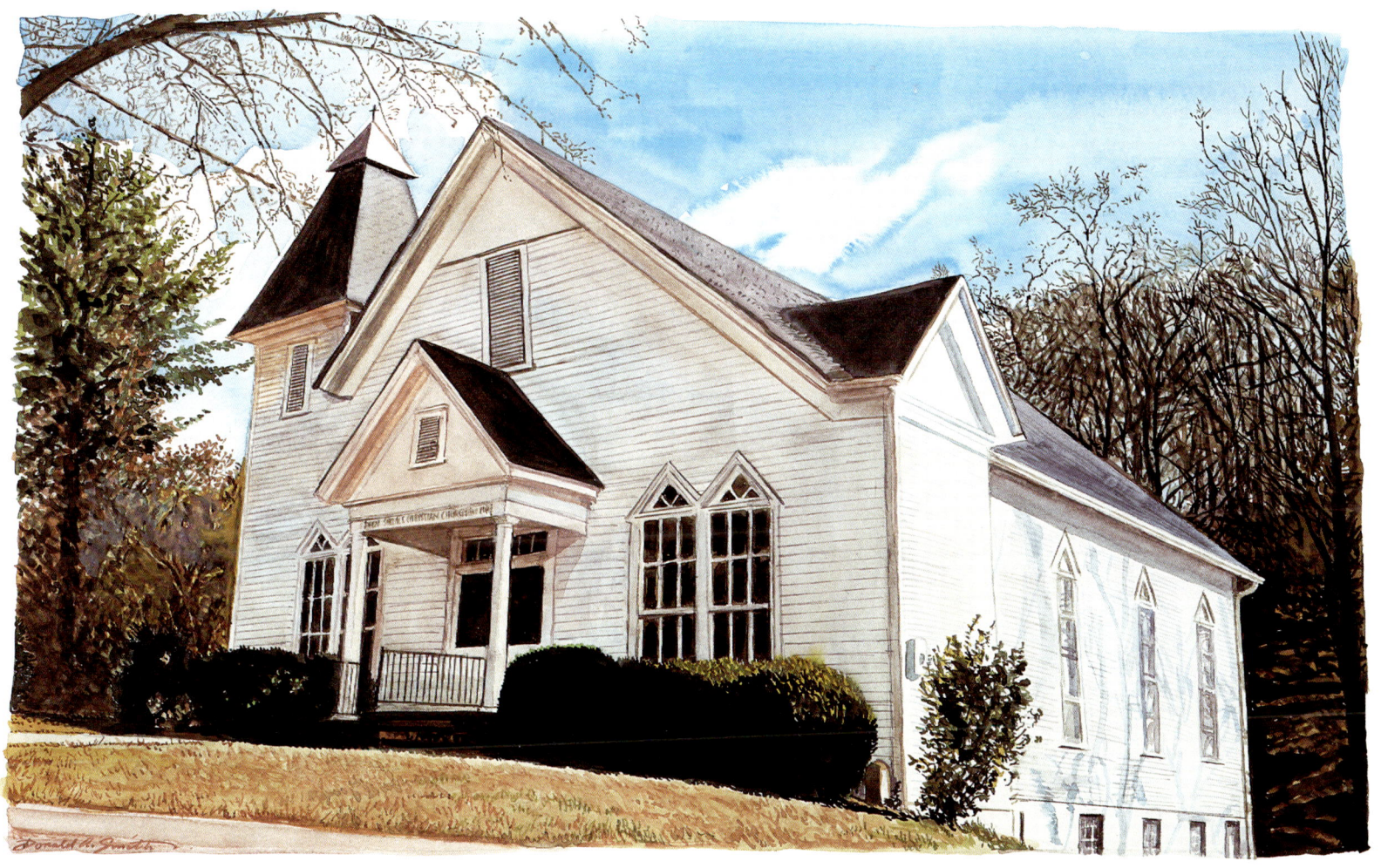

High Shoals

CHURCHES

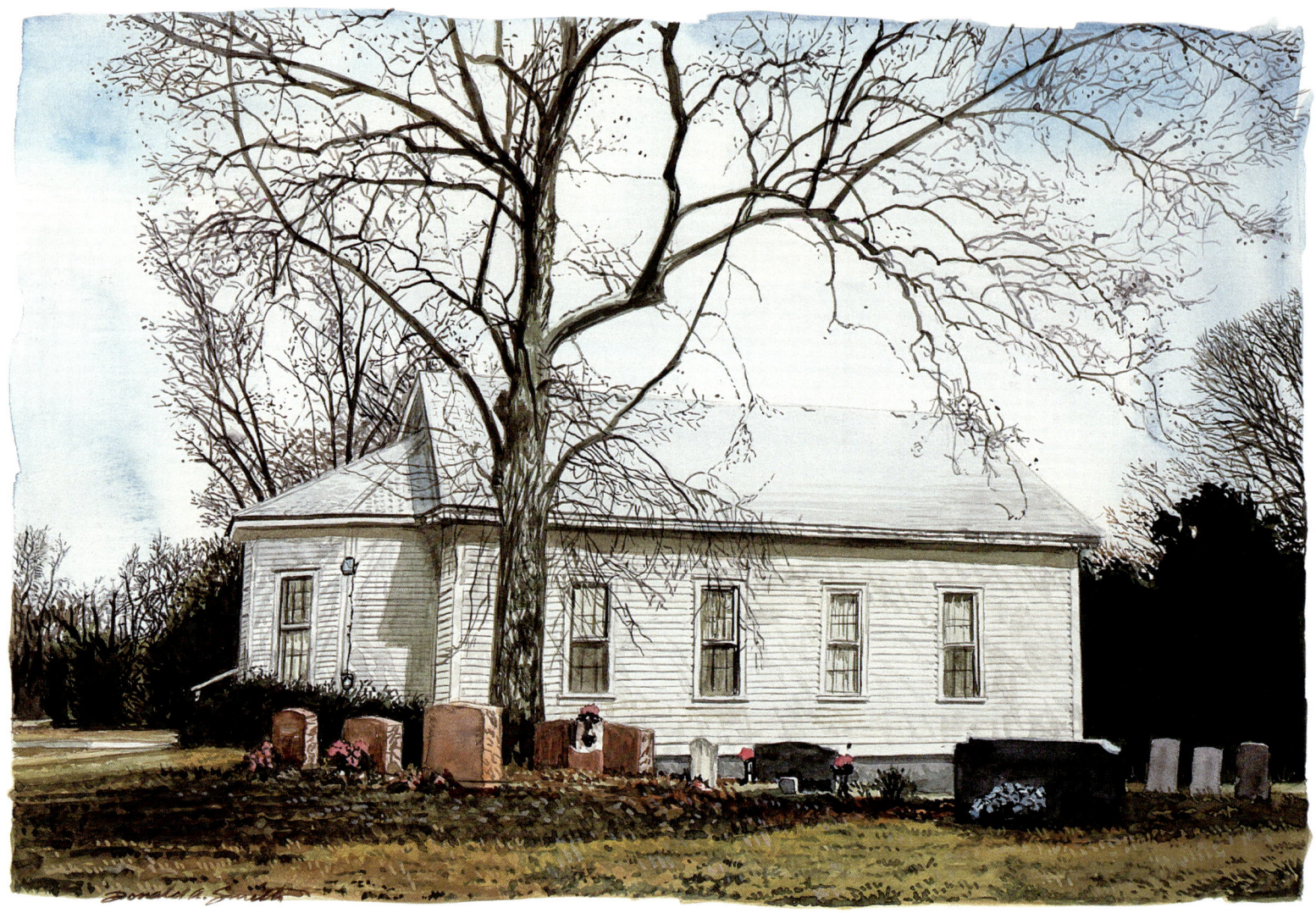

High Shoals

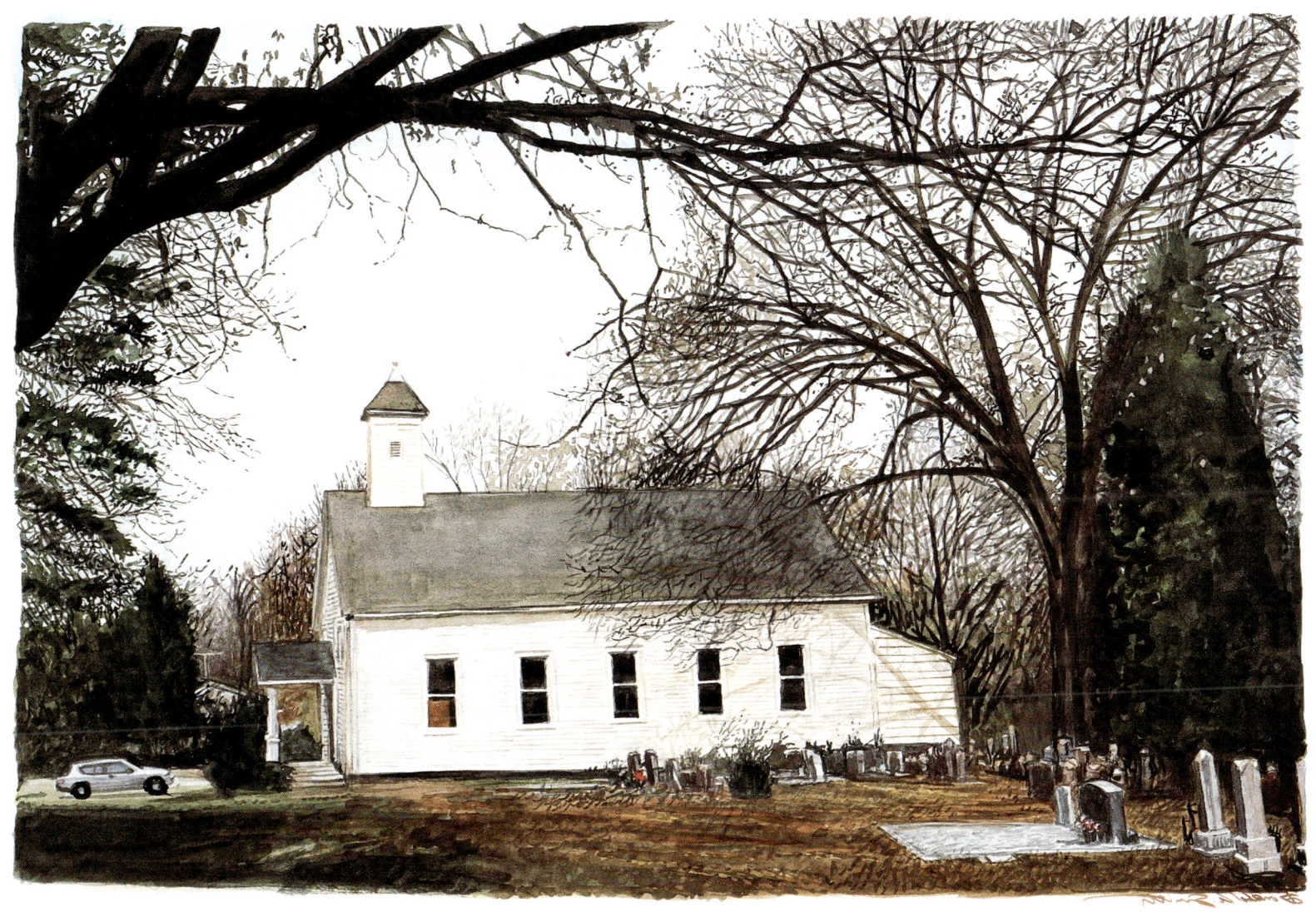

High Shoals

CHURCHES

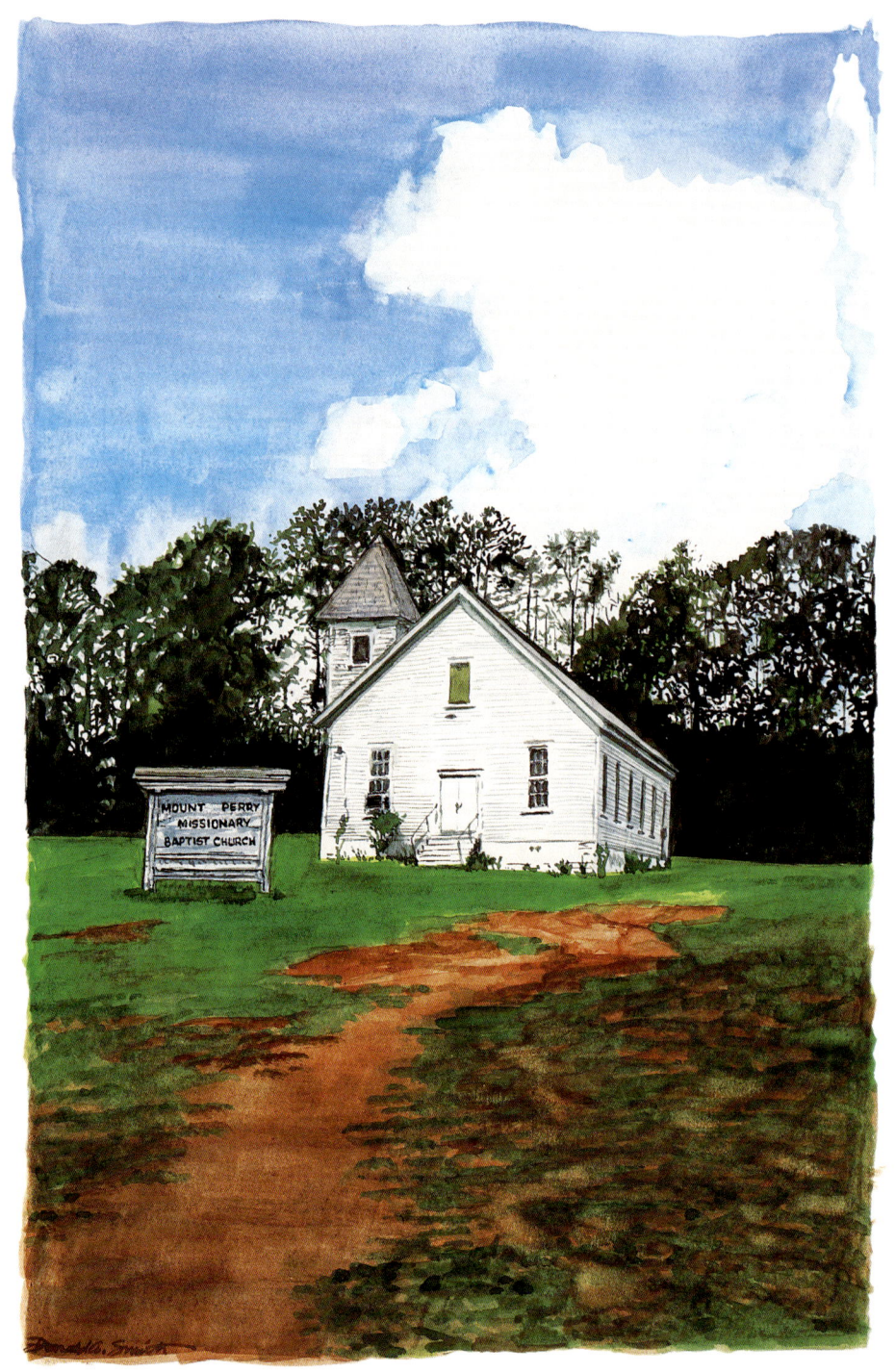

Oconee County

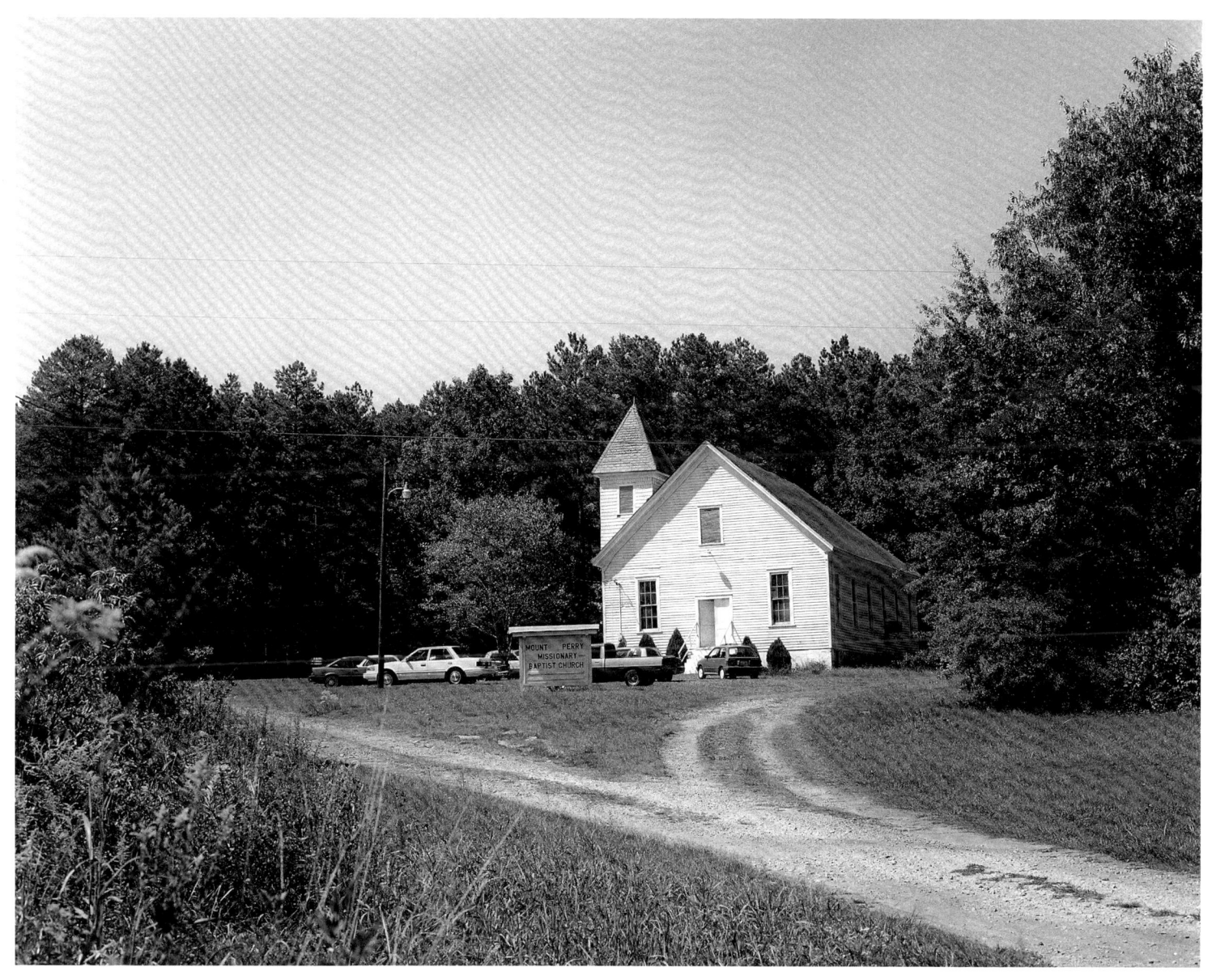

Oconee County

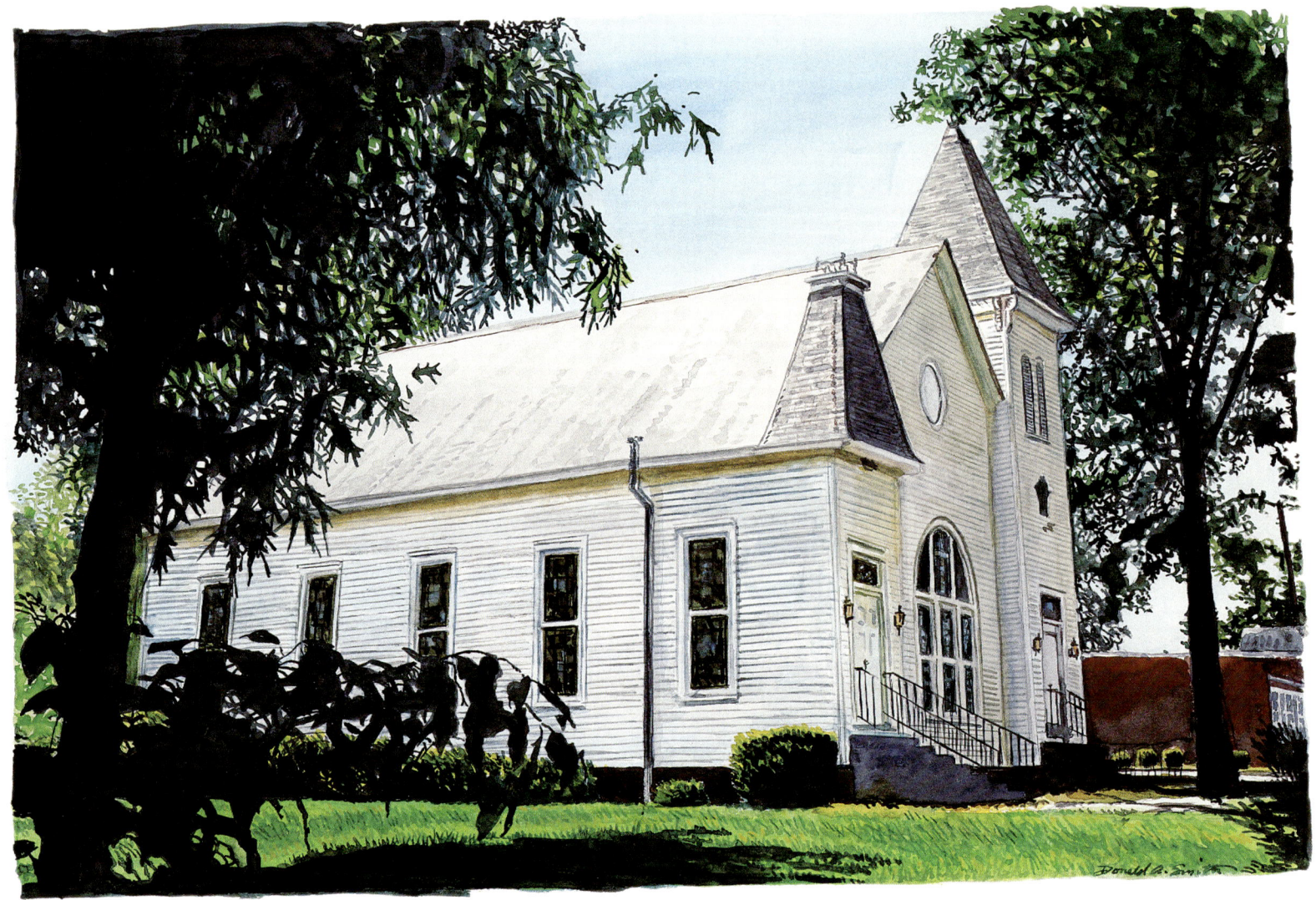

Bostwick

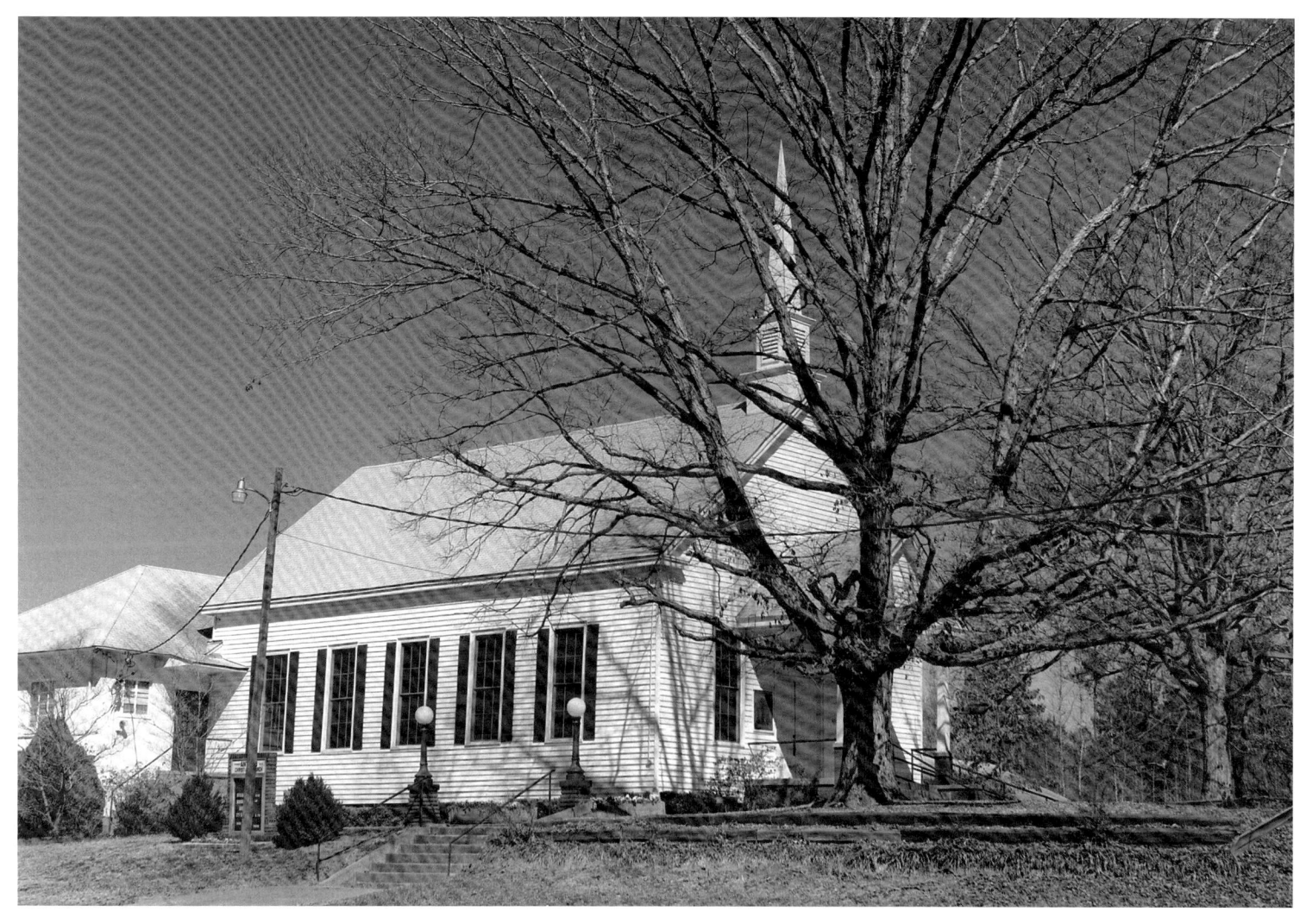

Oconee County

CHURCHES

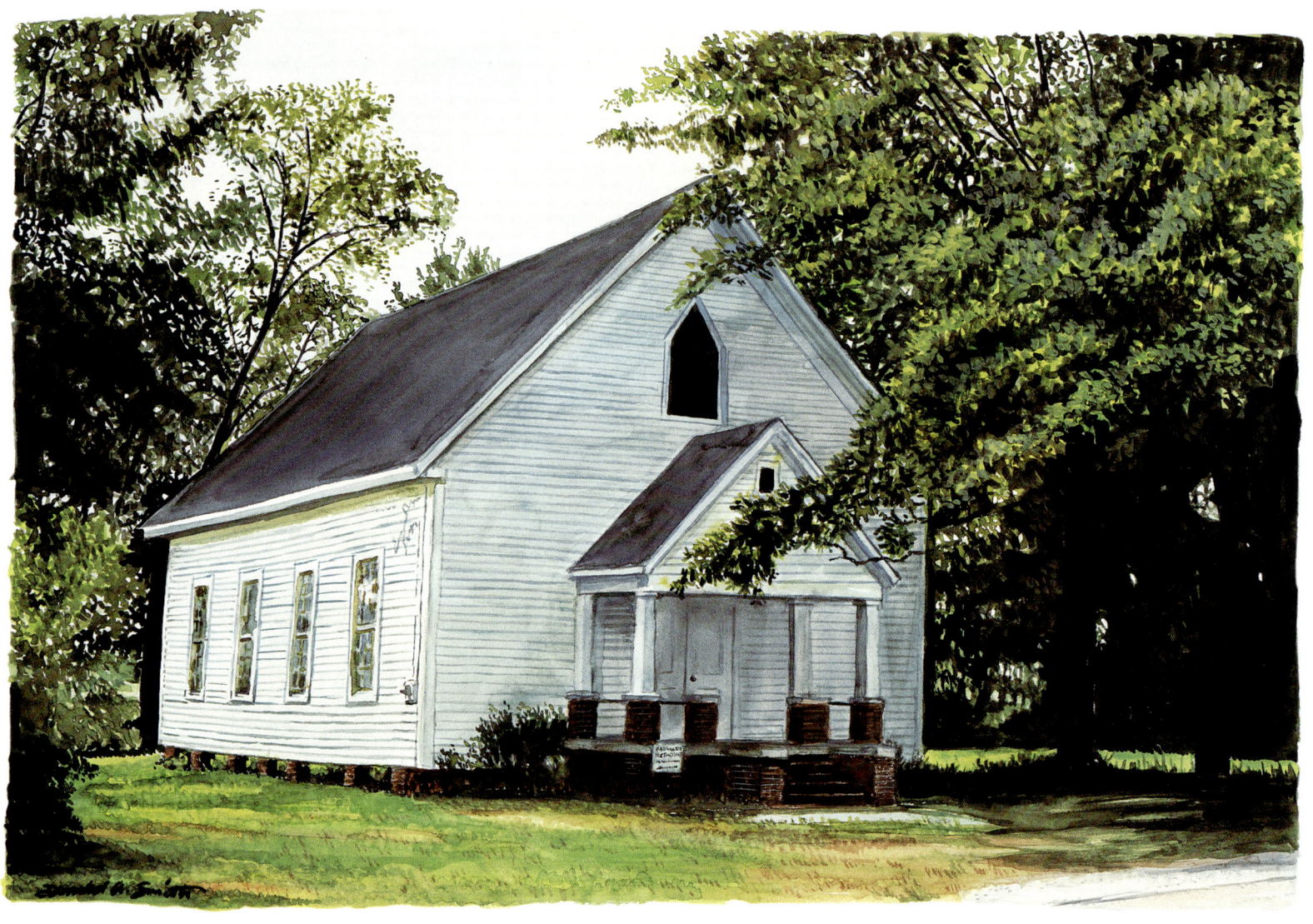

Farmington

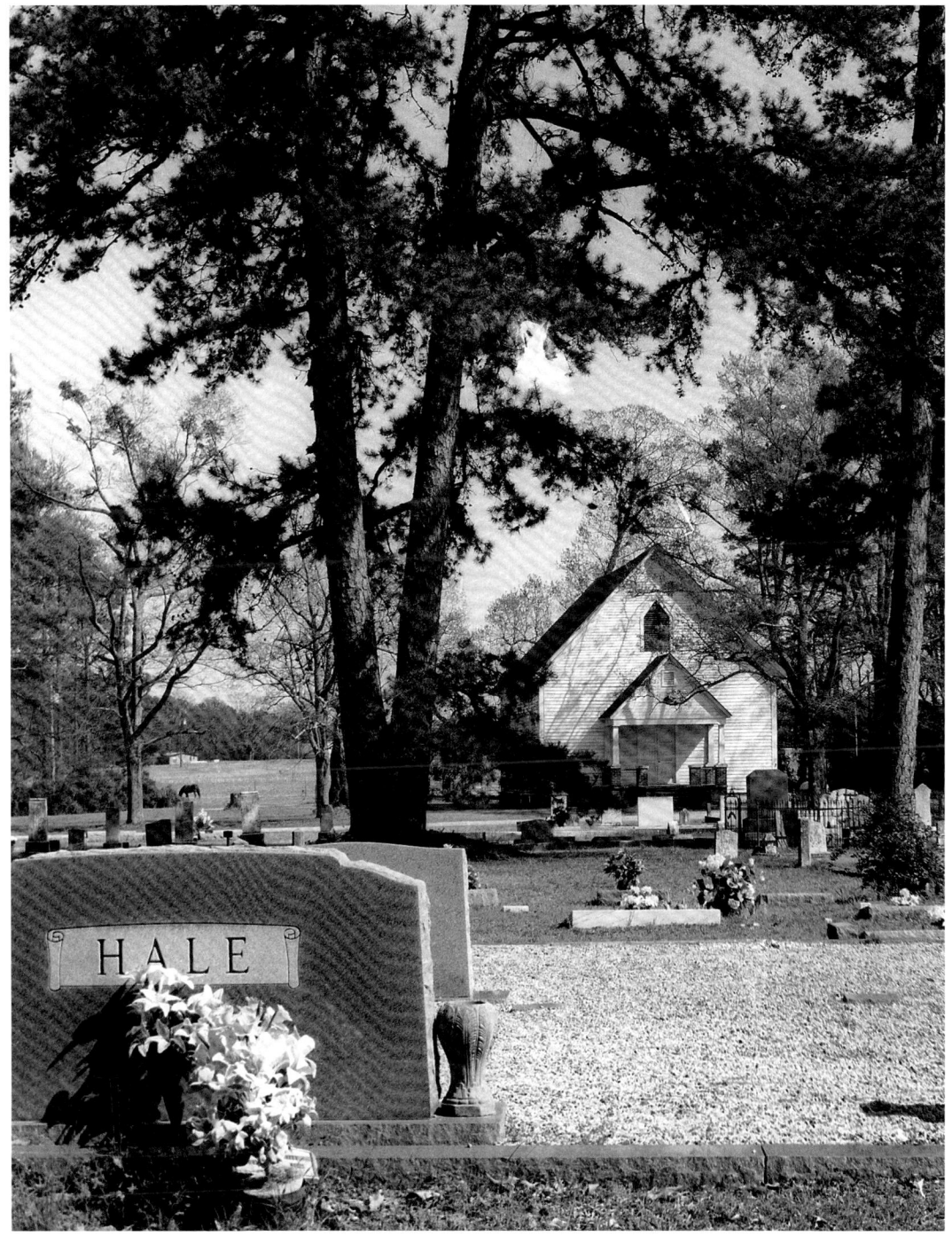

Farmington

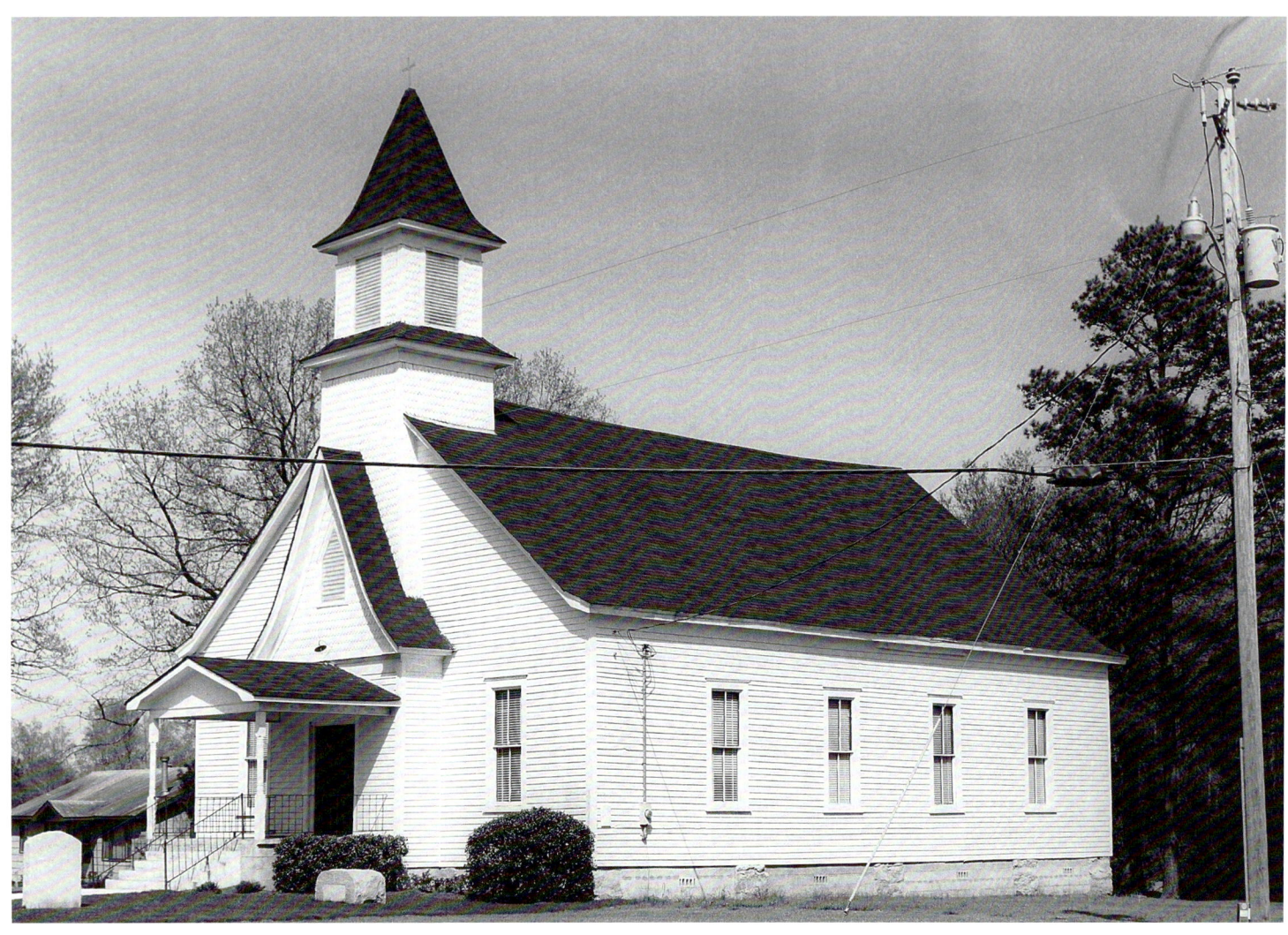

Farmington

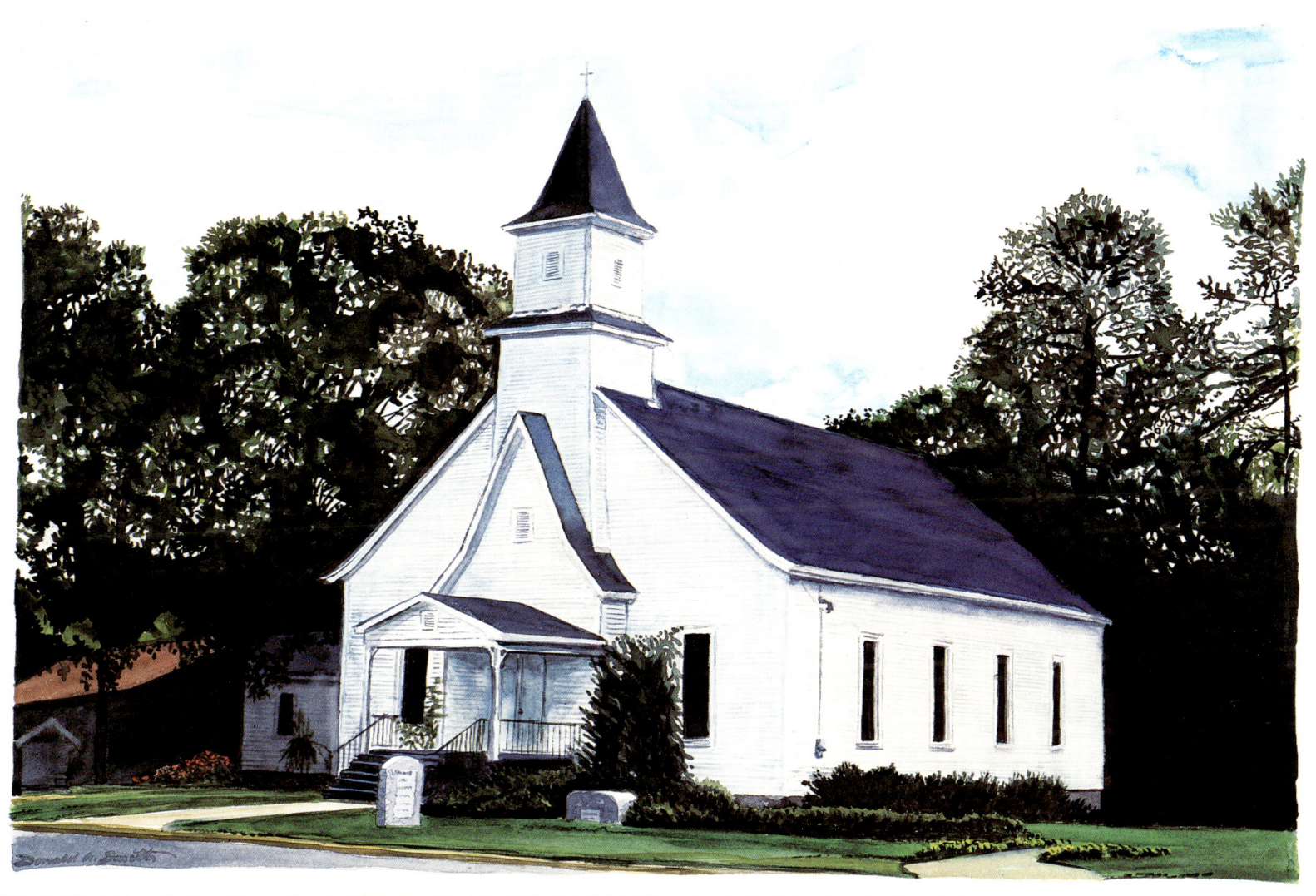

Farmington

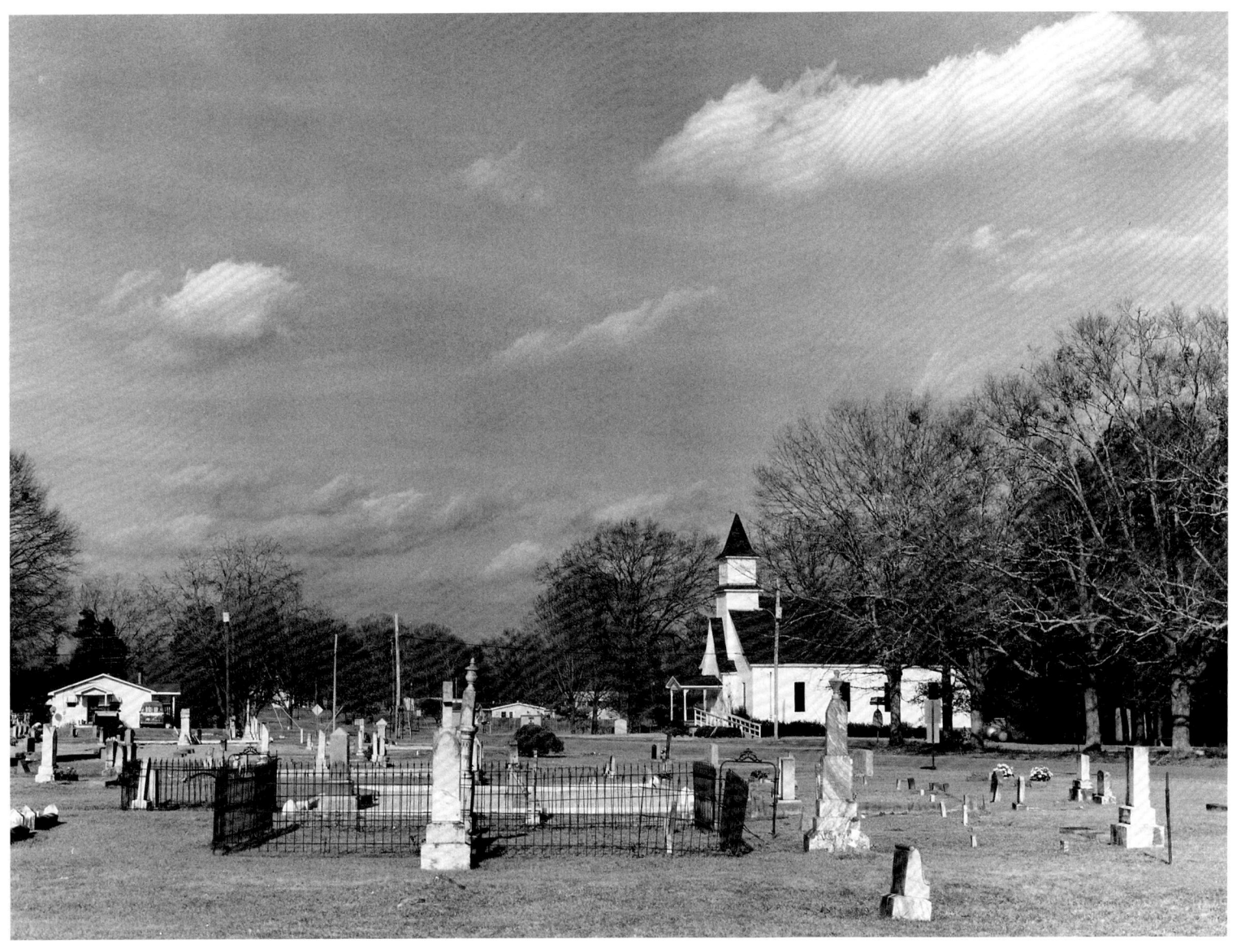

Farmington

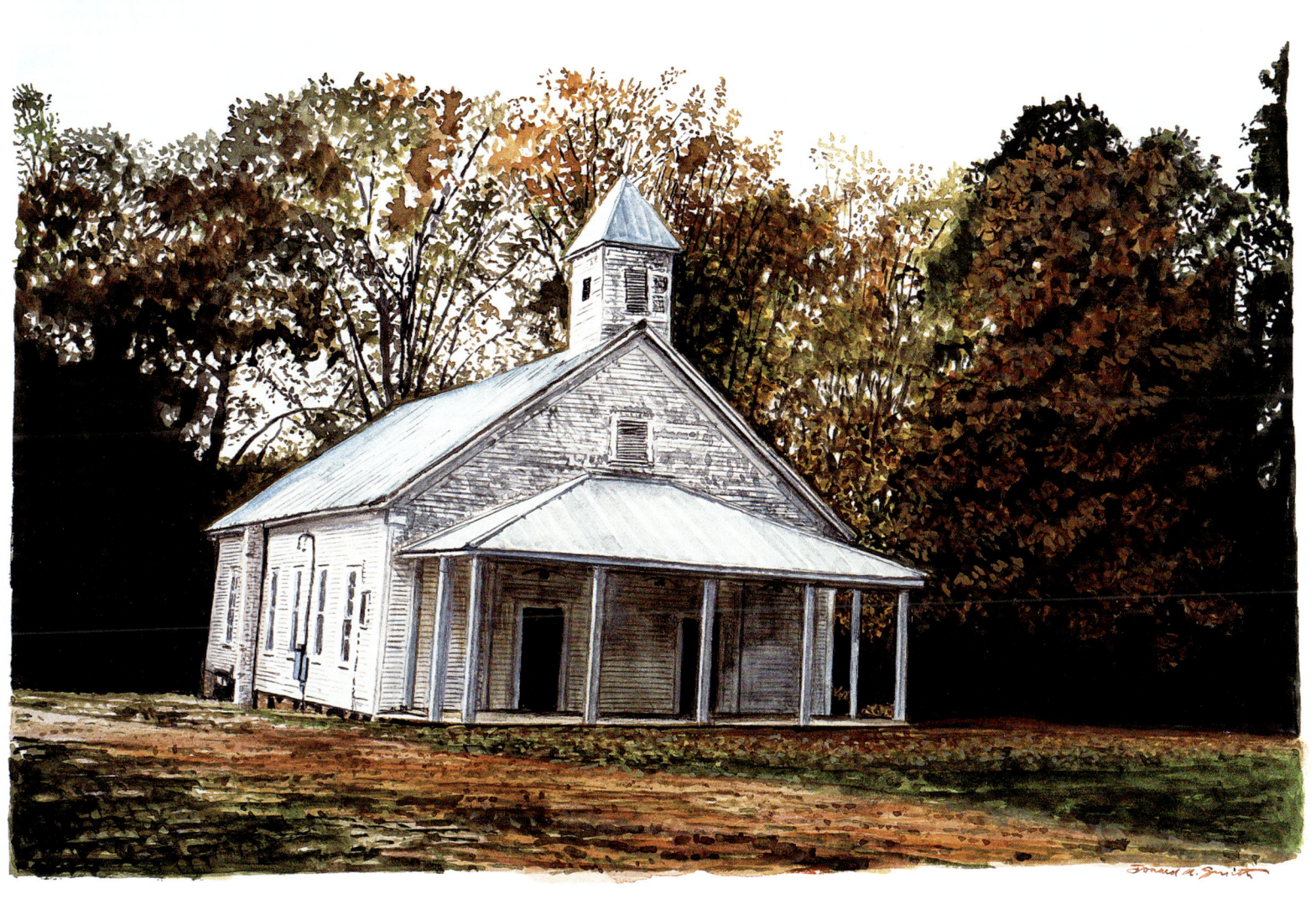

Between Farmington and Greshamville

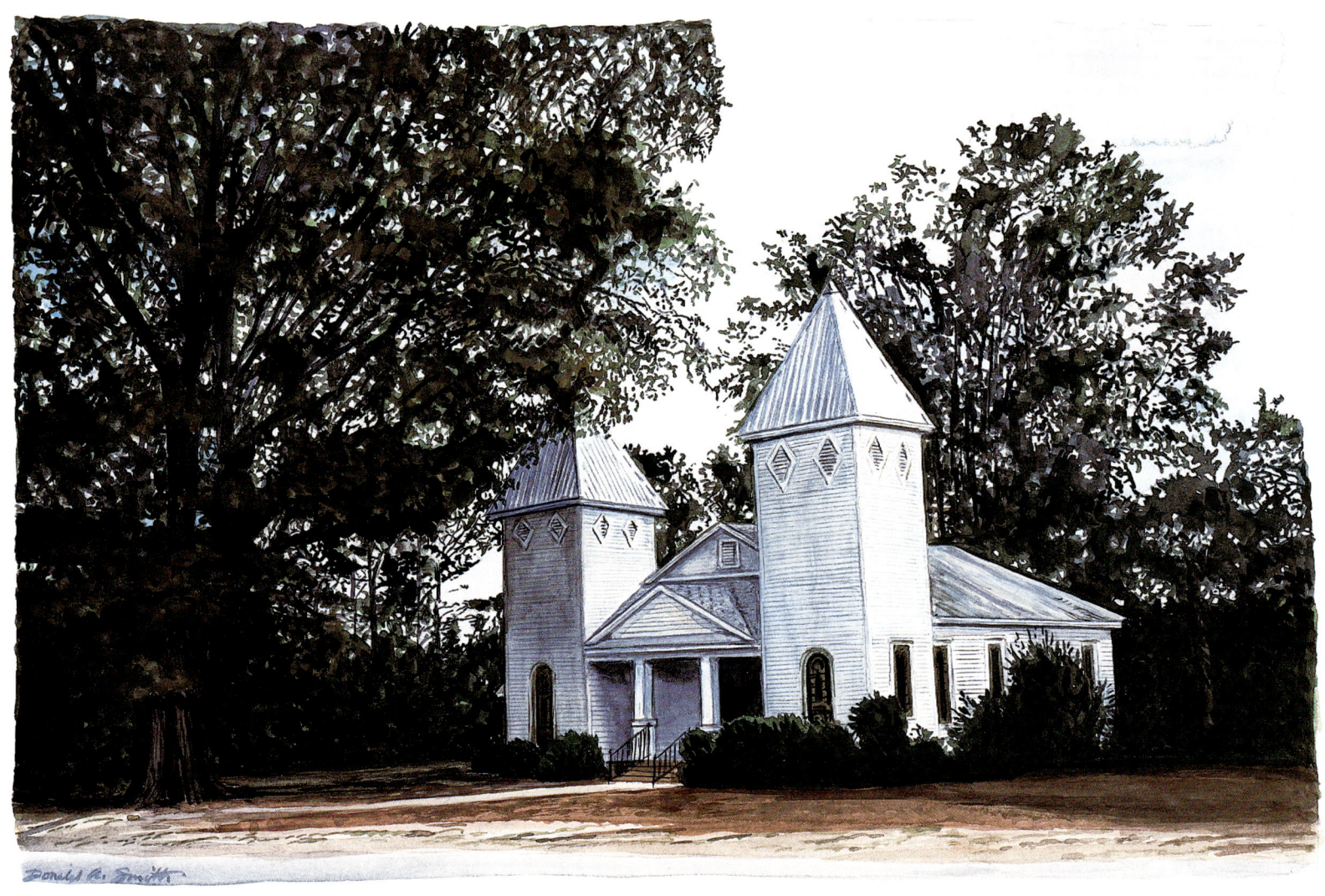

Greshamville

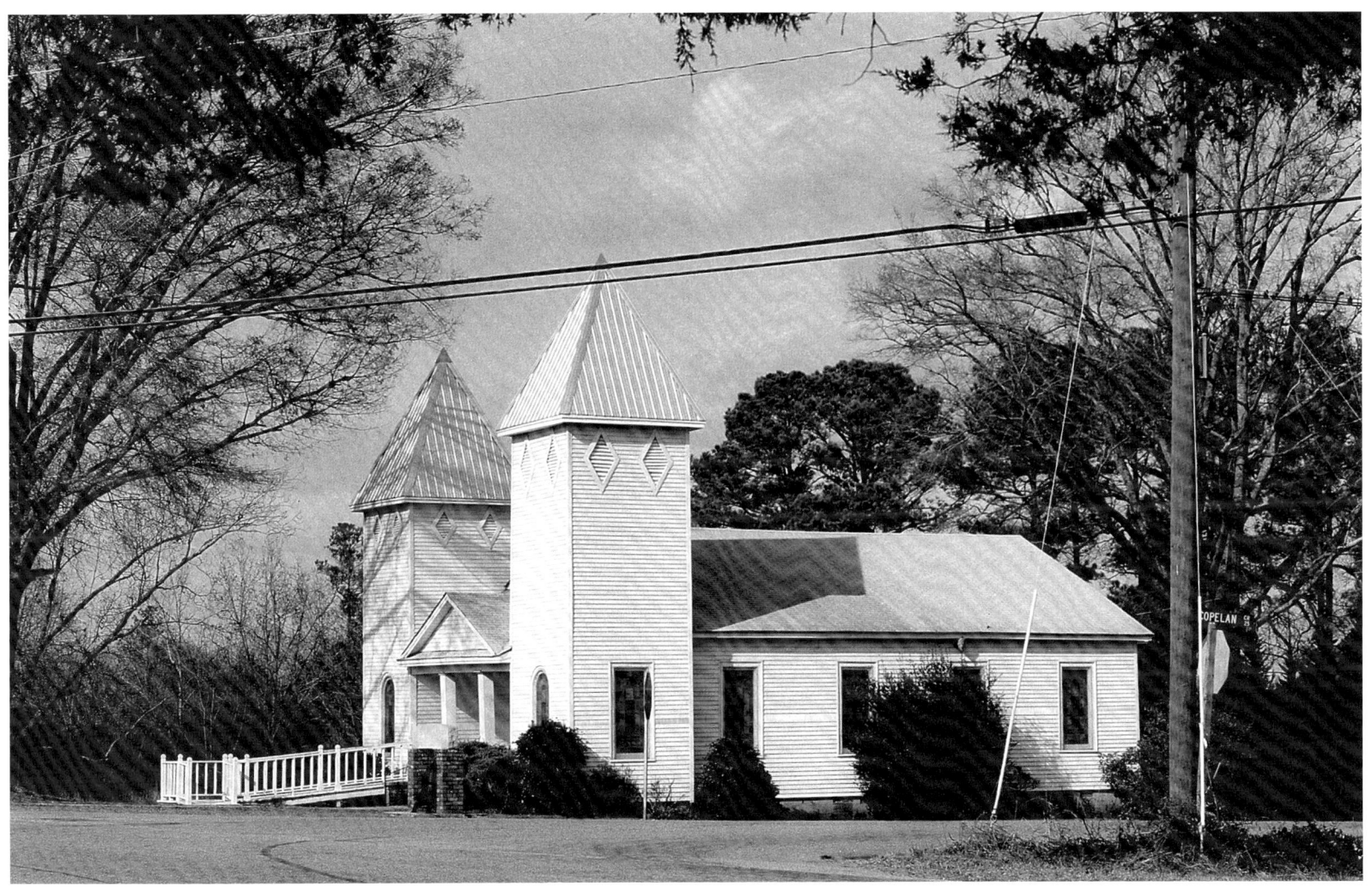

Greshamville

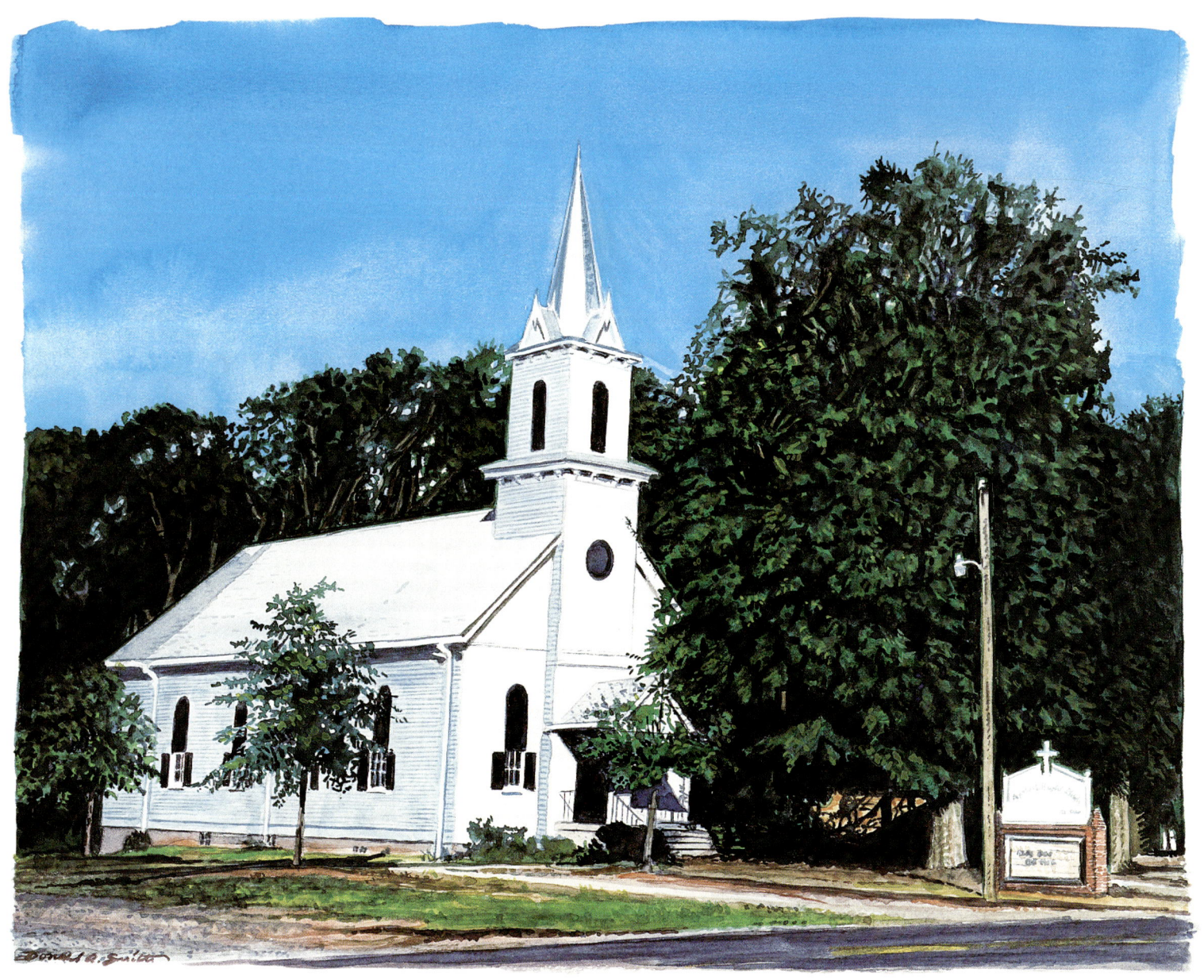

Apalachee

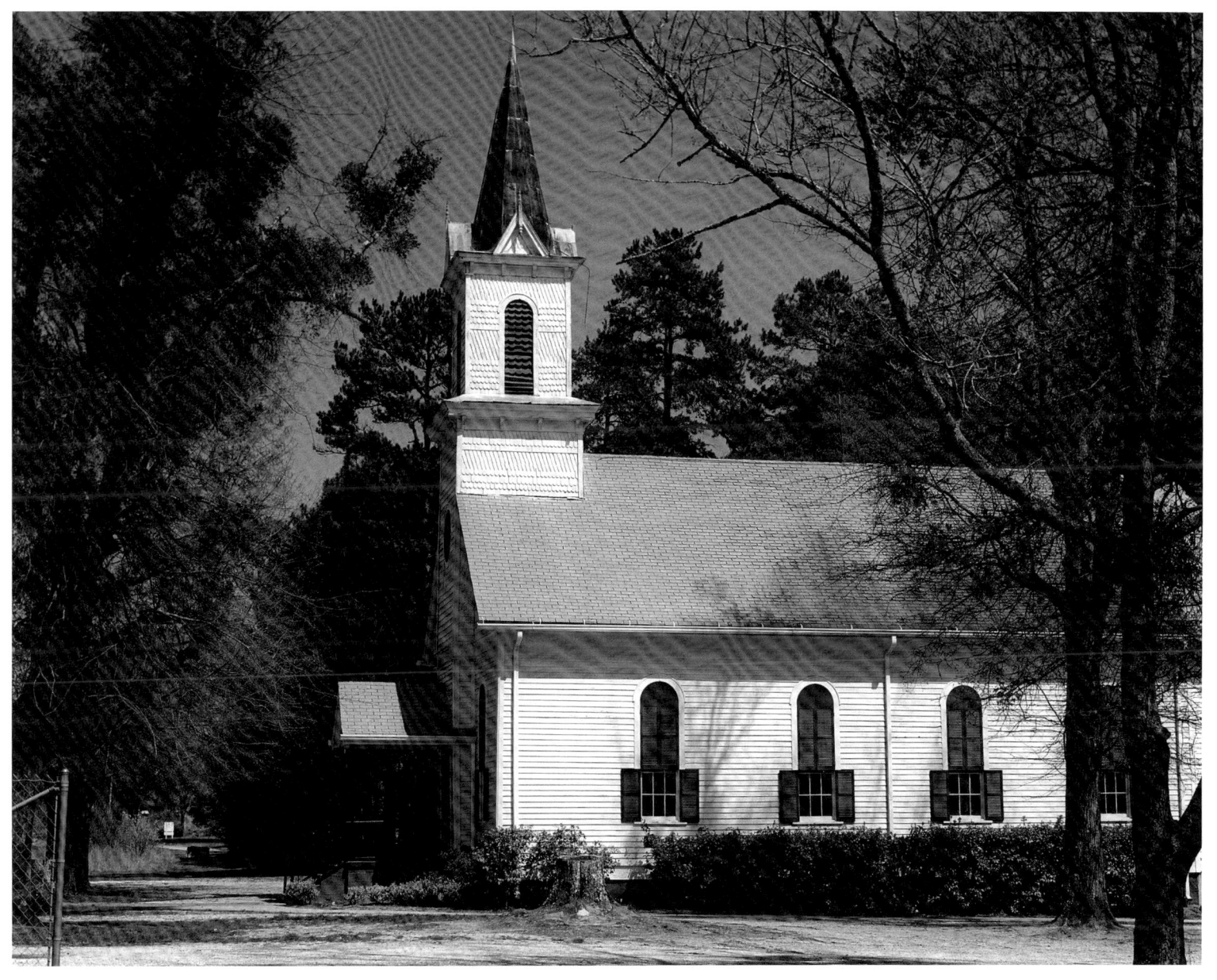

Apalachee

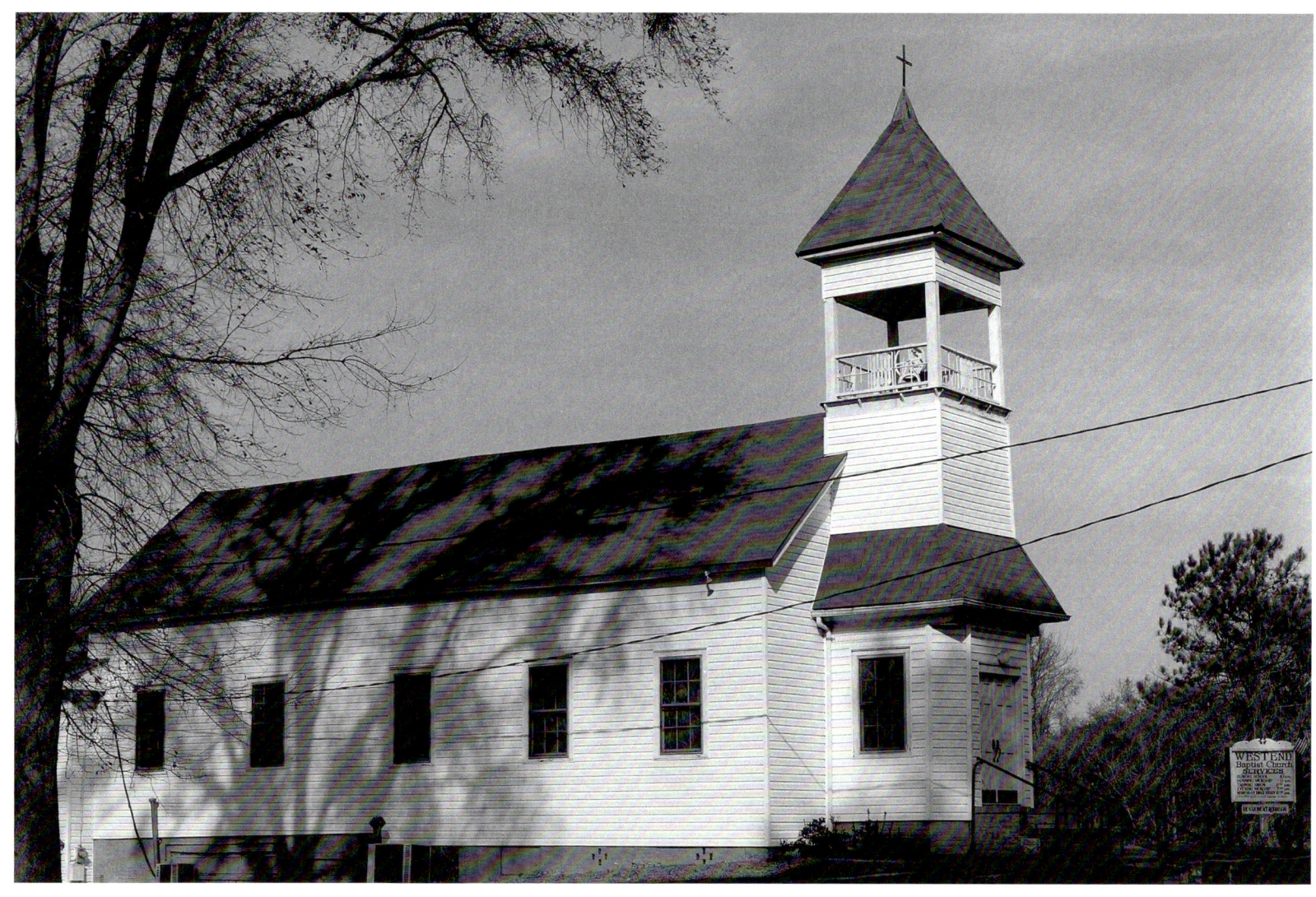

Greensboro

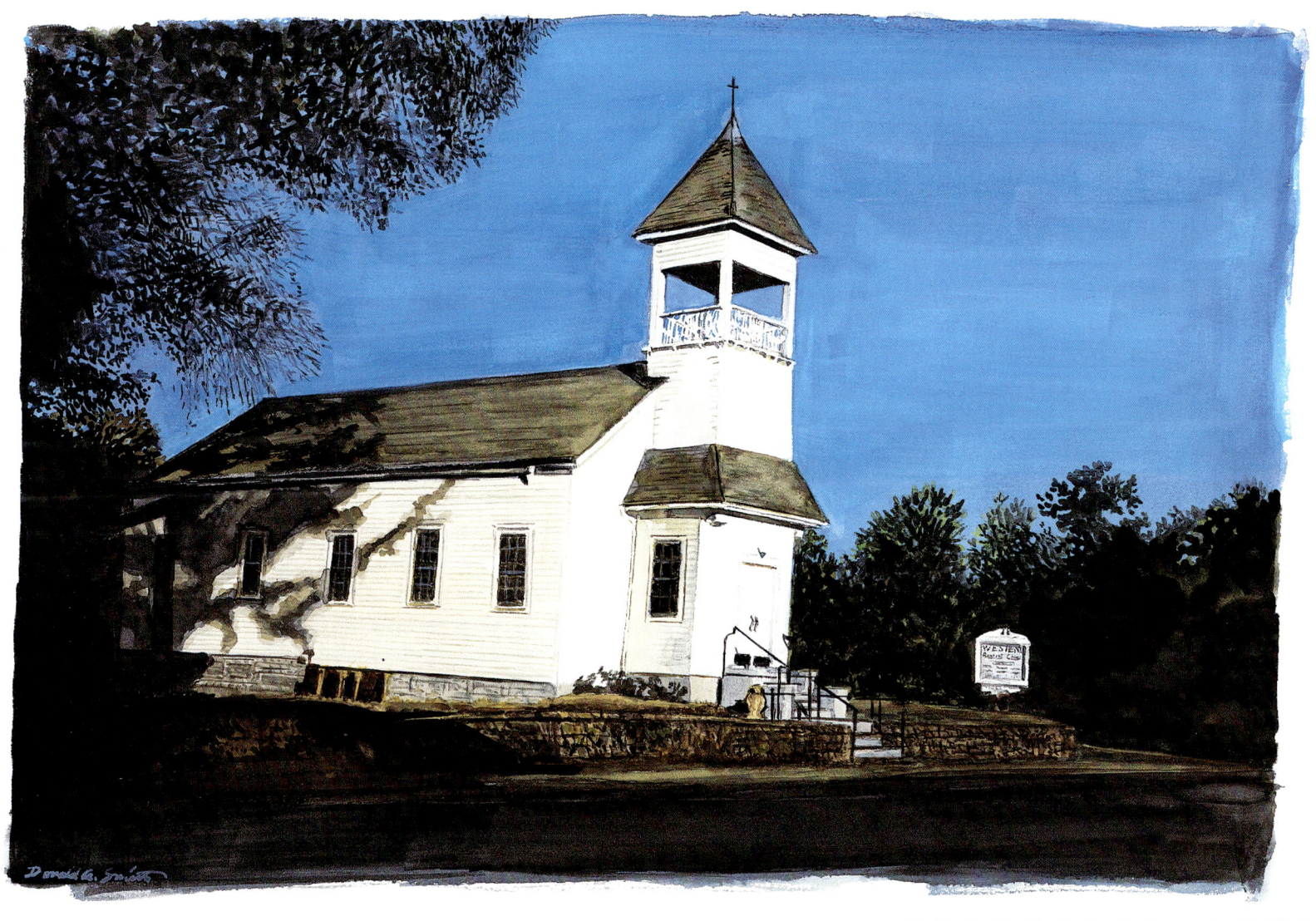

Greensboro

CHURCHES

37

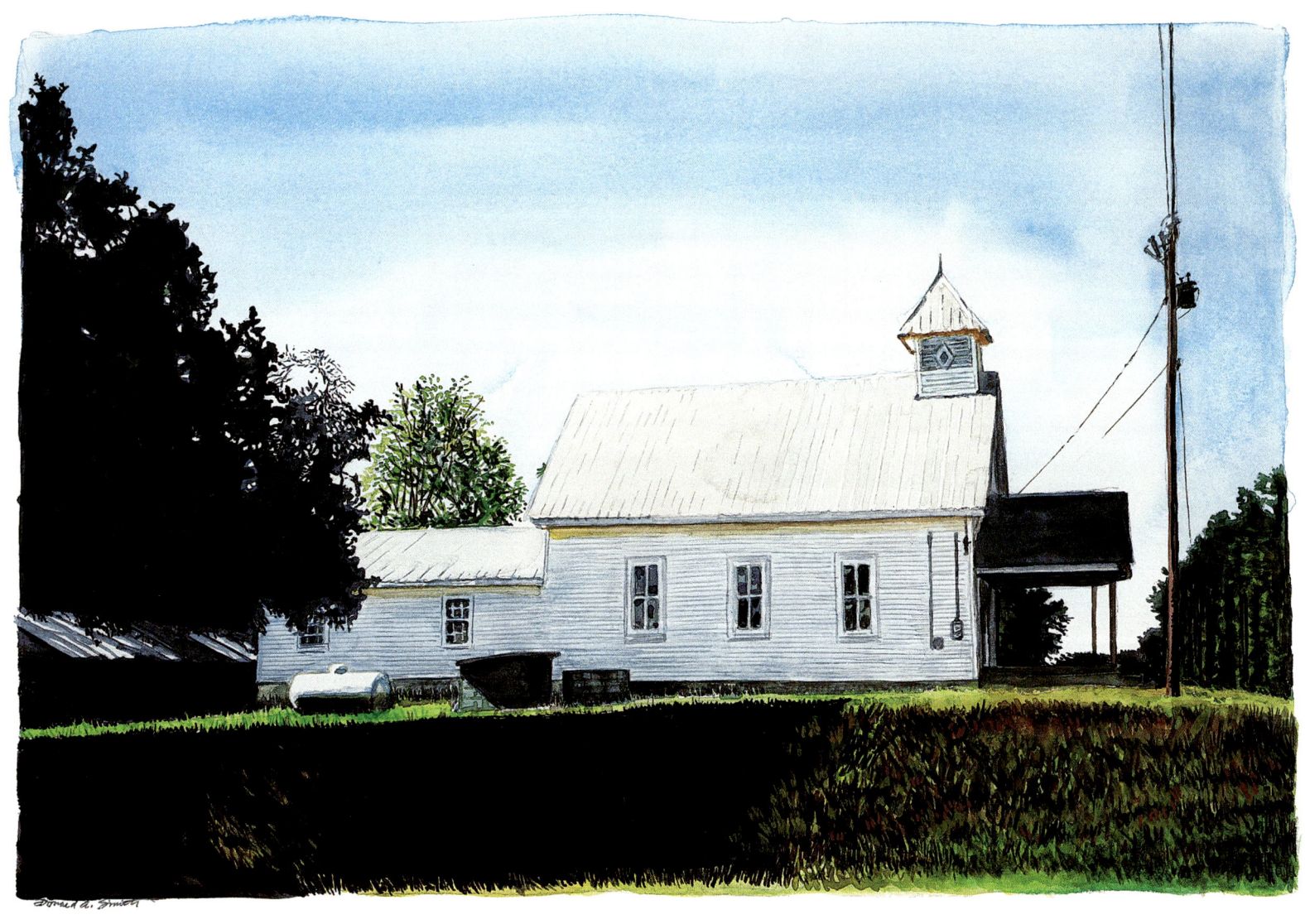

Near Buckhead

CHURCHES

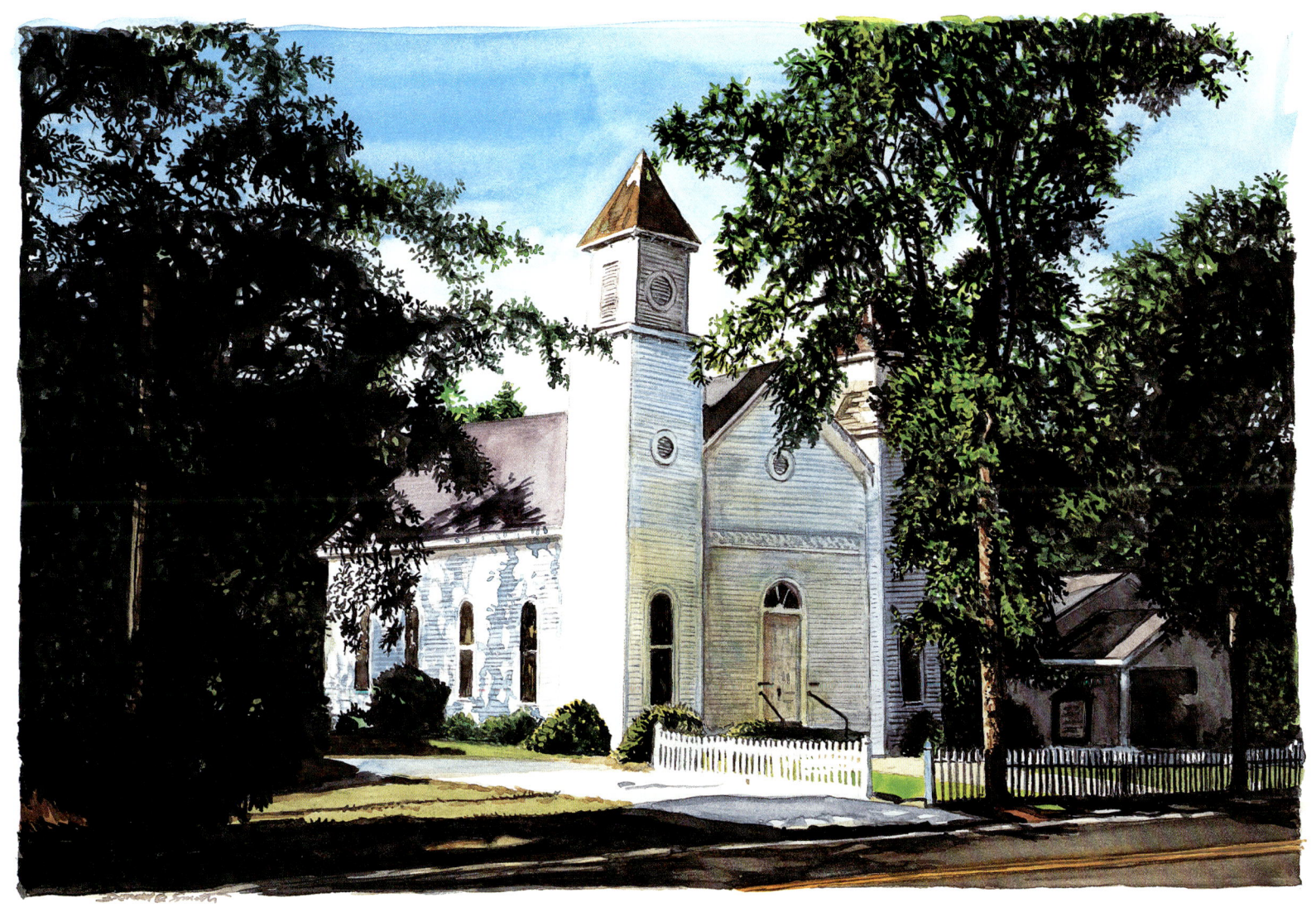

Buckhead

CHURCHES

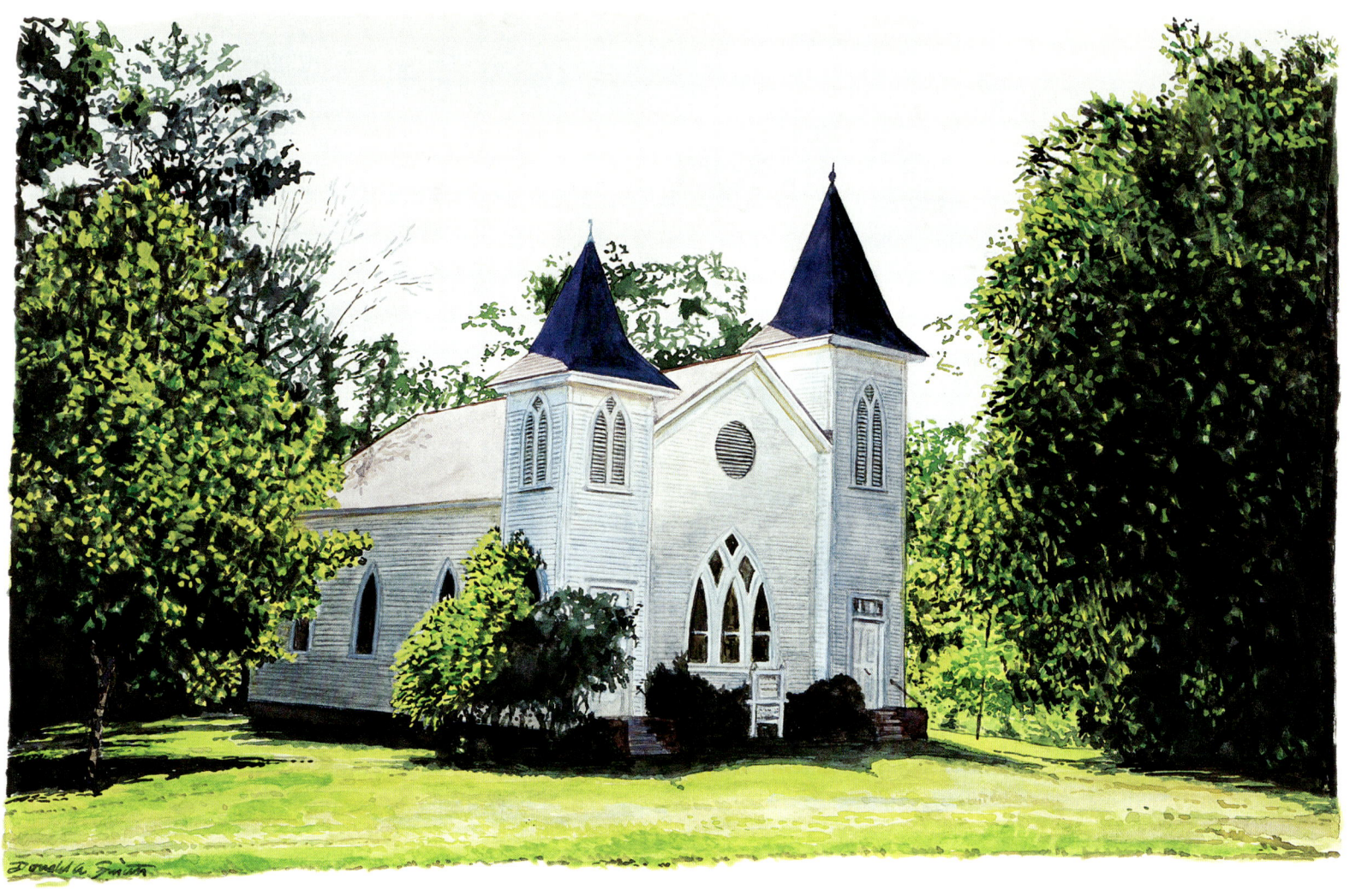

Swords 2002

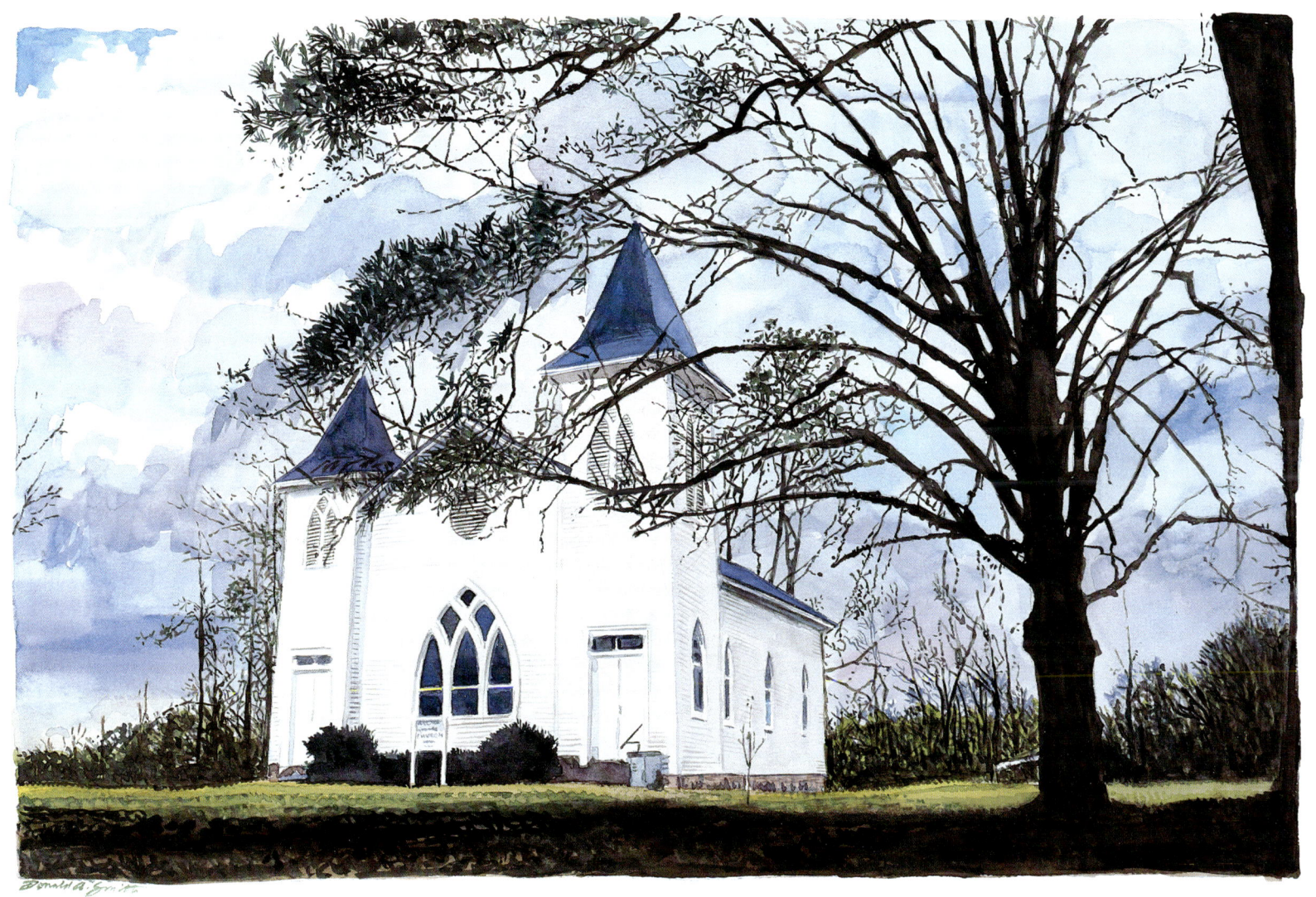

Swords 1995

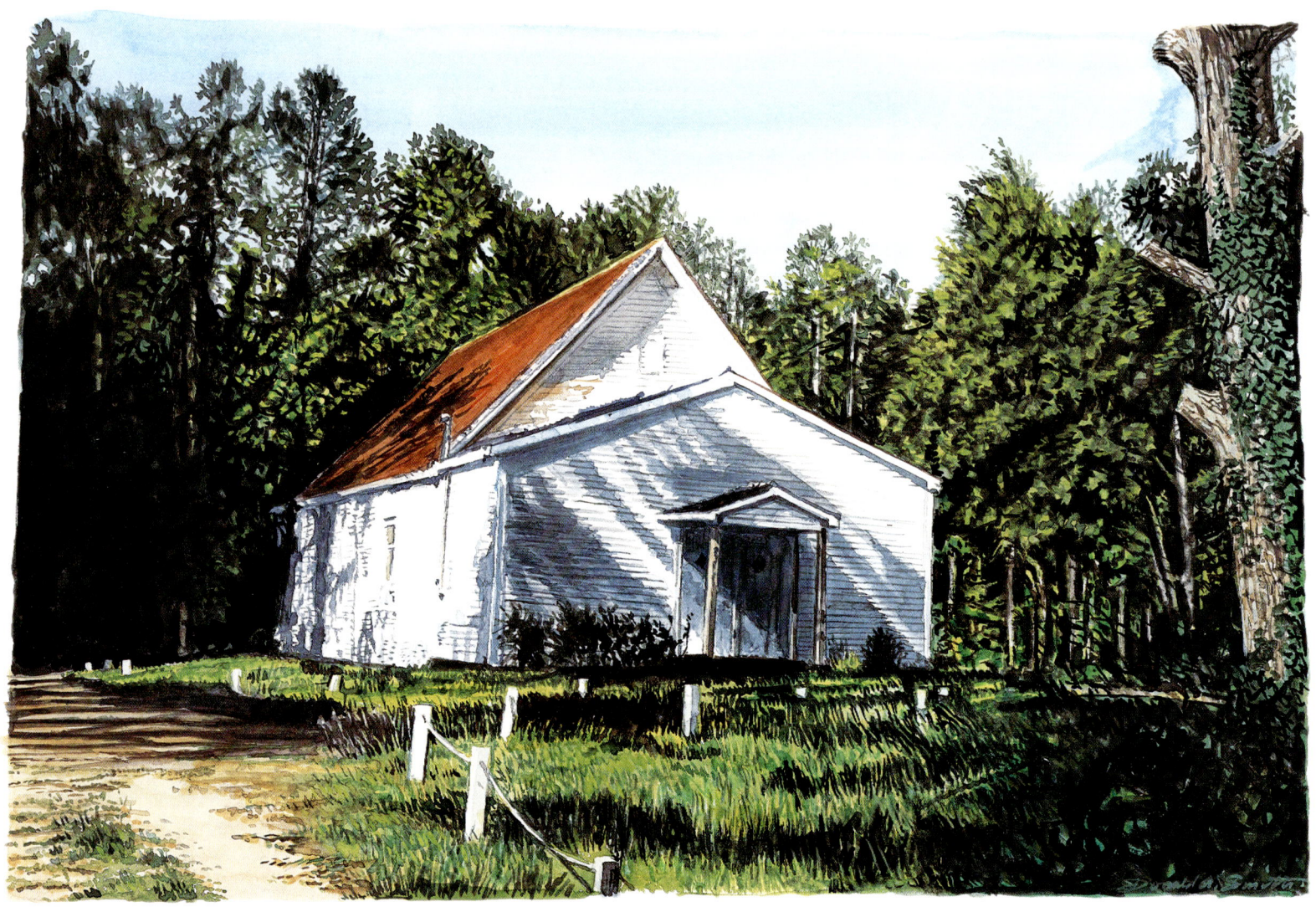

Siloam

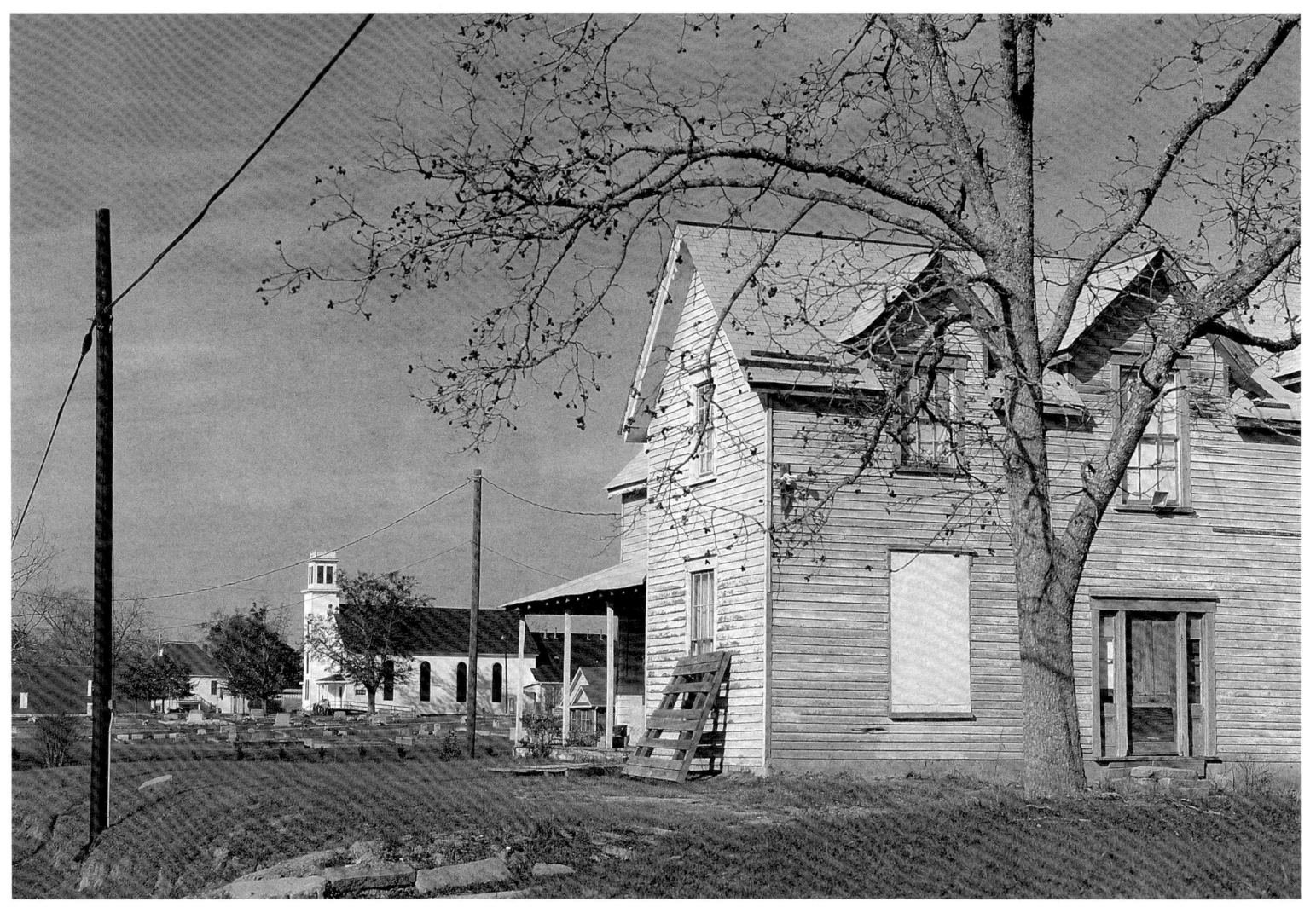

White Plains

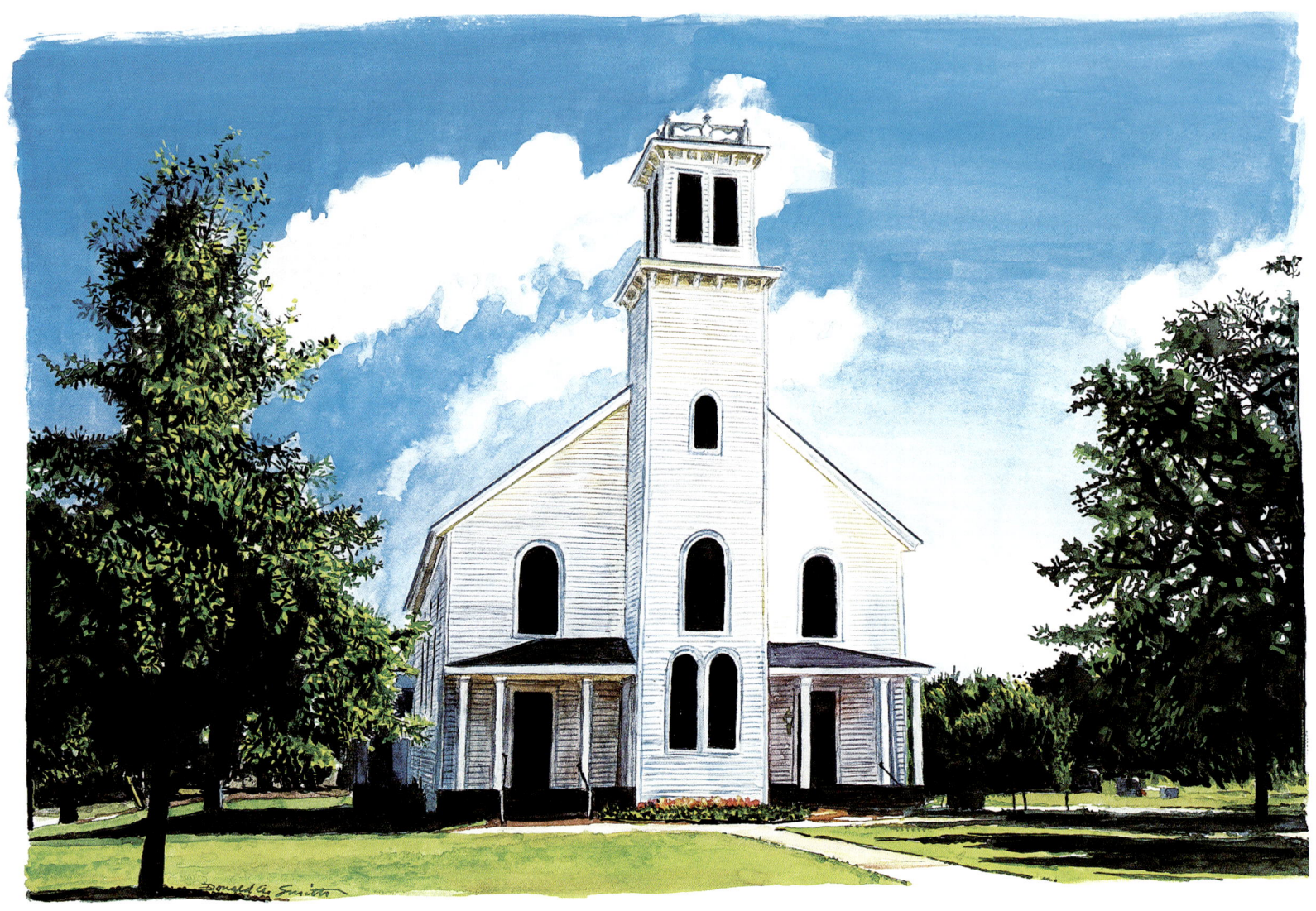

White Plains

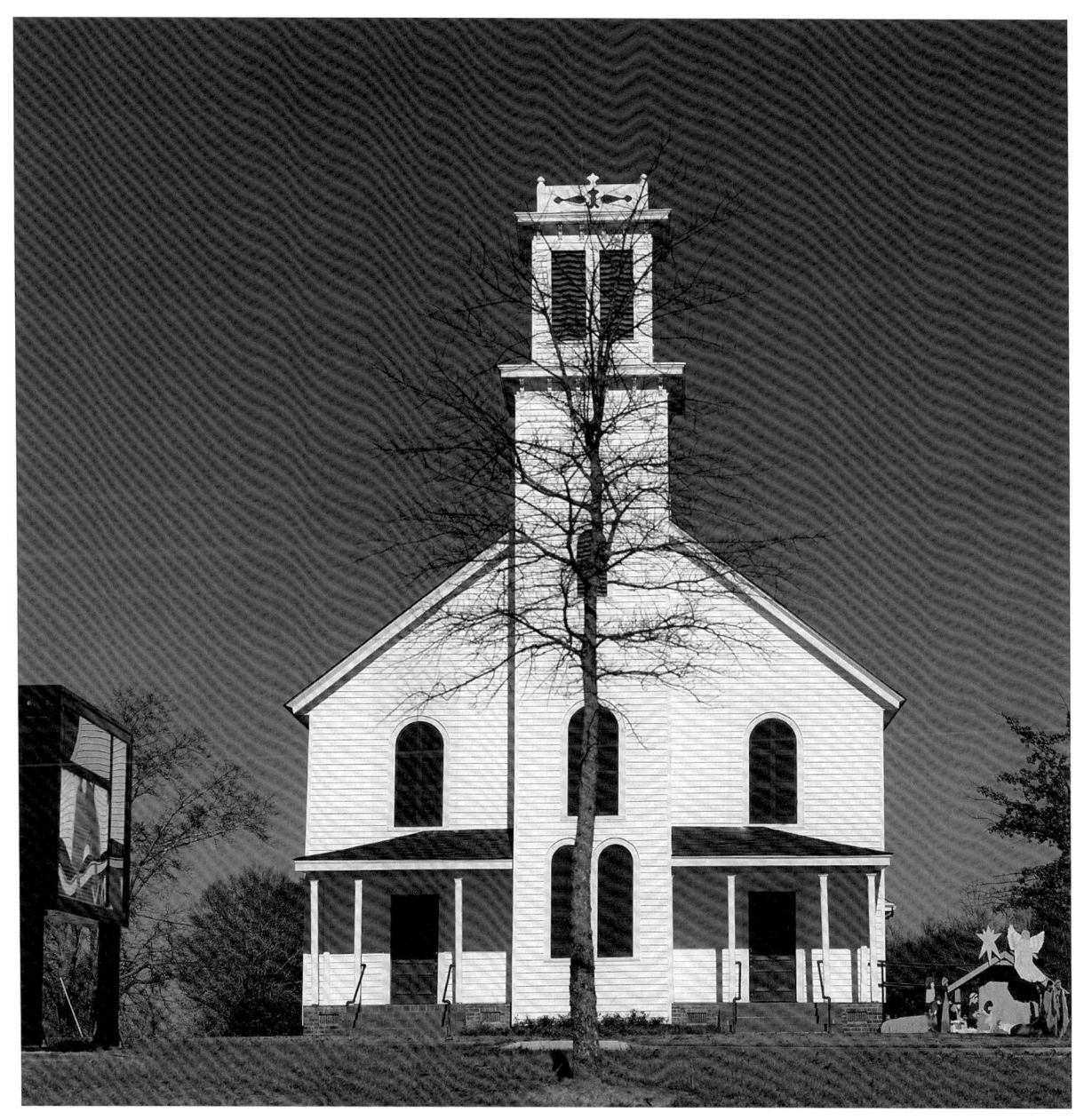

White Plains

CHURCHES

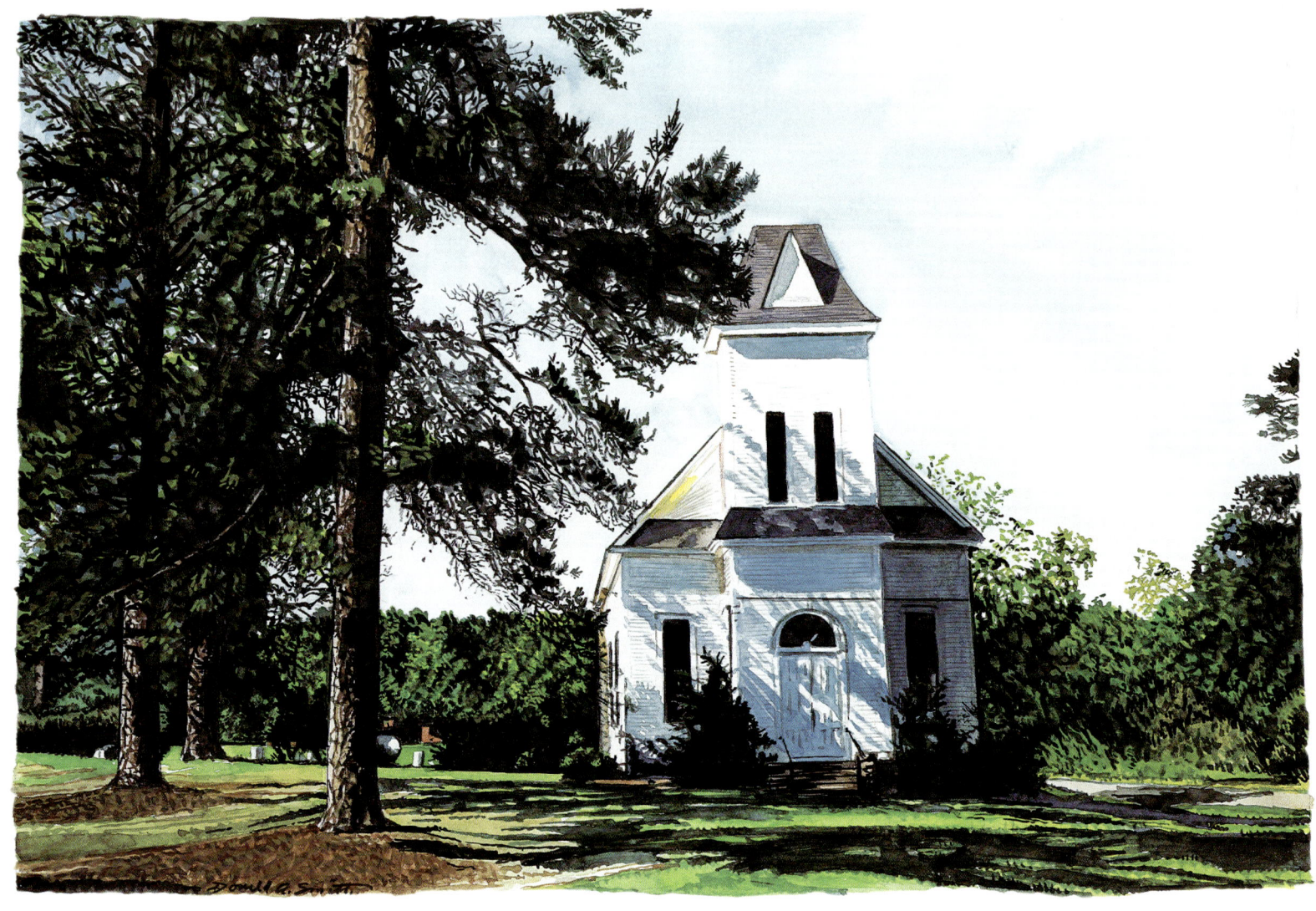

Siloam

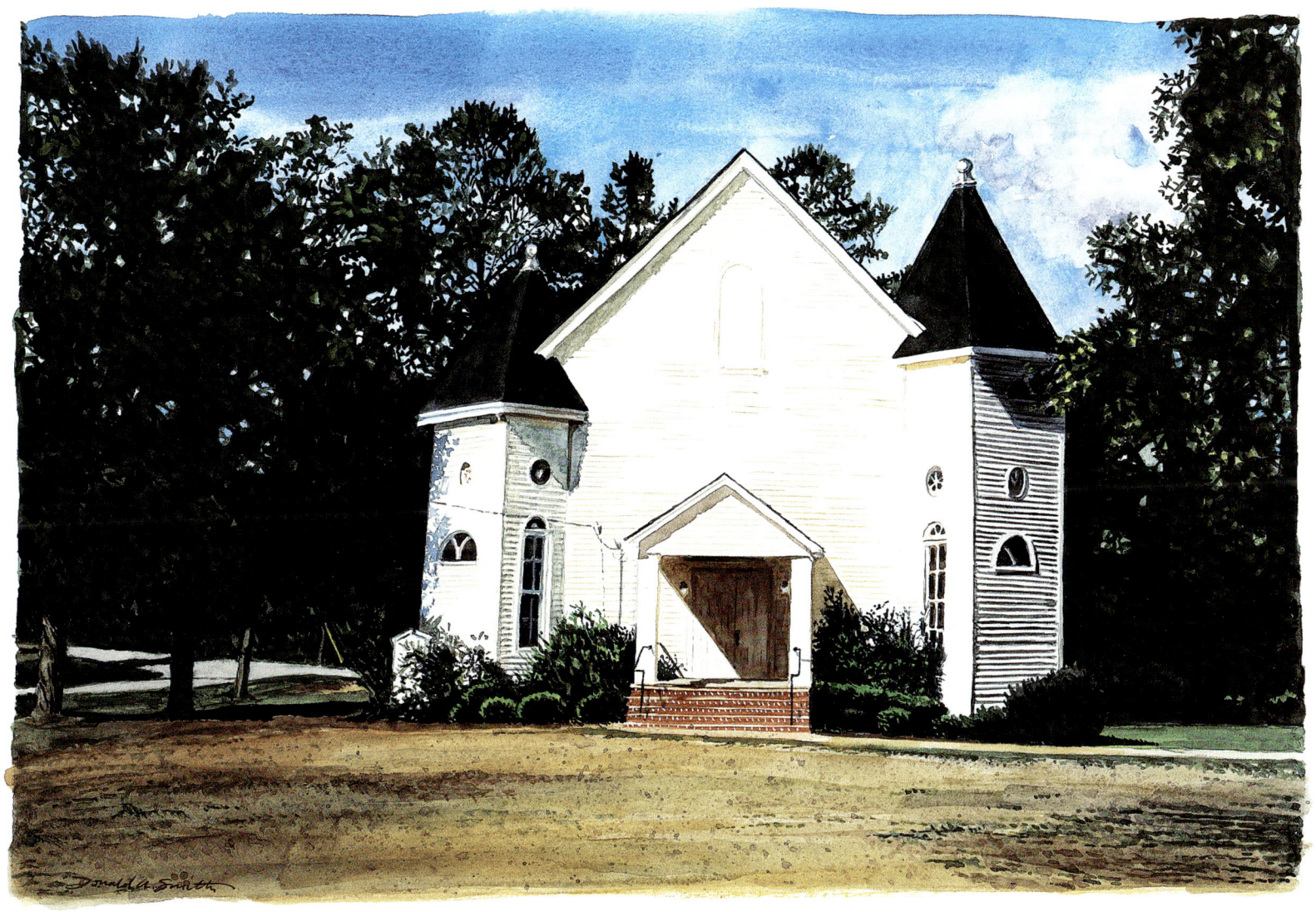

Siloam

CHURCHES

47

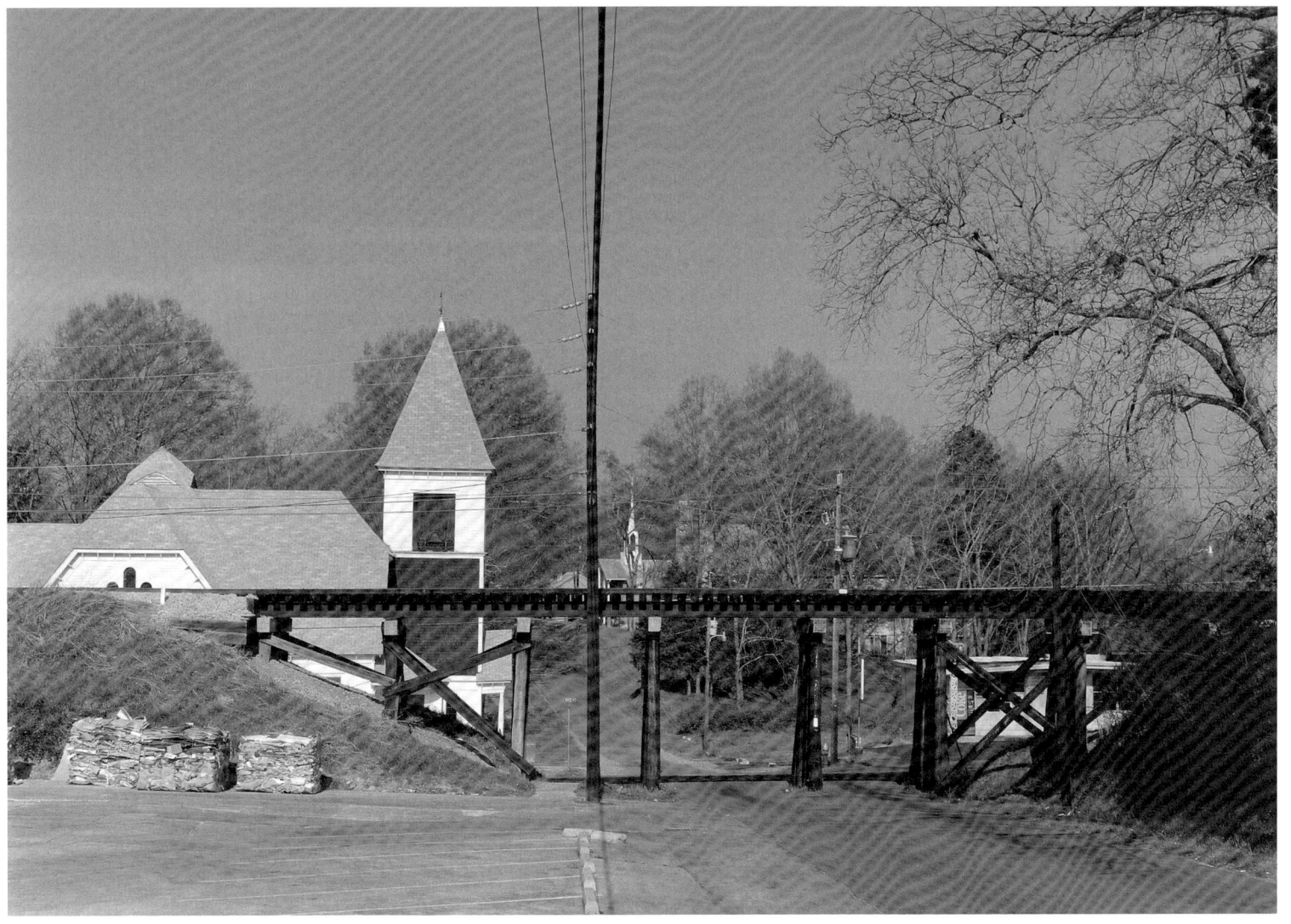

Eatonton

CHURCHES

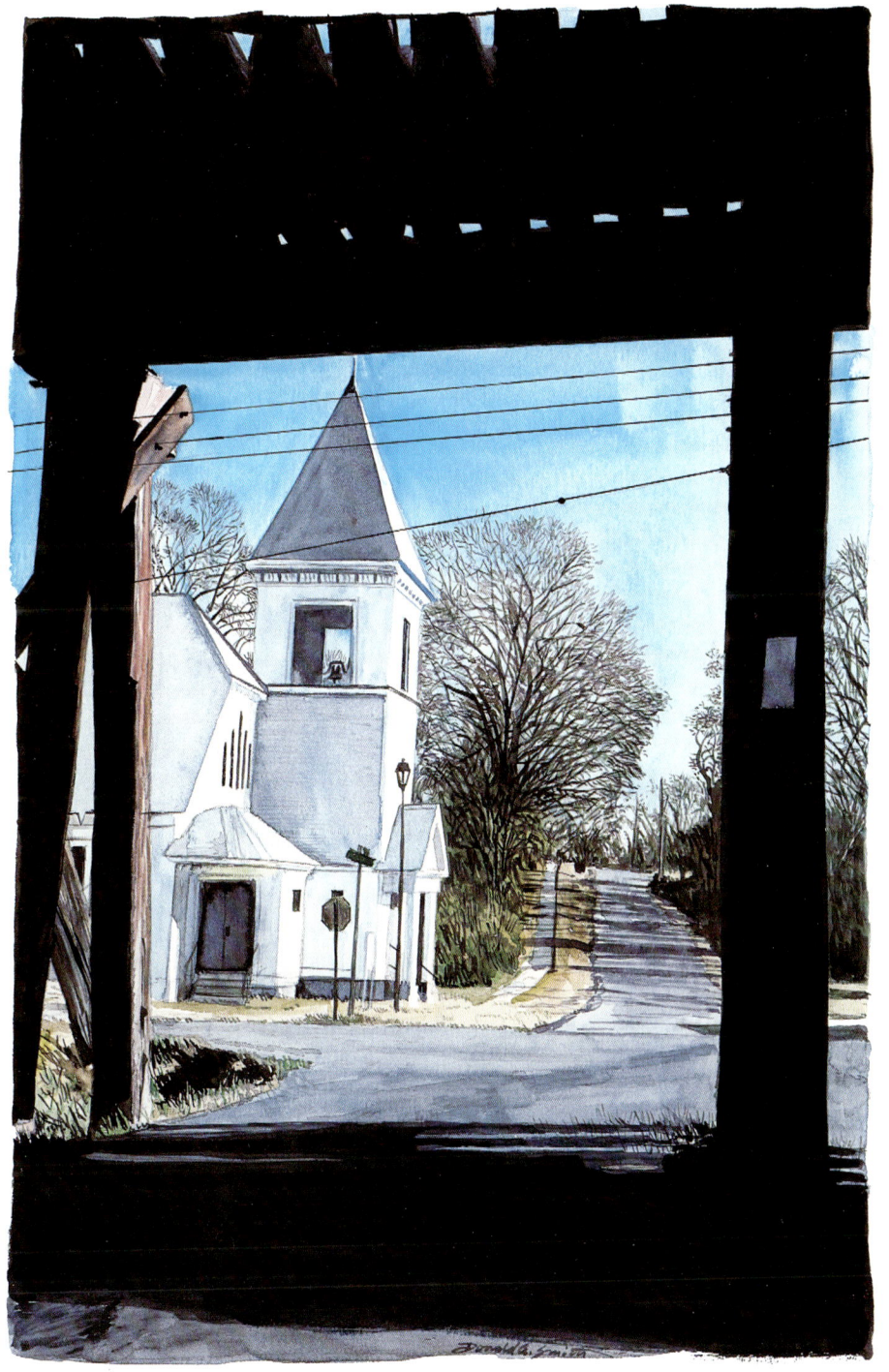

Eatonton

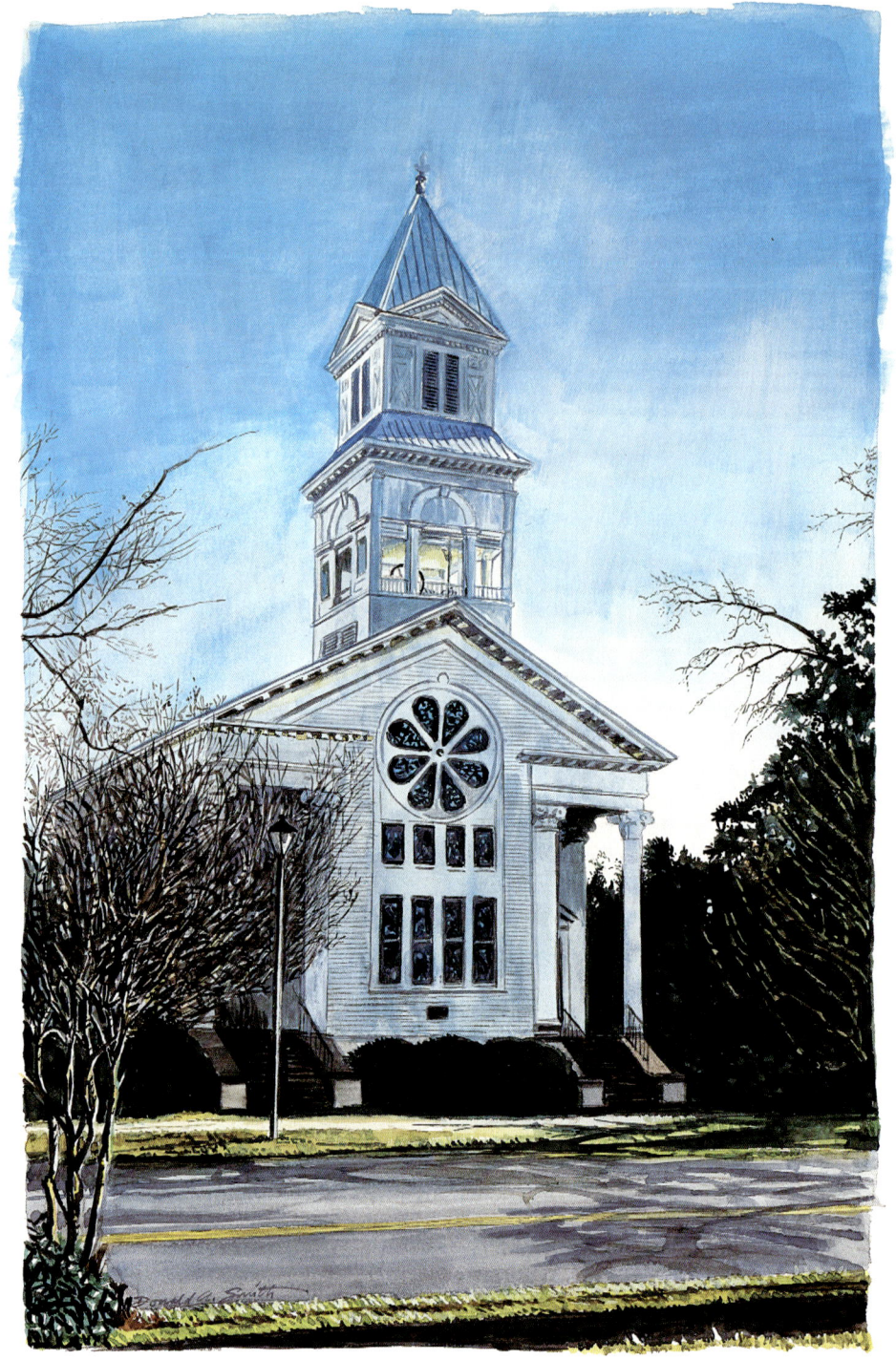

Eatonton

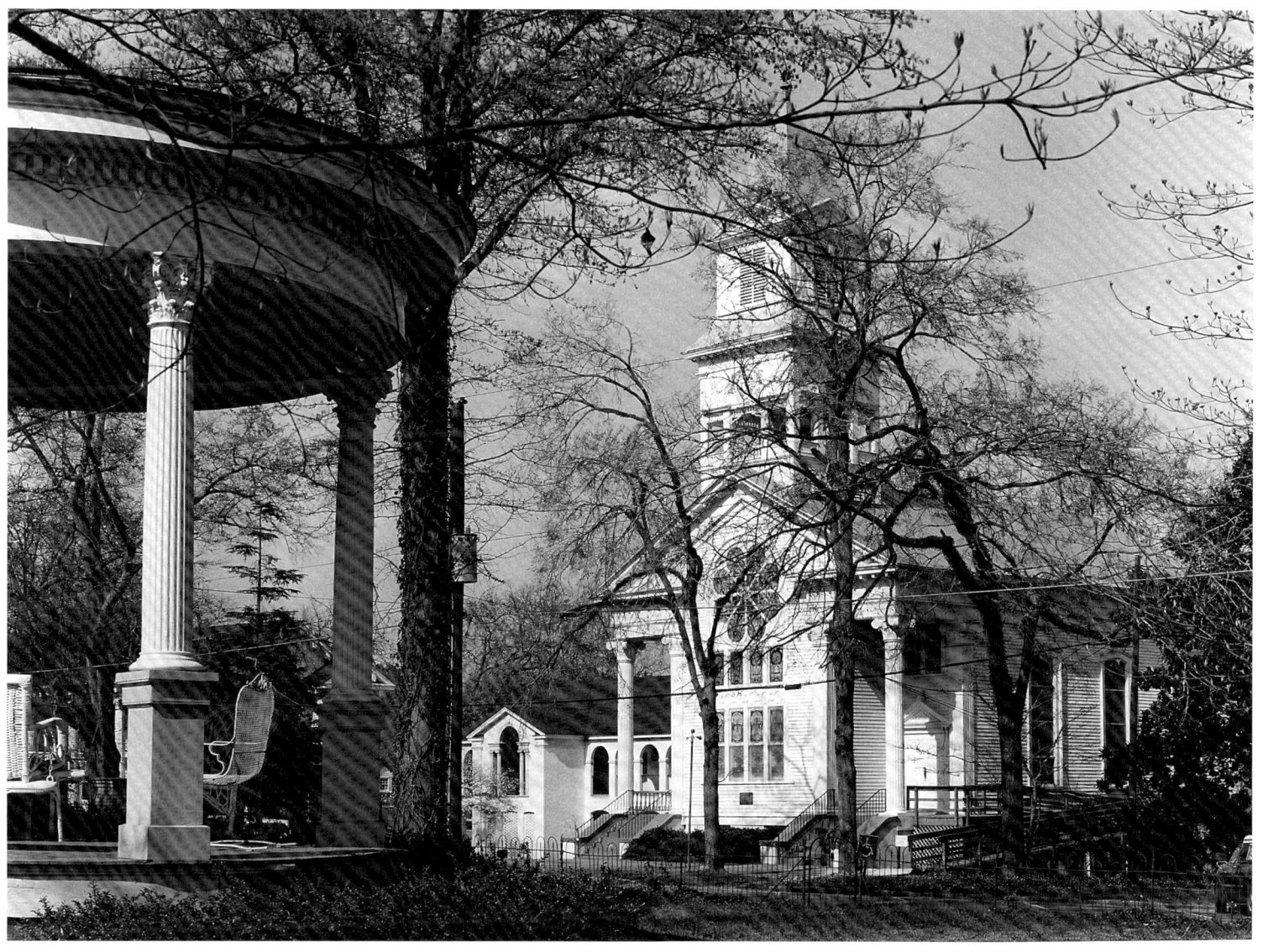

Eatonton

CHURCHES

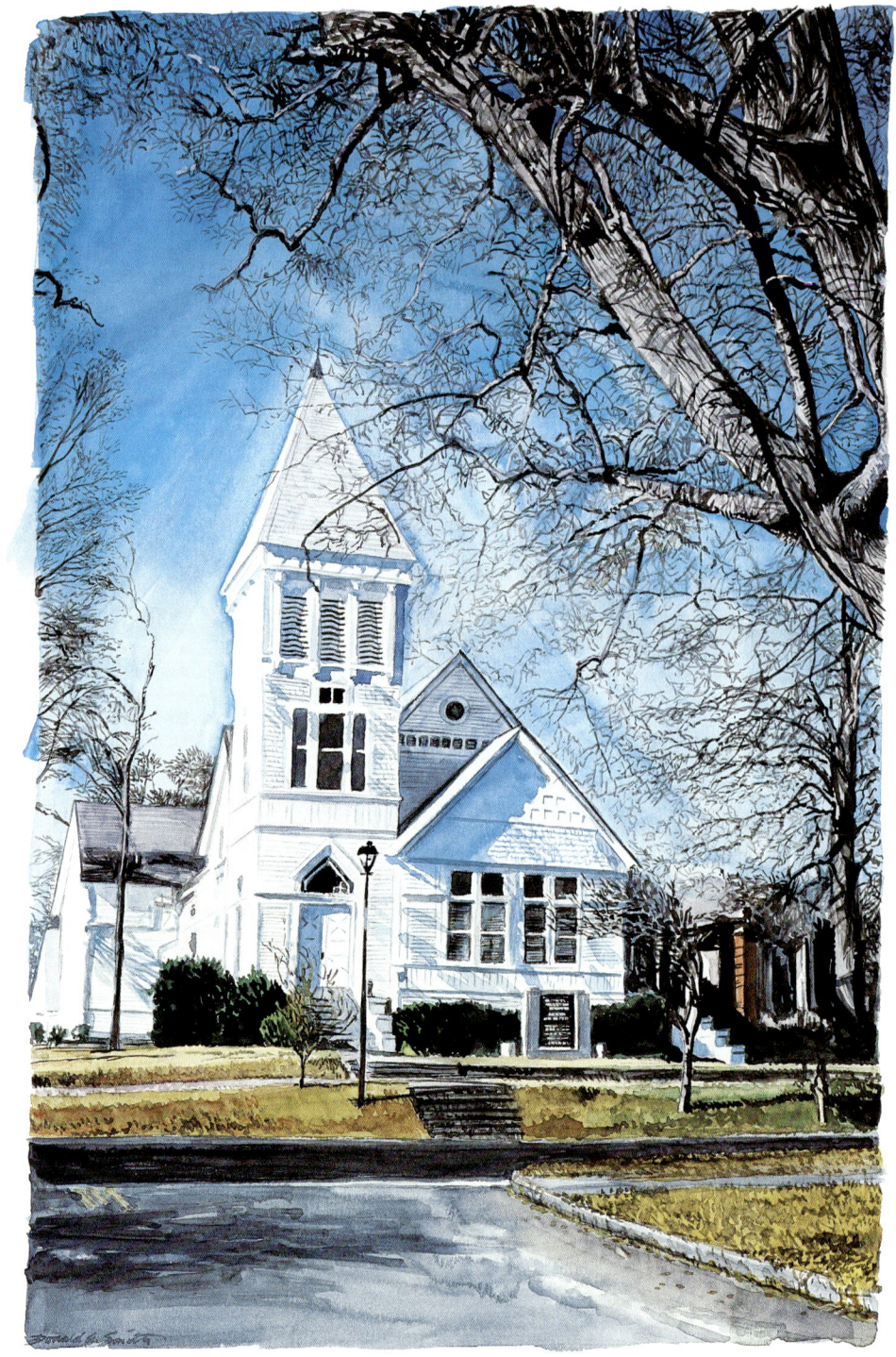

Eatonton

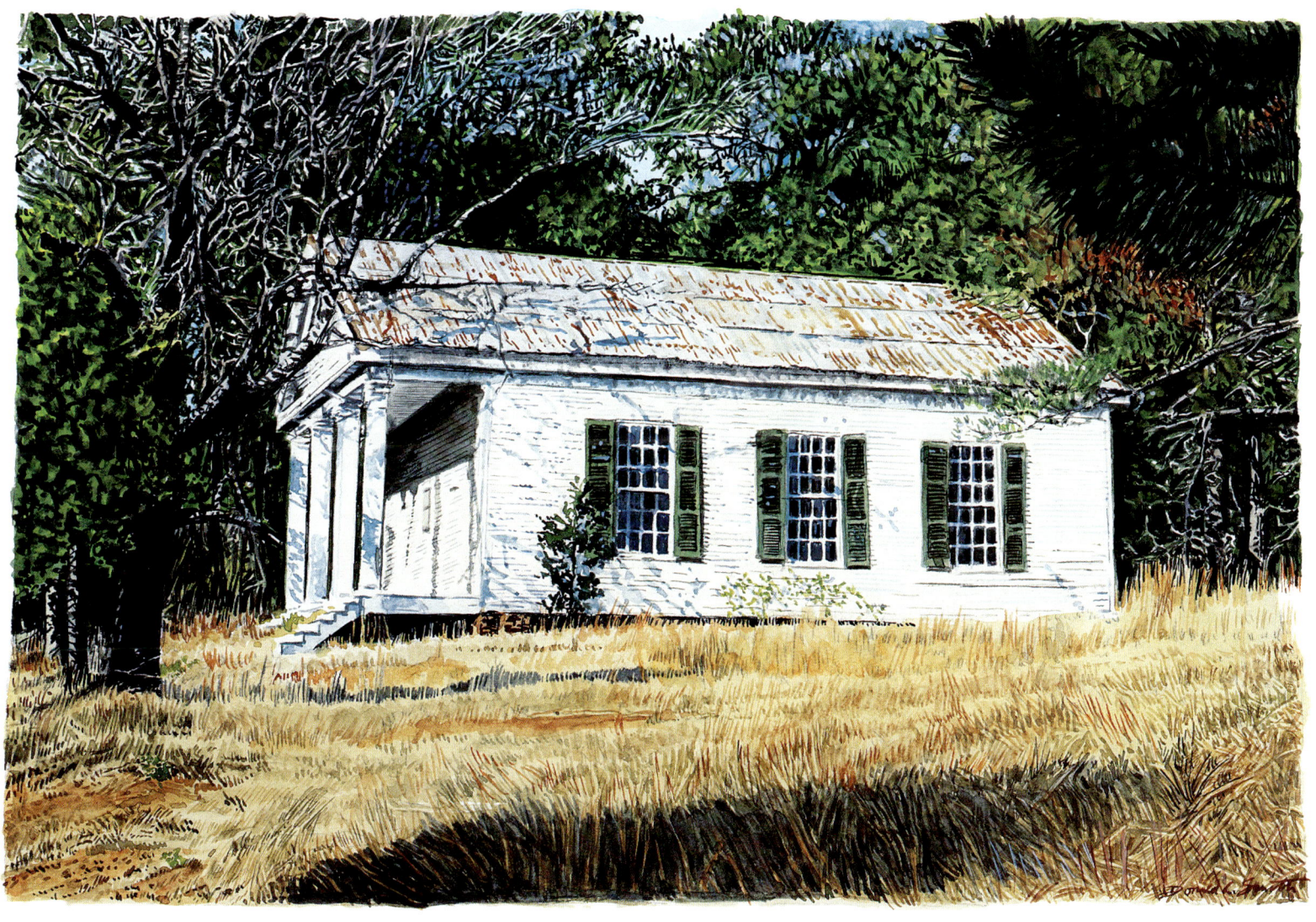

Near Sparta

CHURCHES

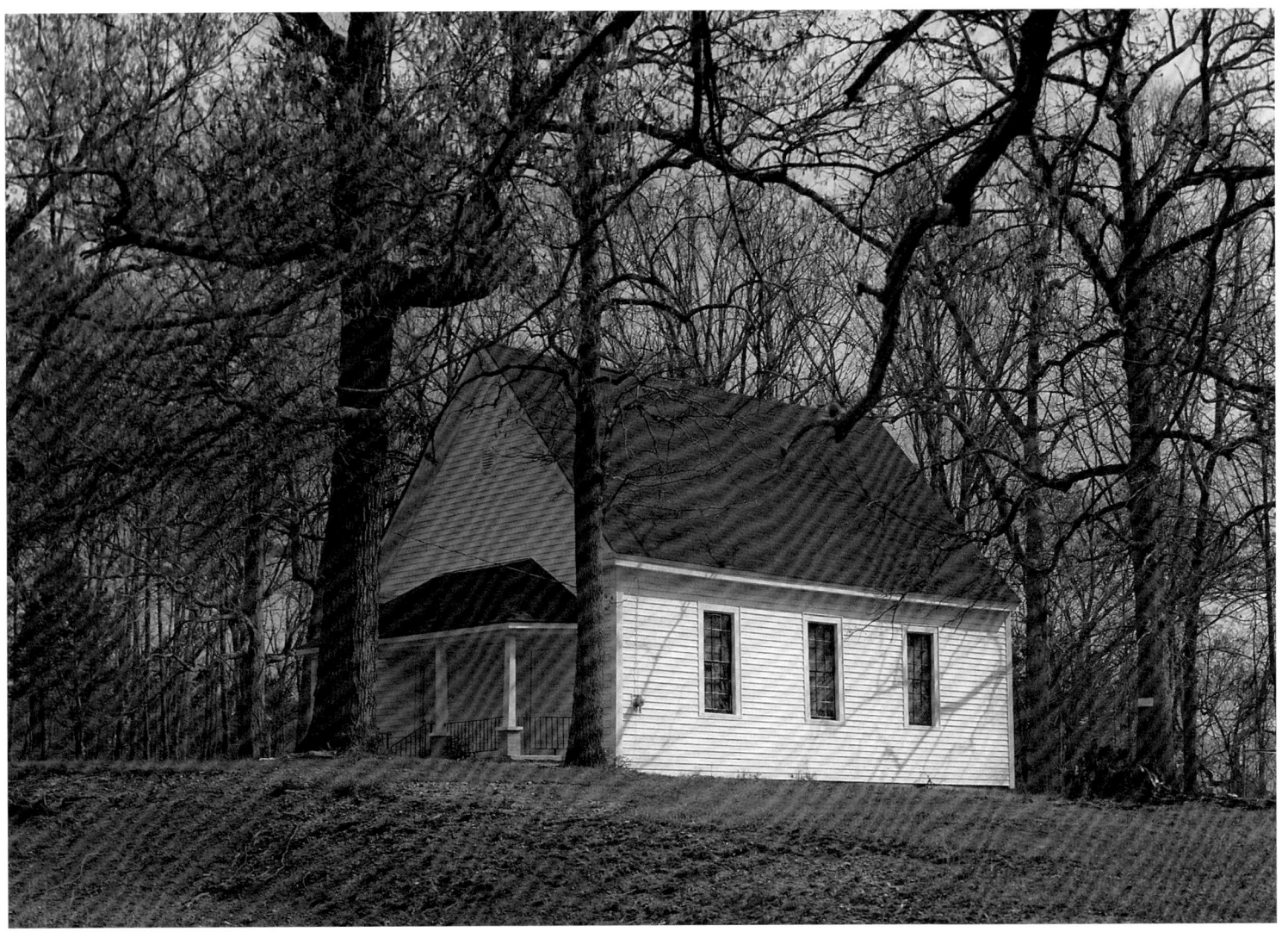

Near Eatonton

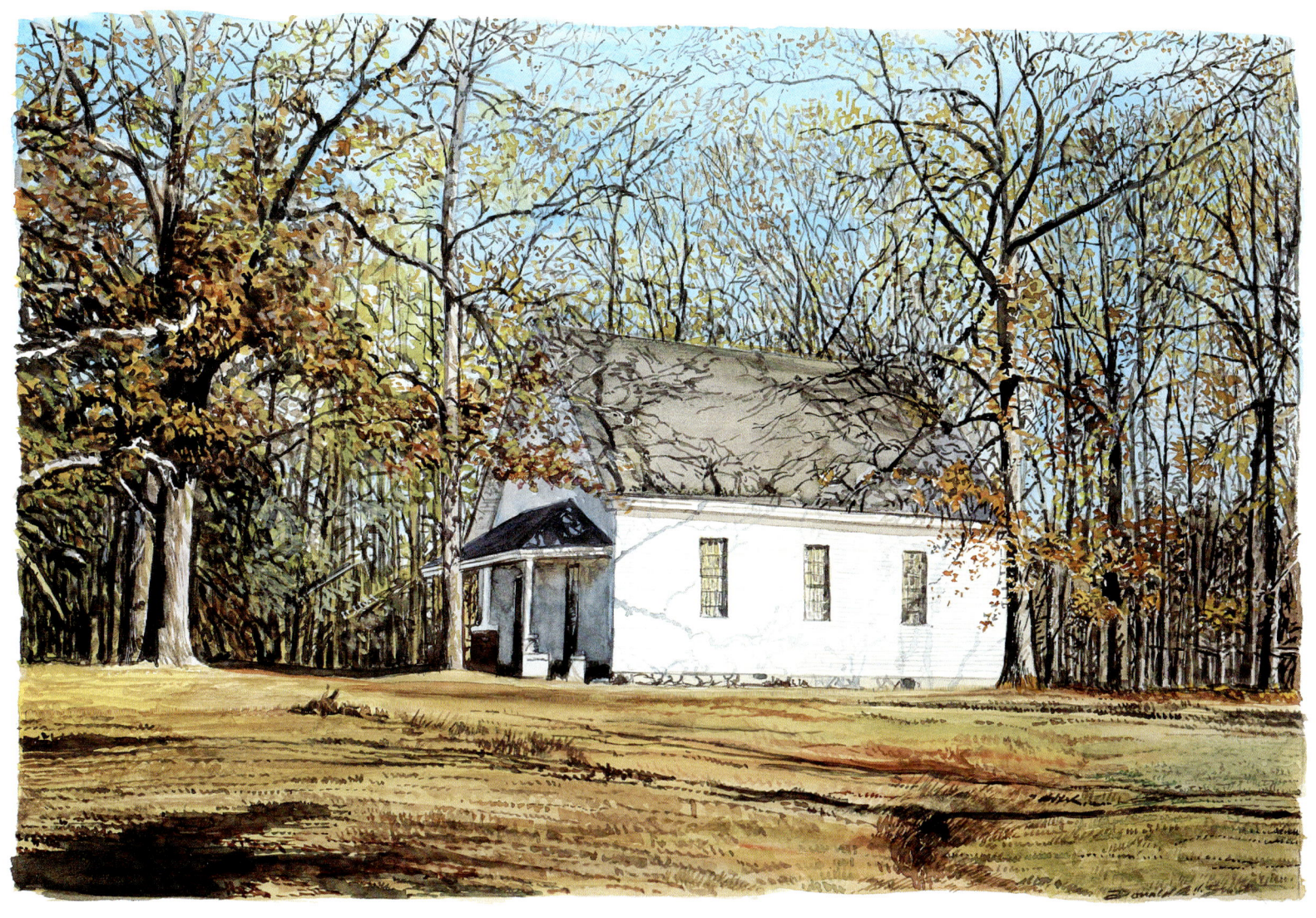

Near Eatonton

CHURCHES

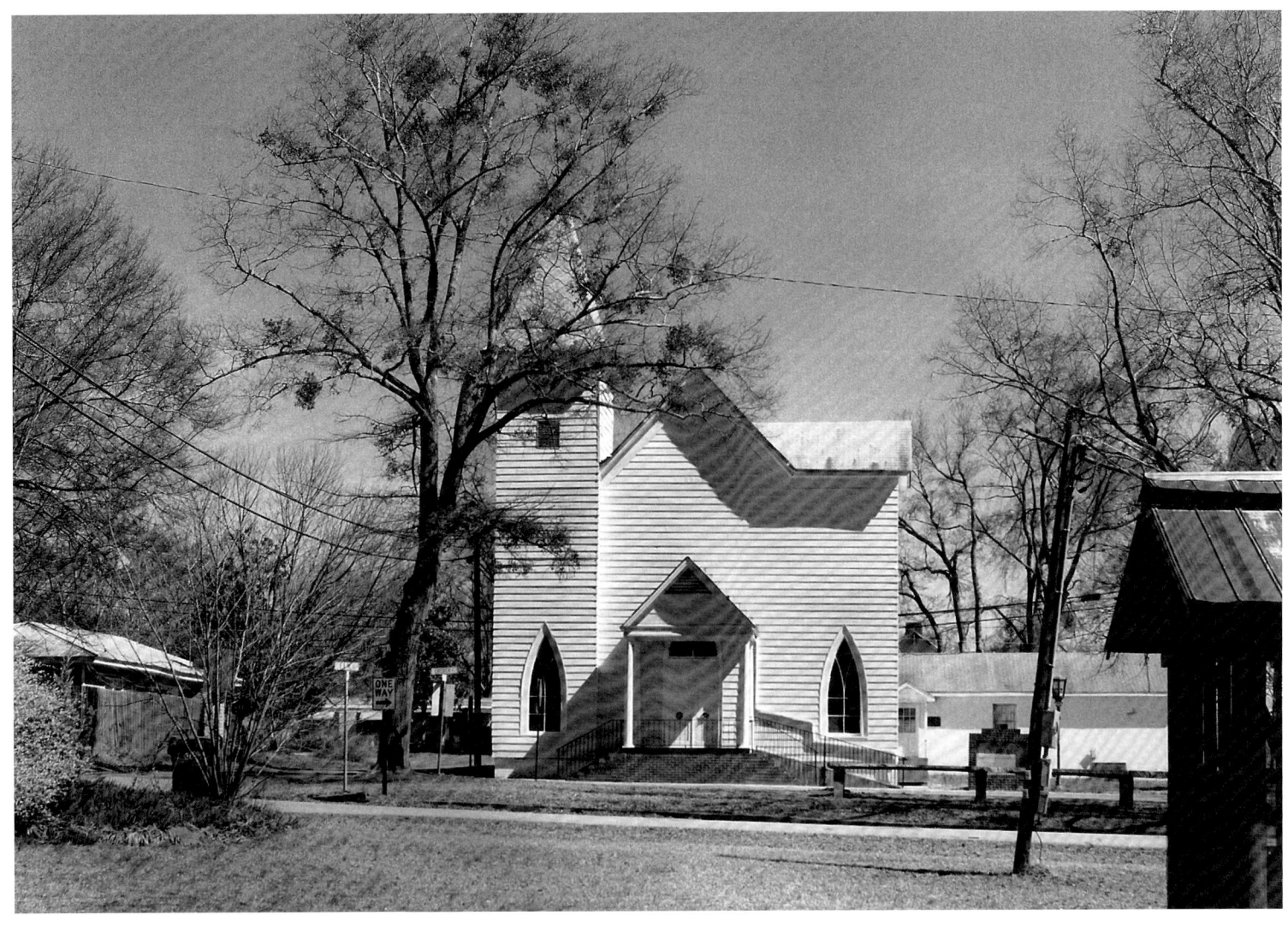

Crawford

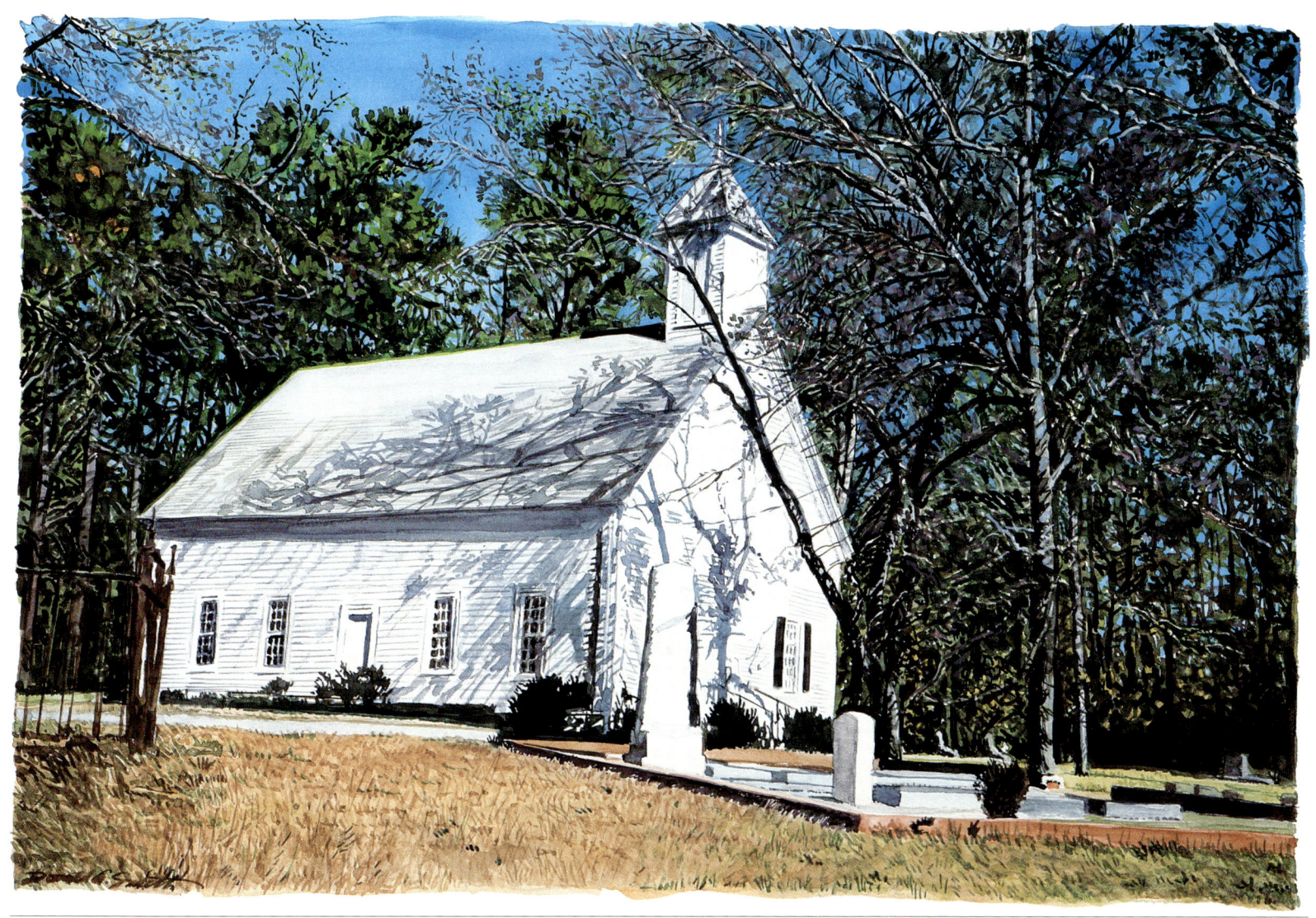

Old Clinton

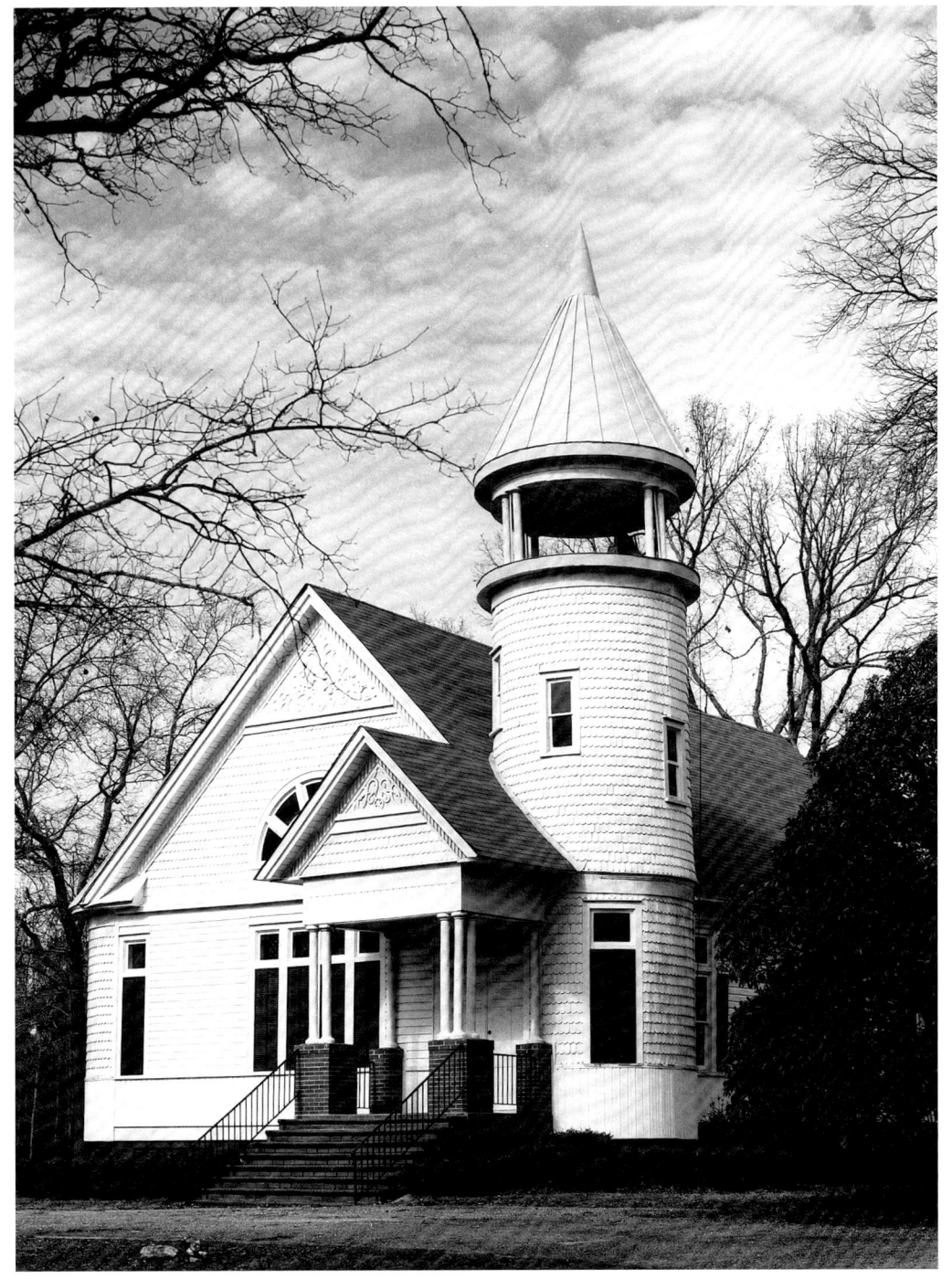

Sharon

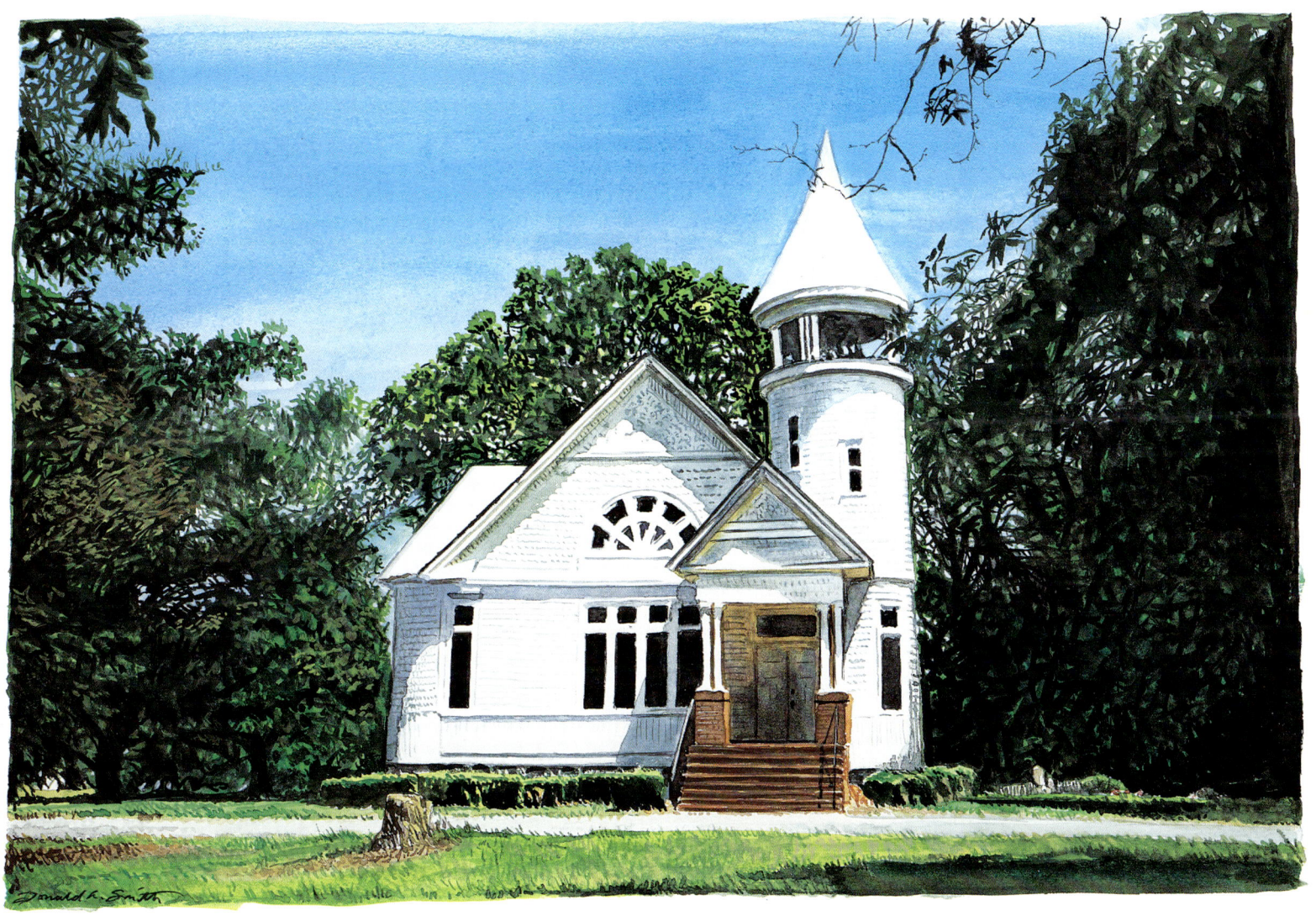

Sharon

CHURCHES

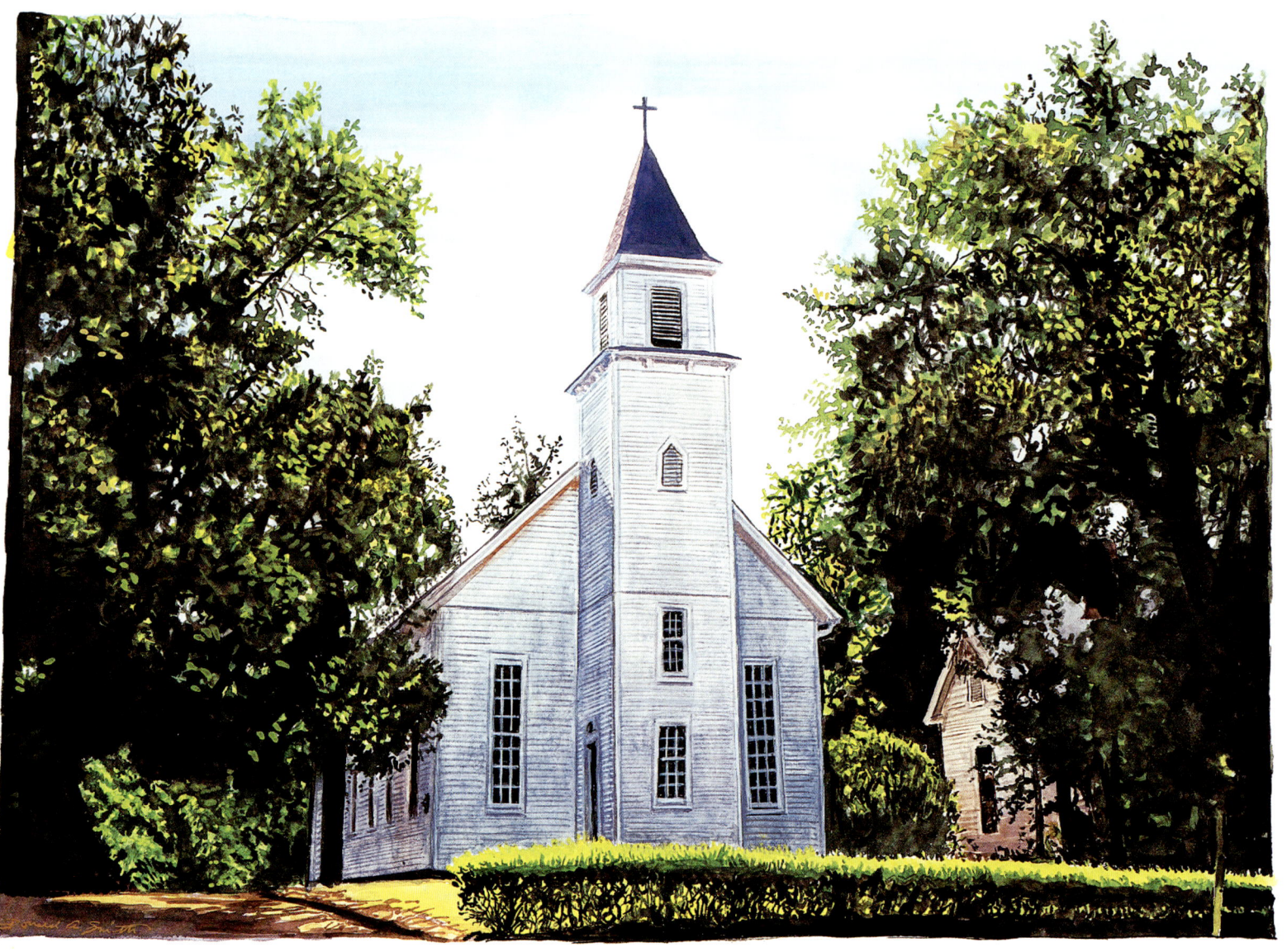

Sharon

CHURCHES

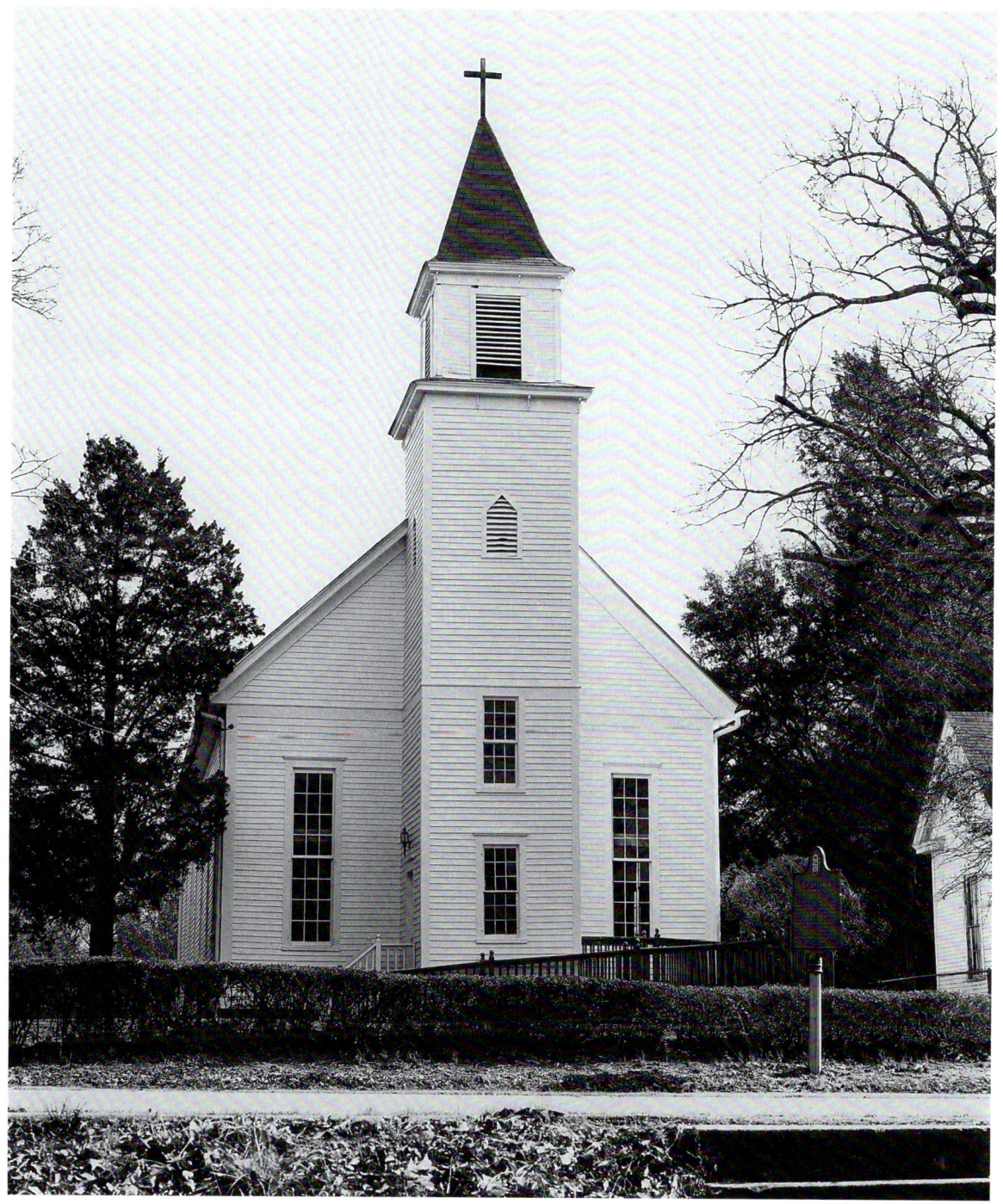

Sharon

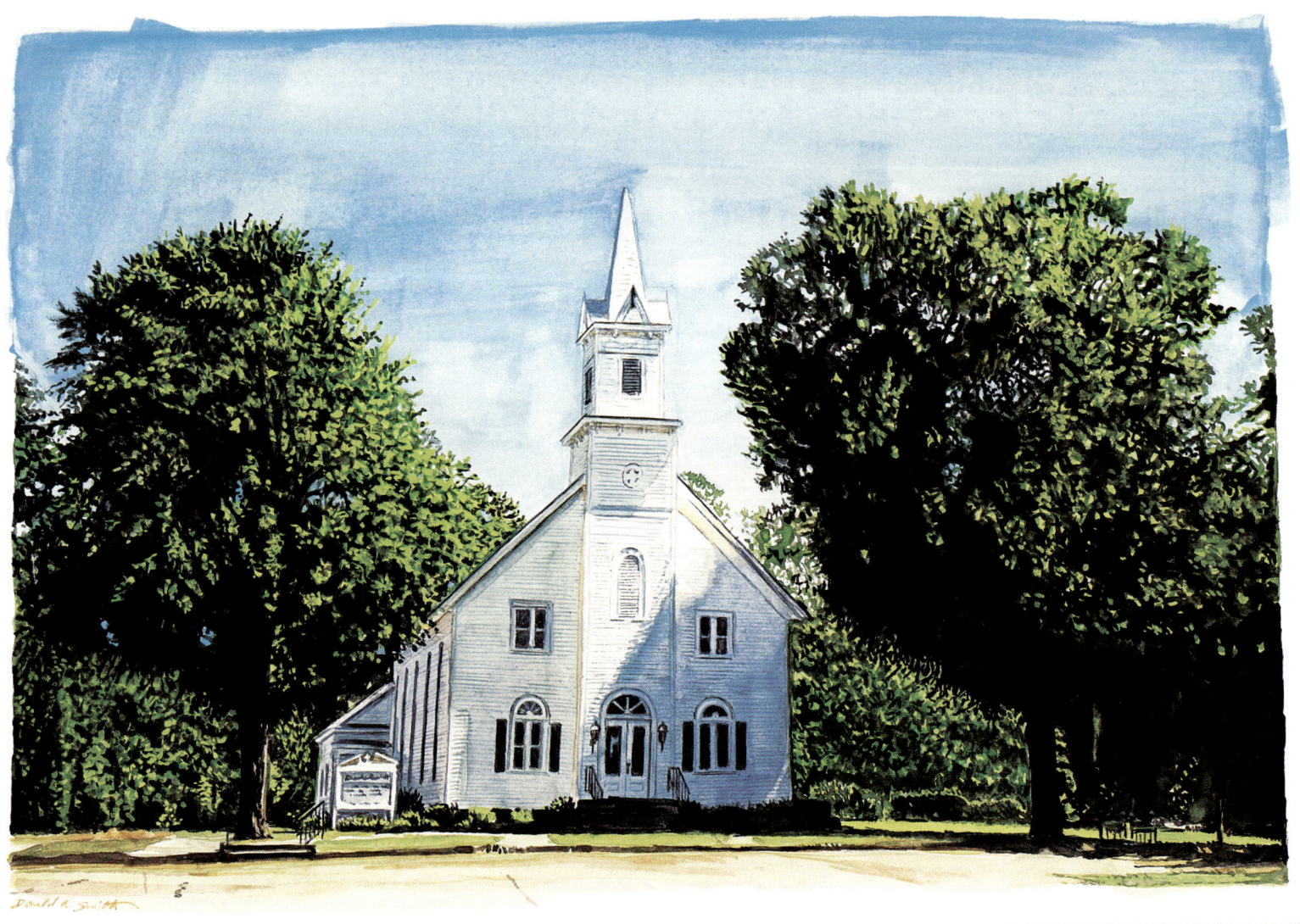

Crawfordville

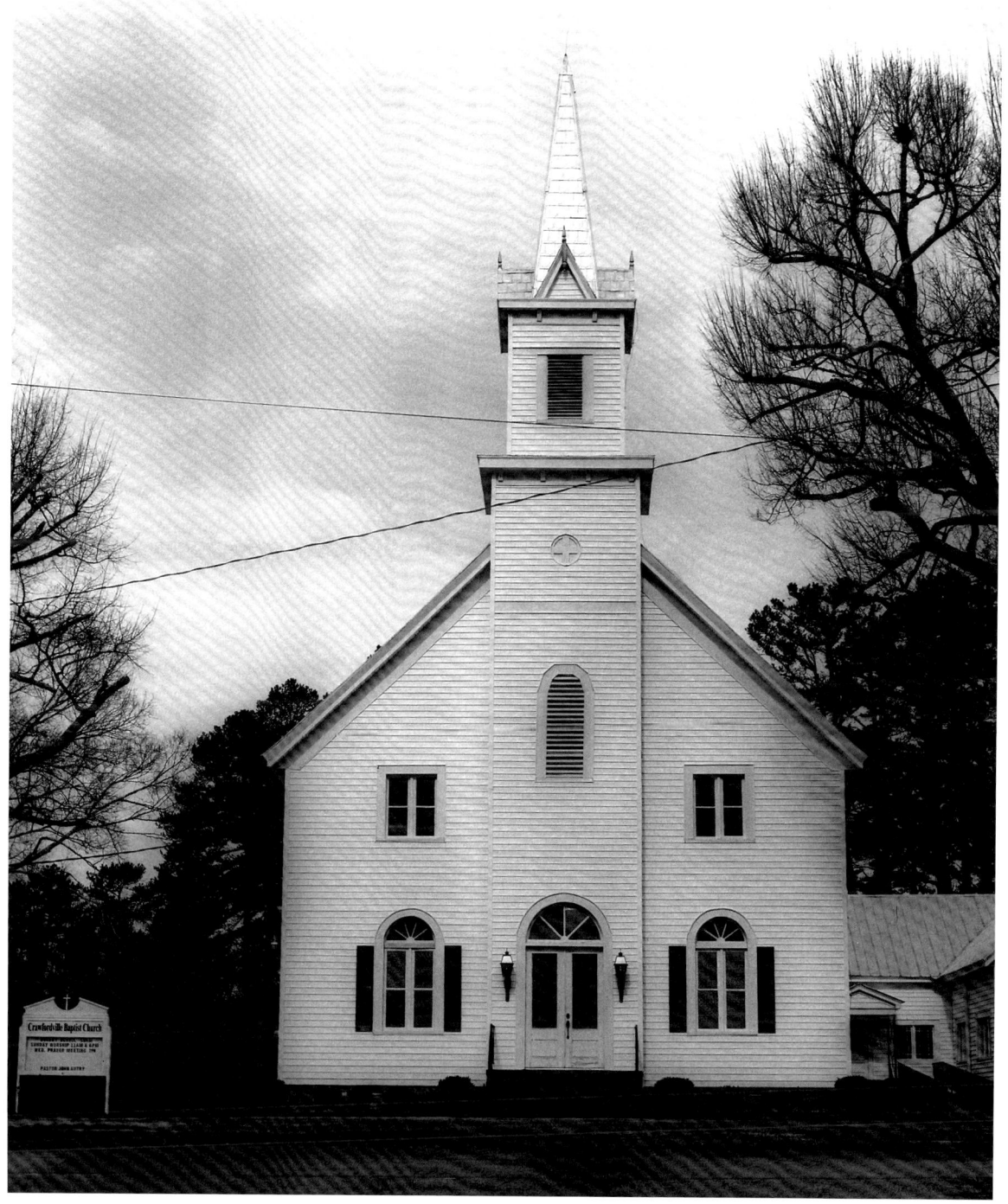

Crawfordville

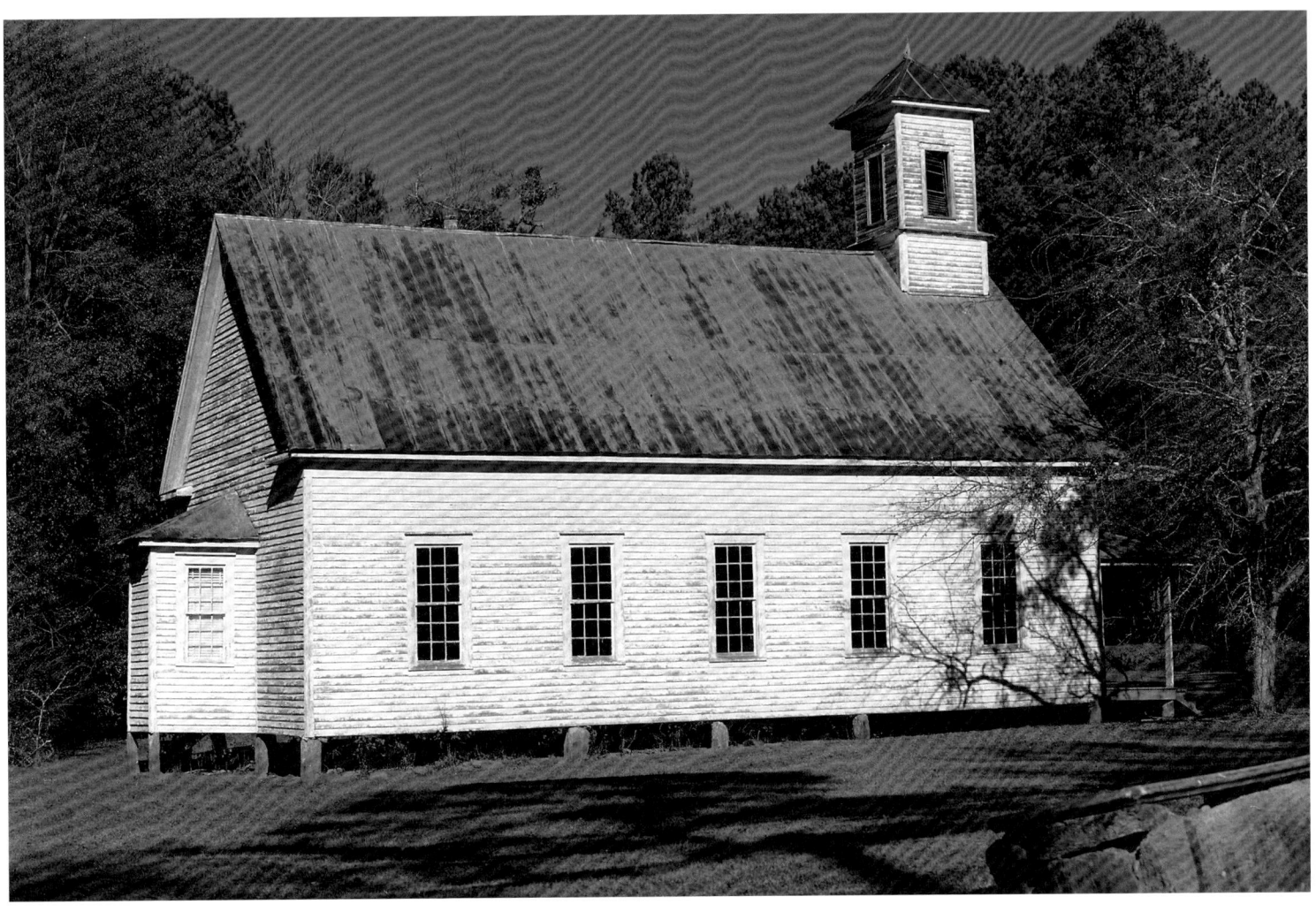

Powellton

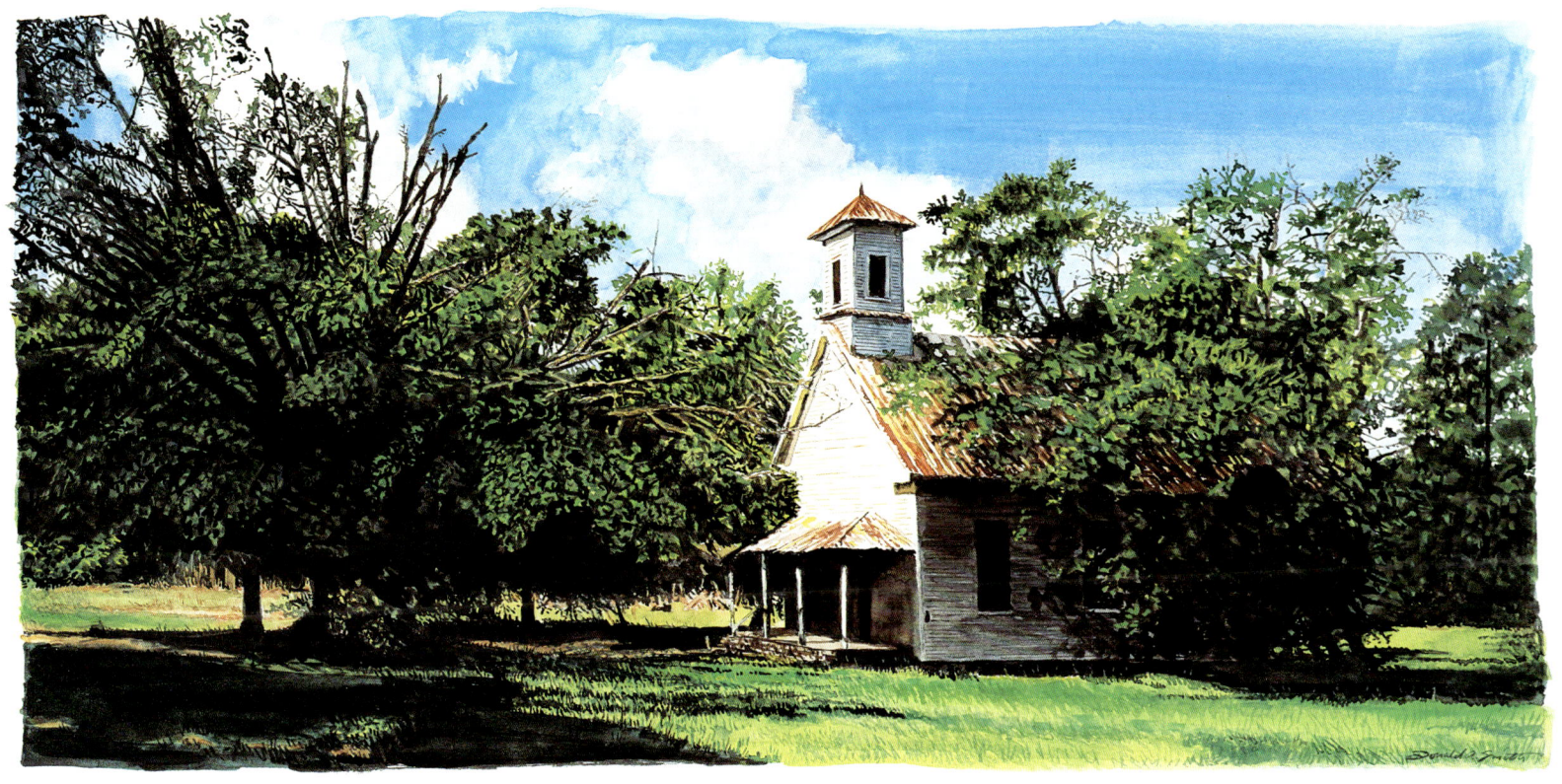

Powellton

CHURCHES

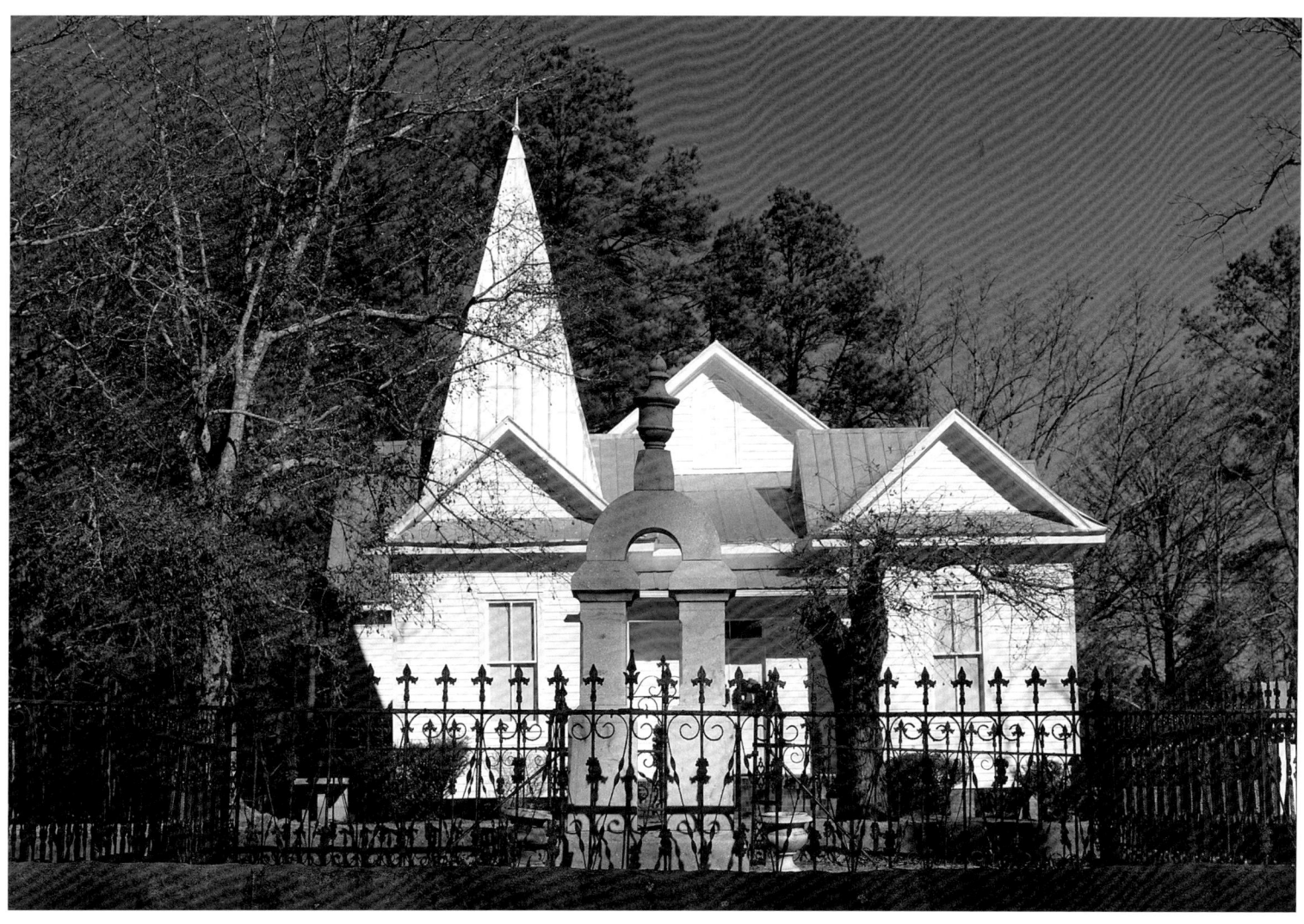

Powellton

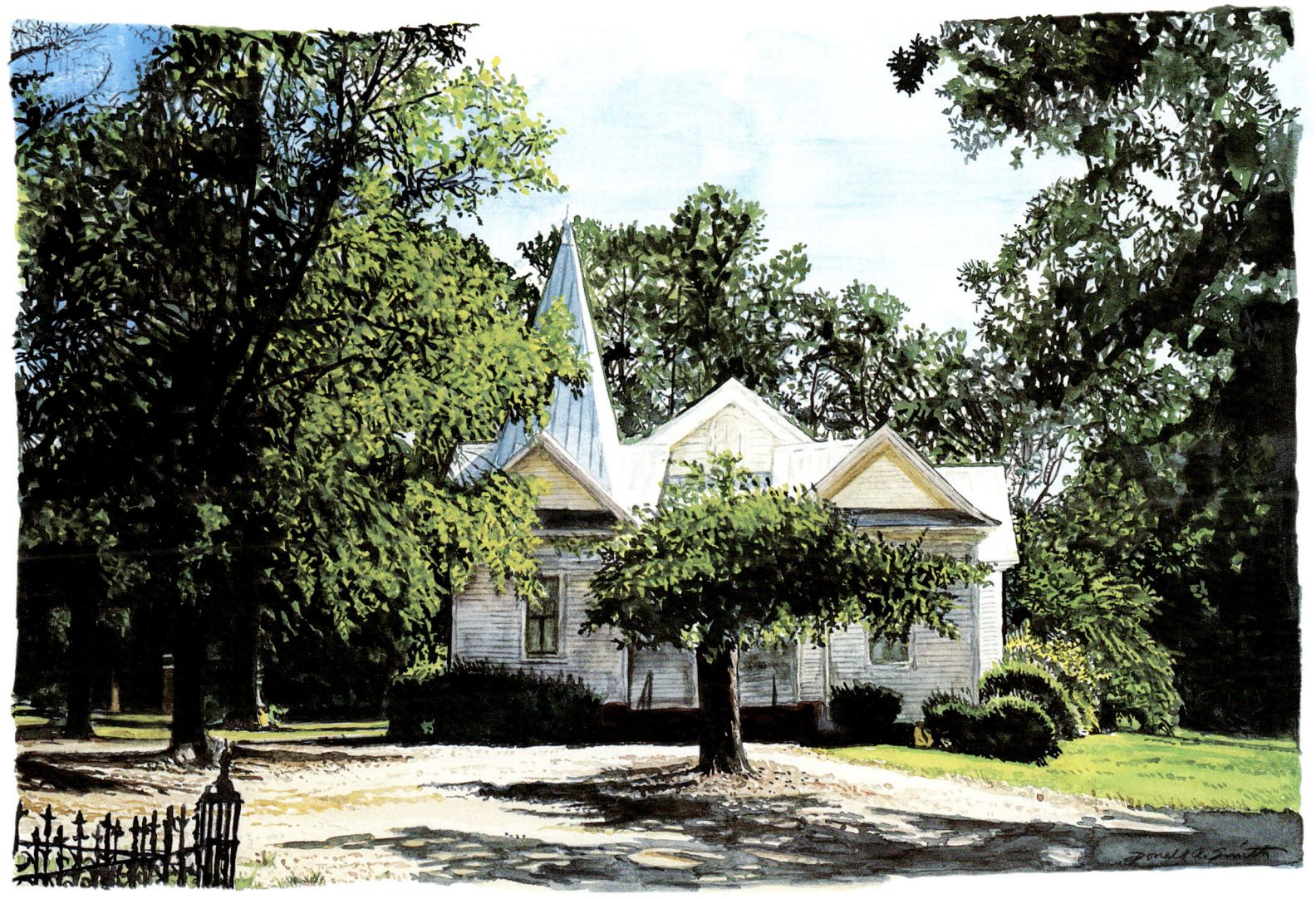

Powellton

CHURCHES

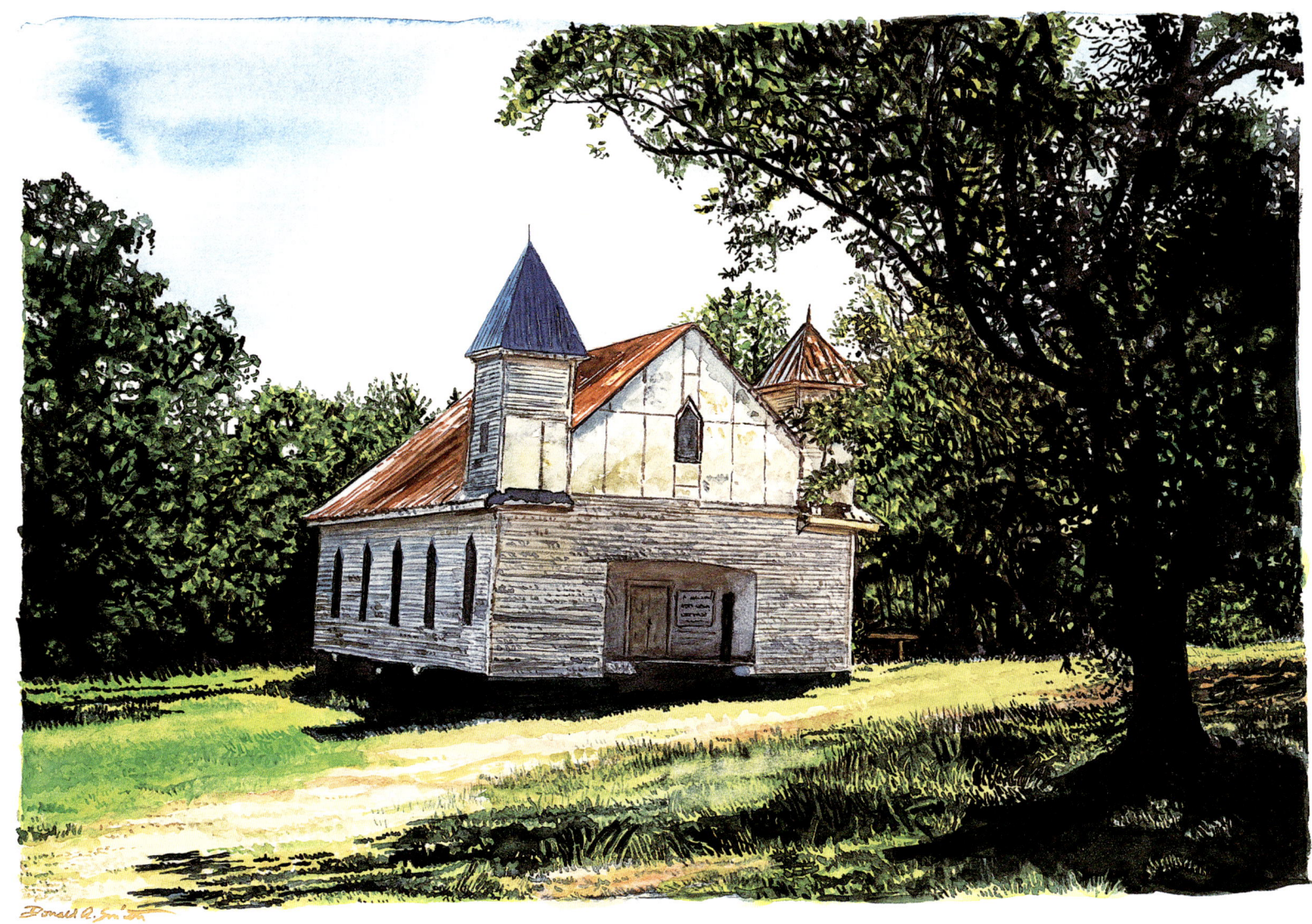

Powellton

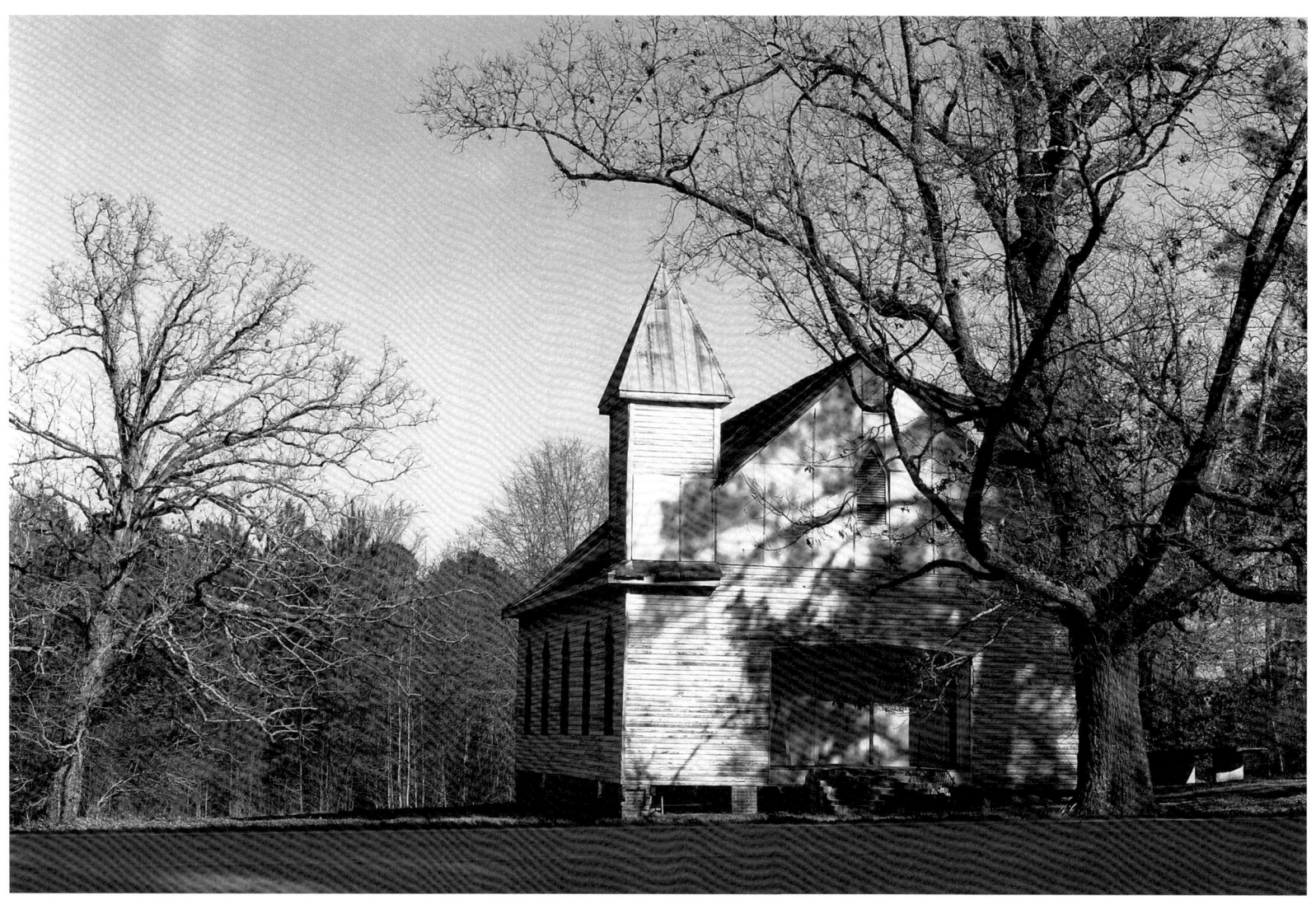

Powellton

CHURCHES

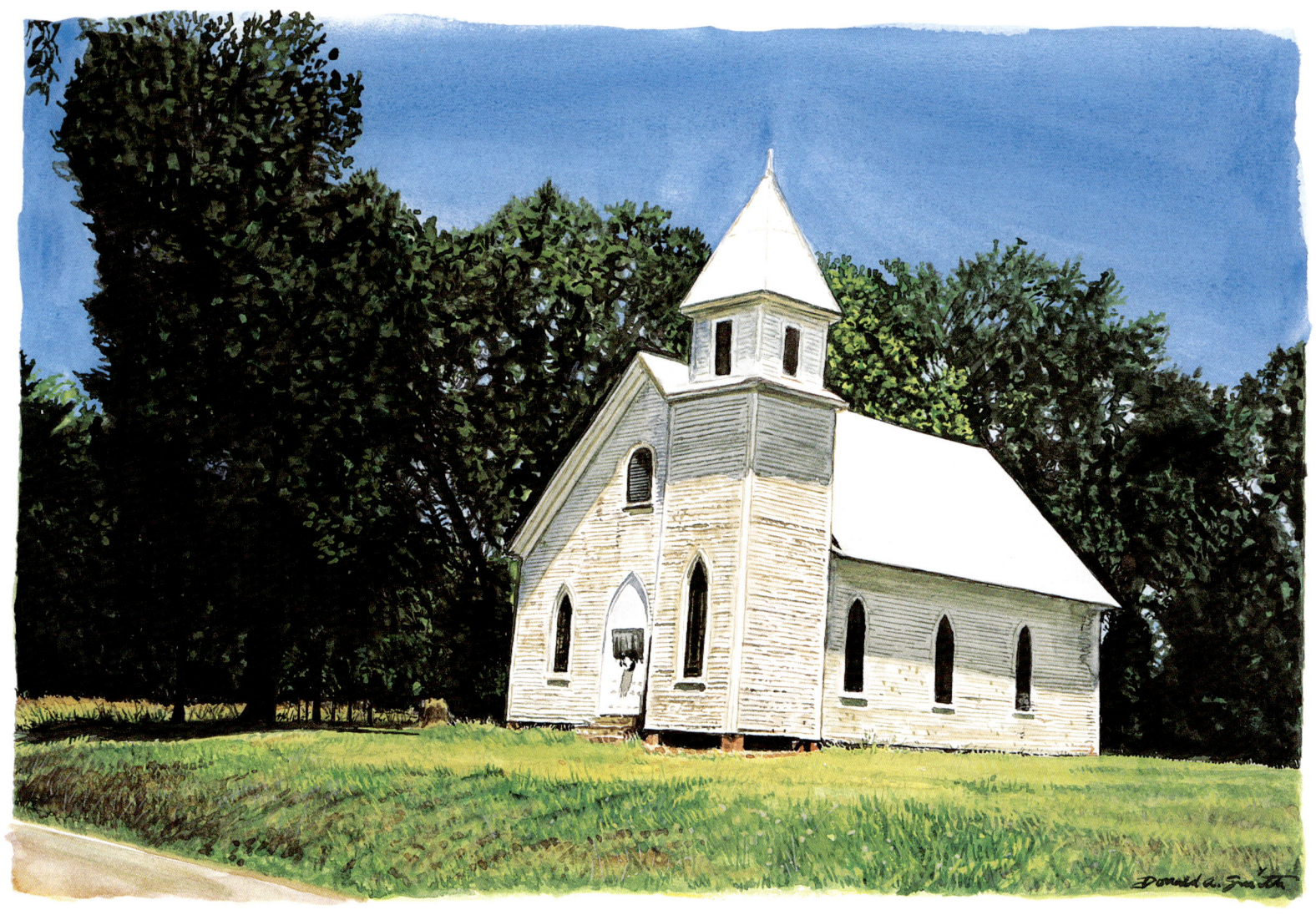

Philomath

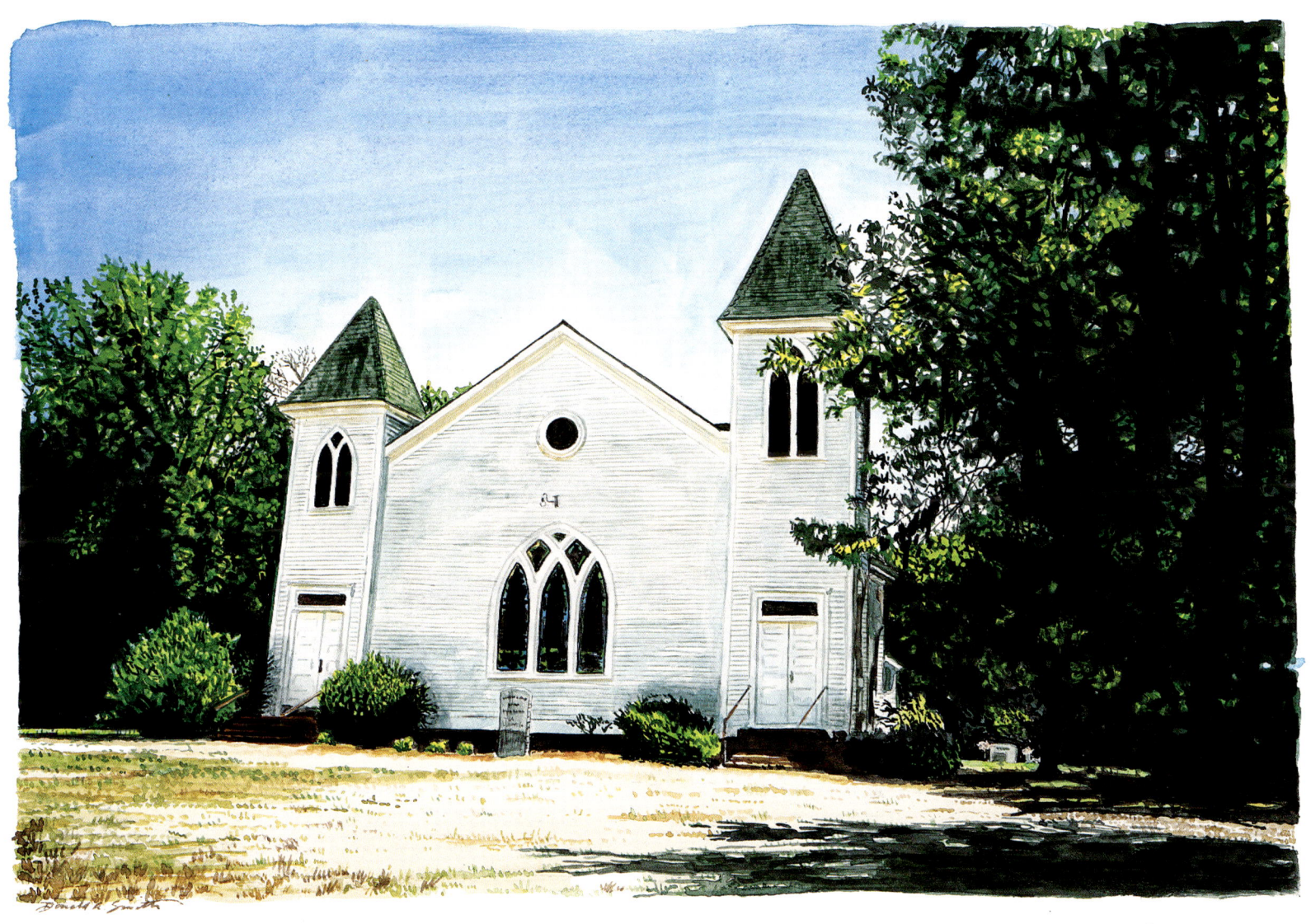

Stephens

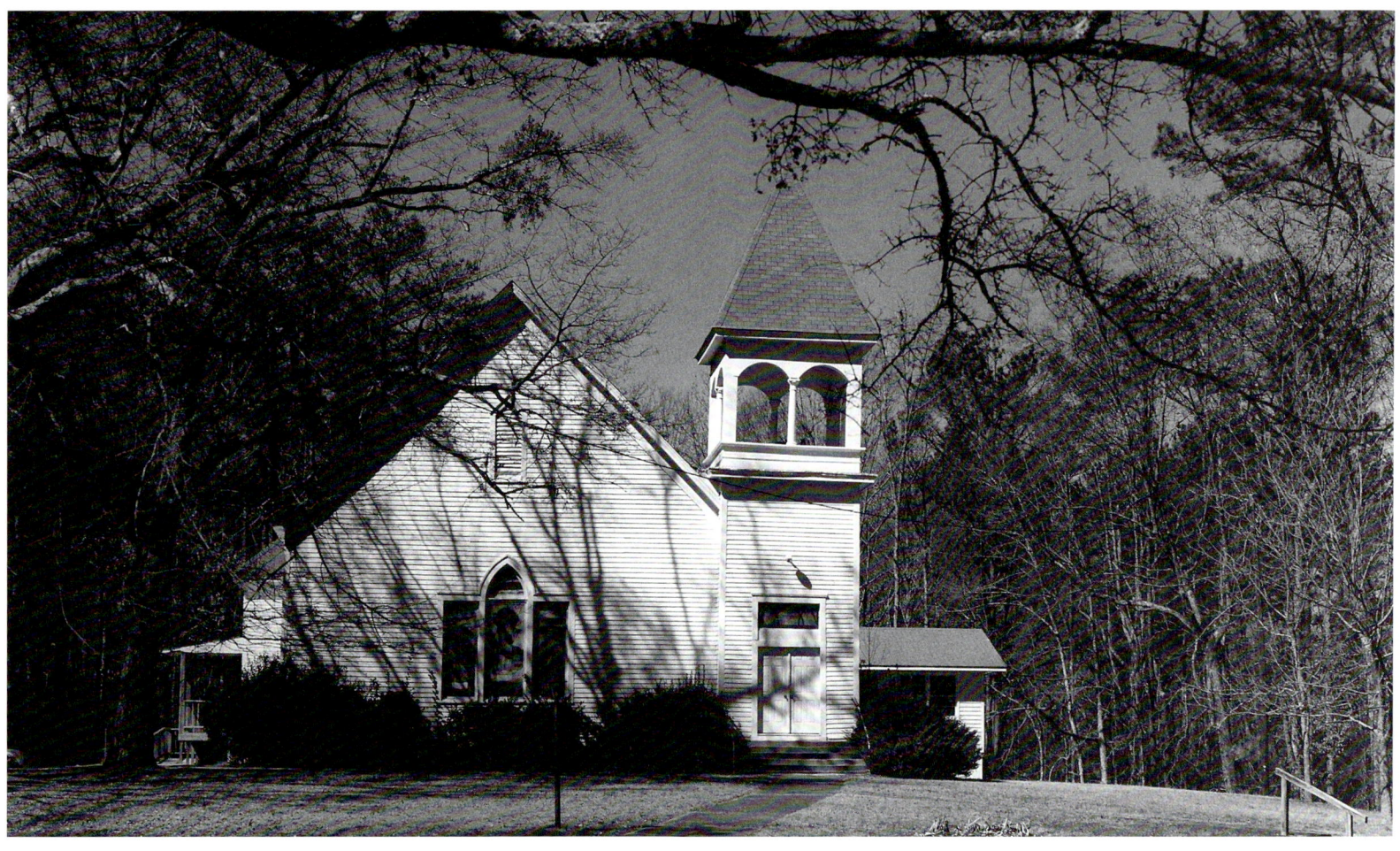

Maxeys

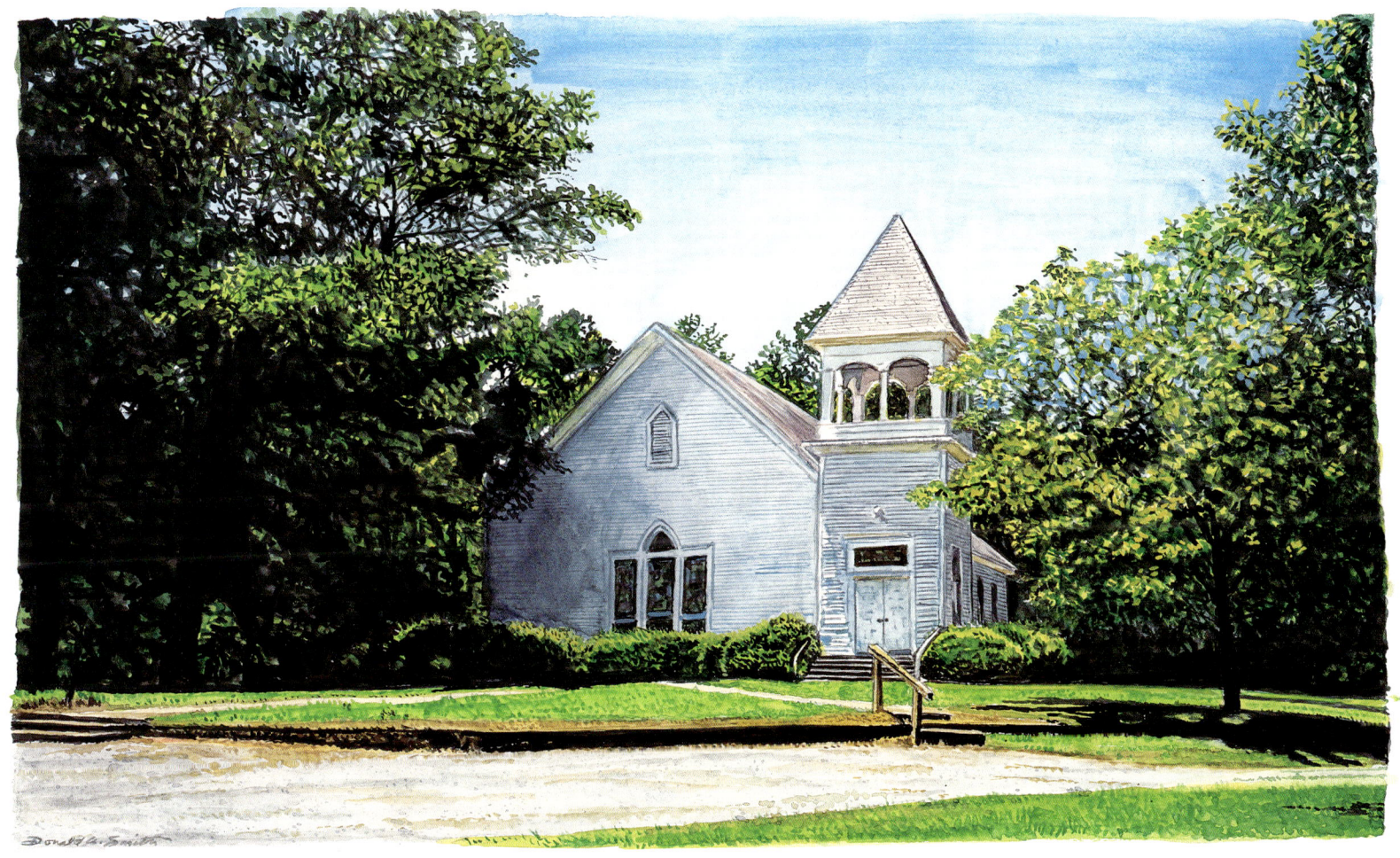

Maxeys

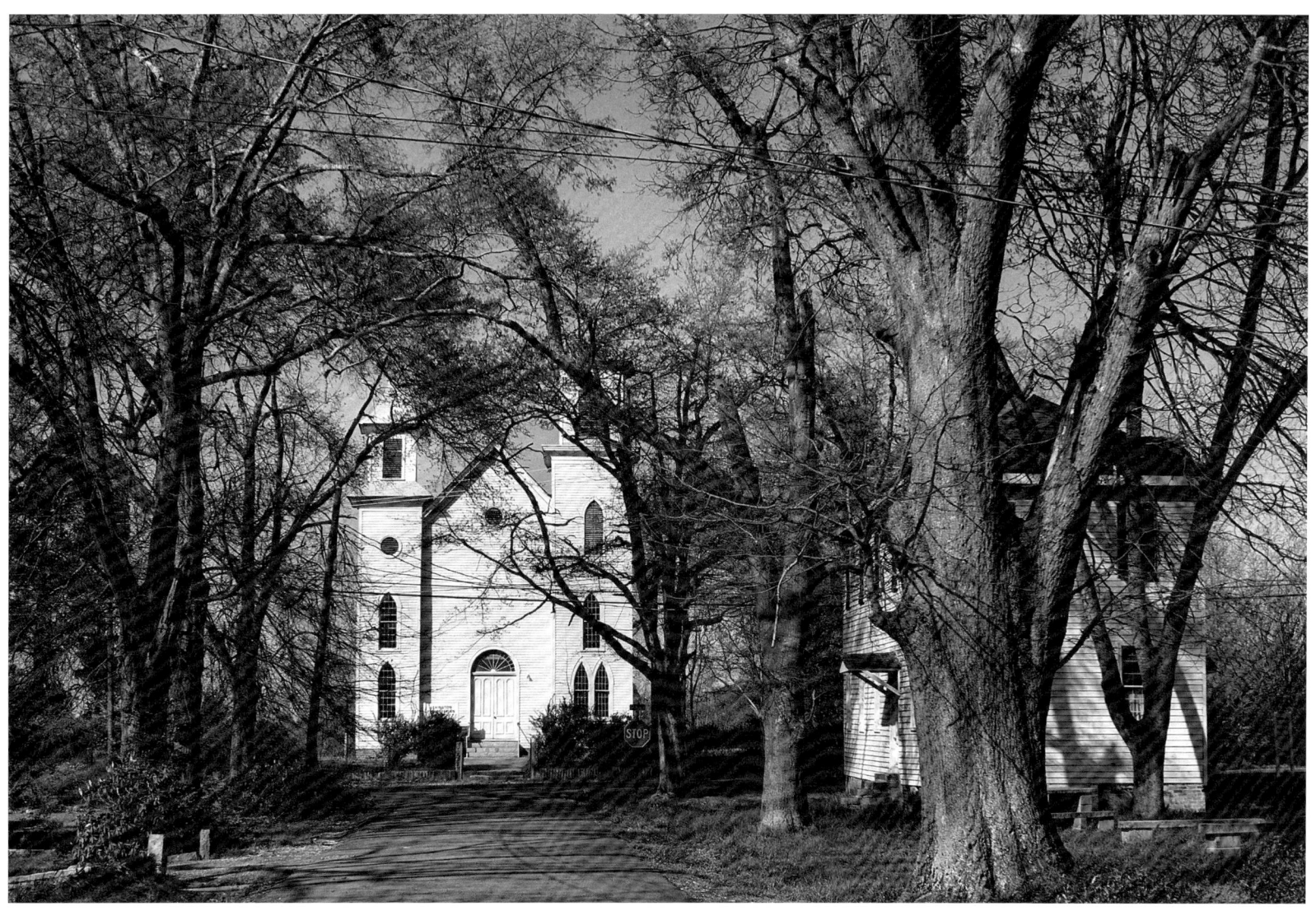

Lexington

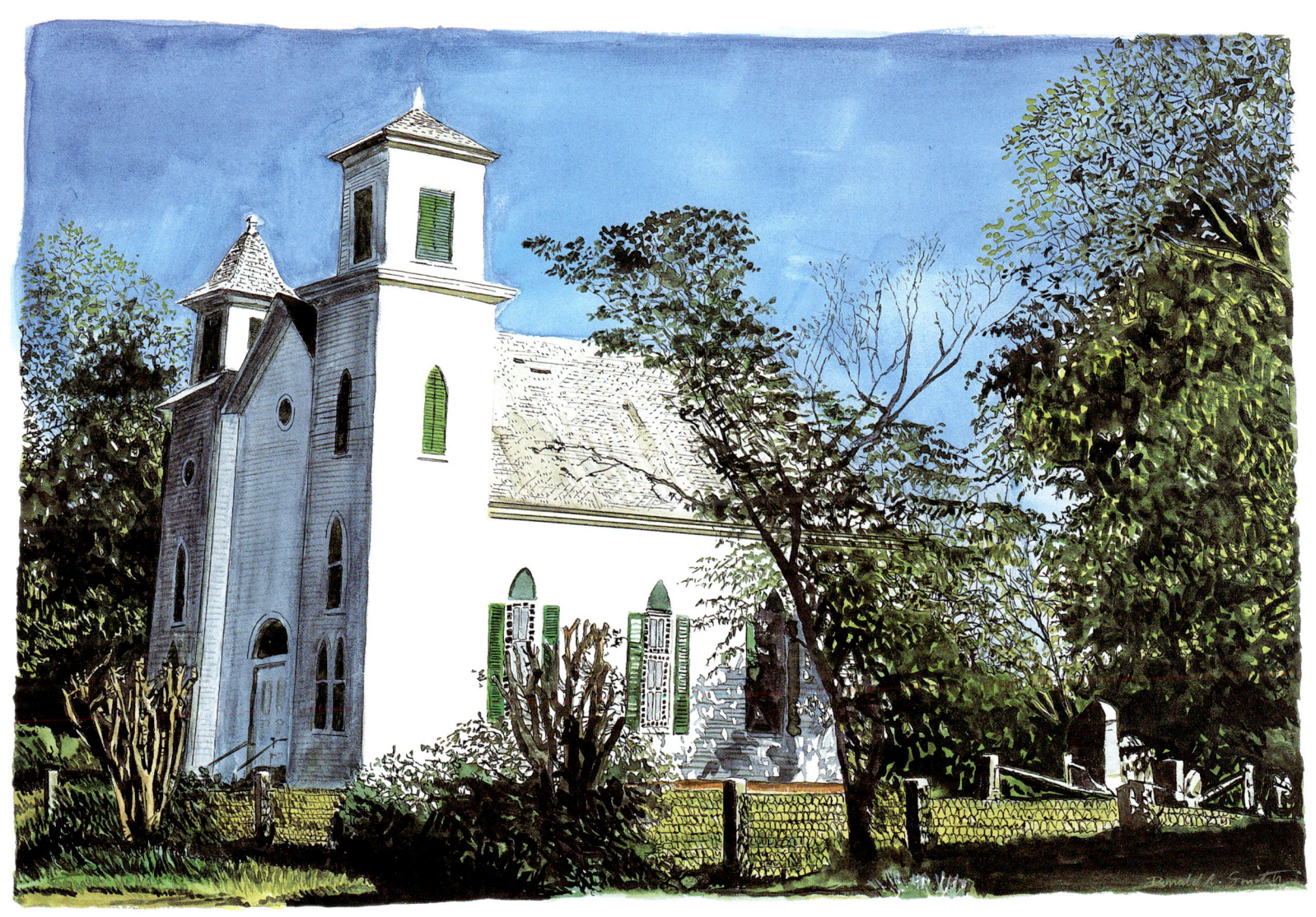

Lexington

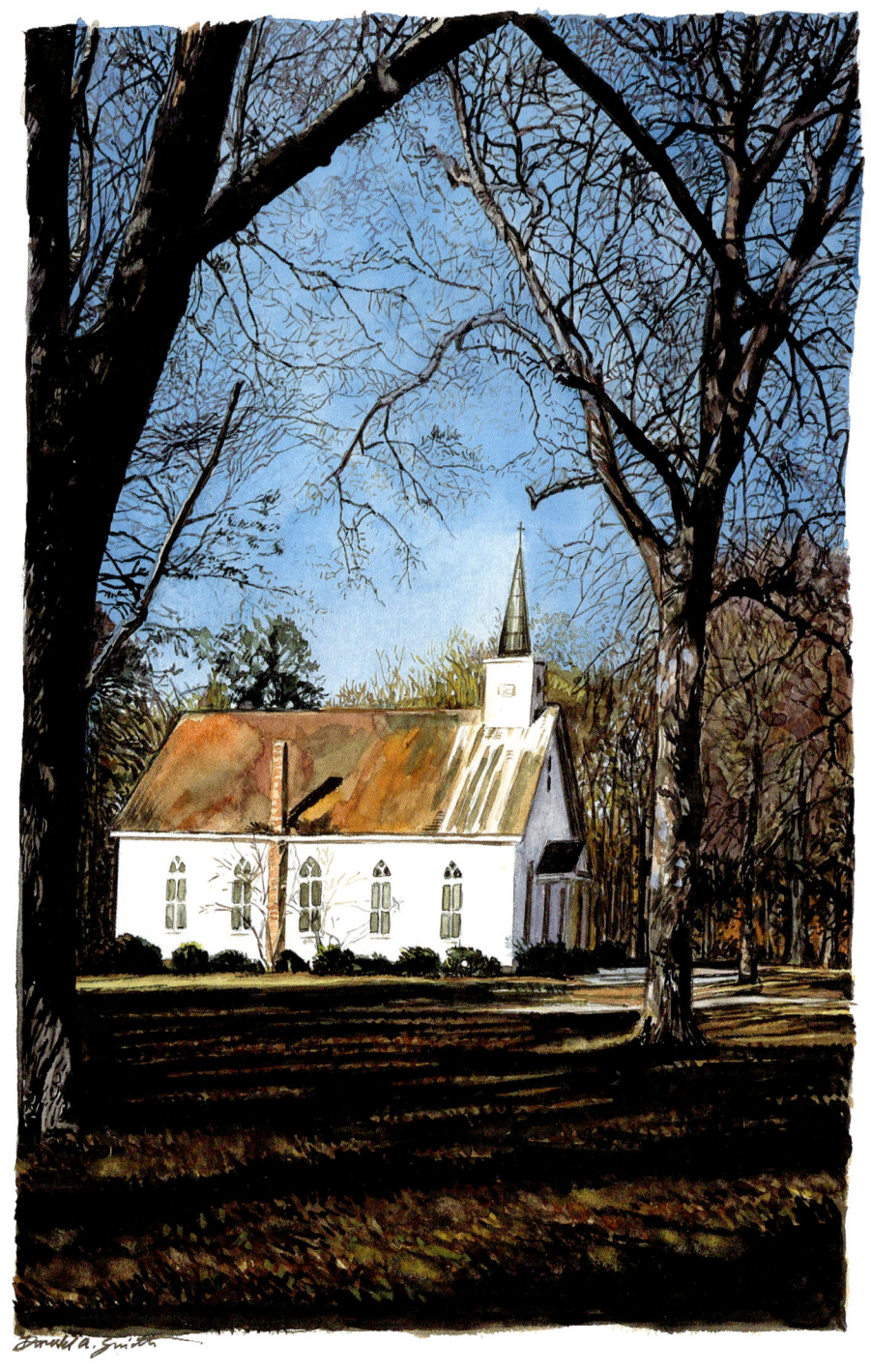

Wilkes County

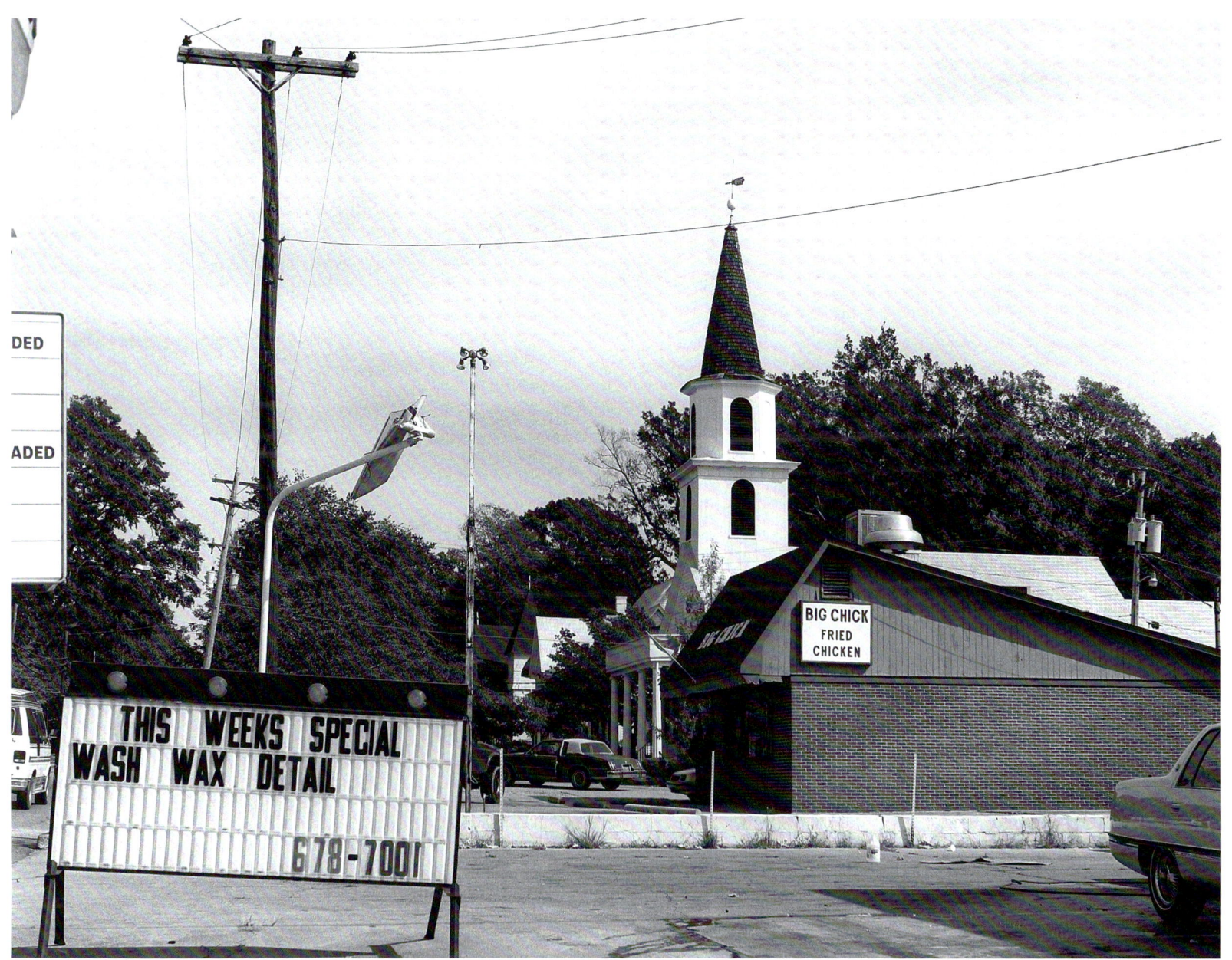

Lincolnton

CHURCHES

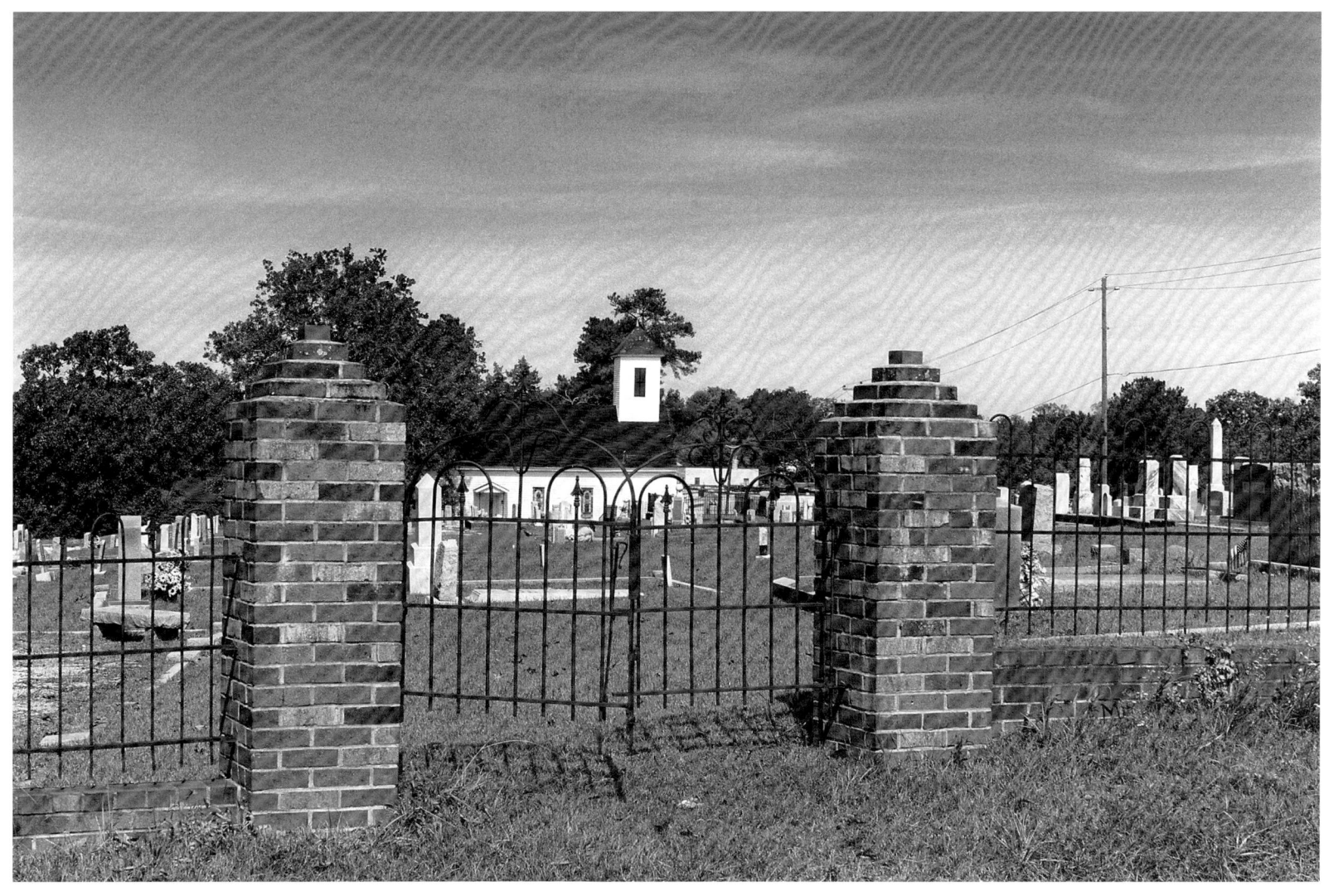

Lincolnton

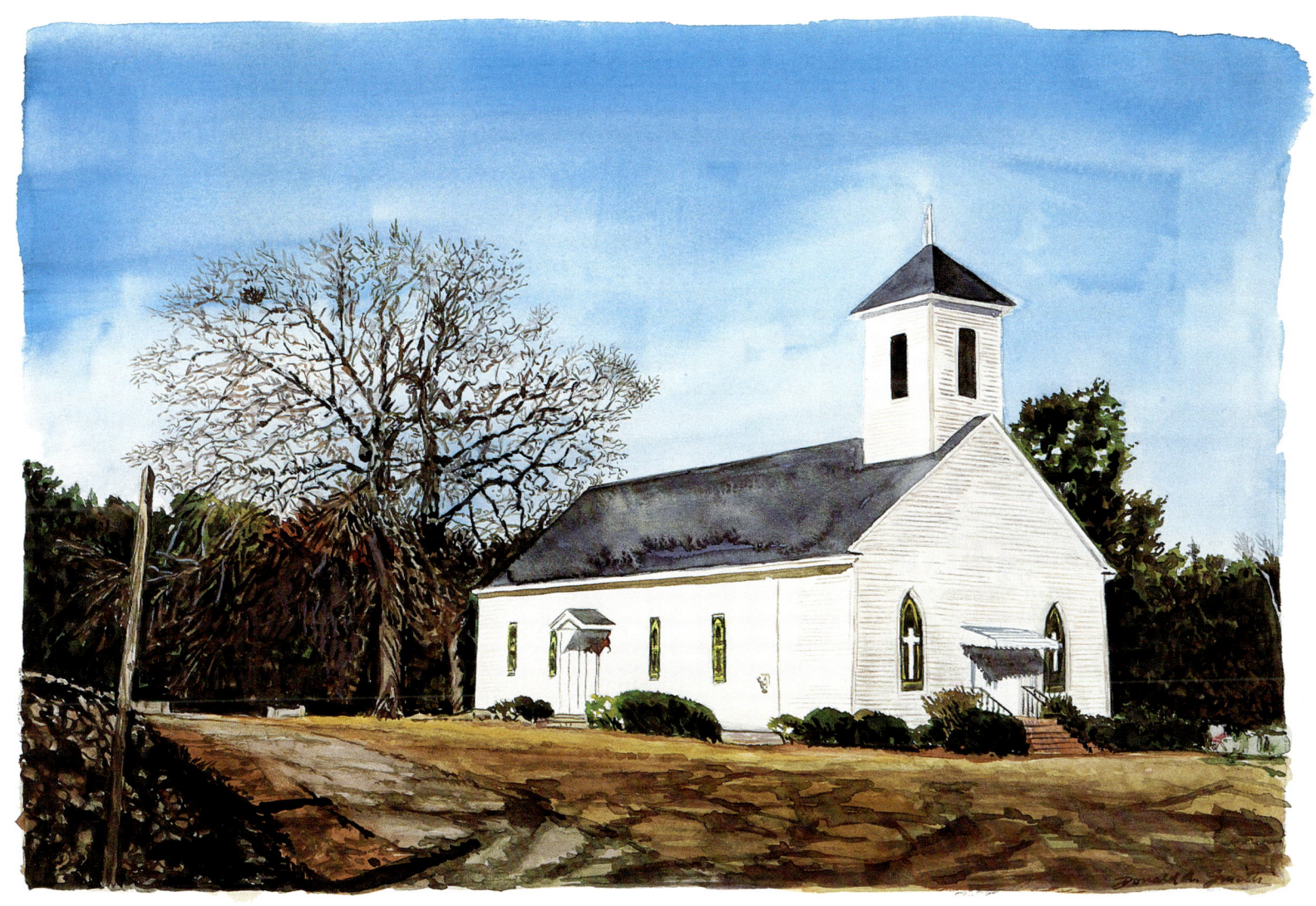

Lincolnton

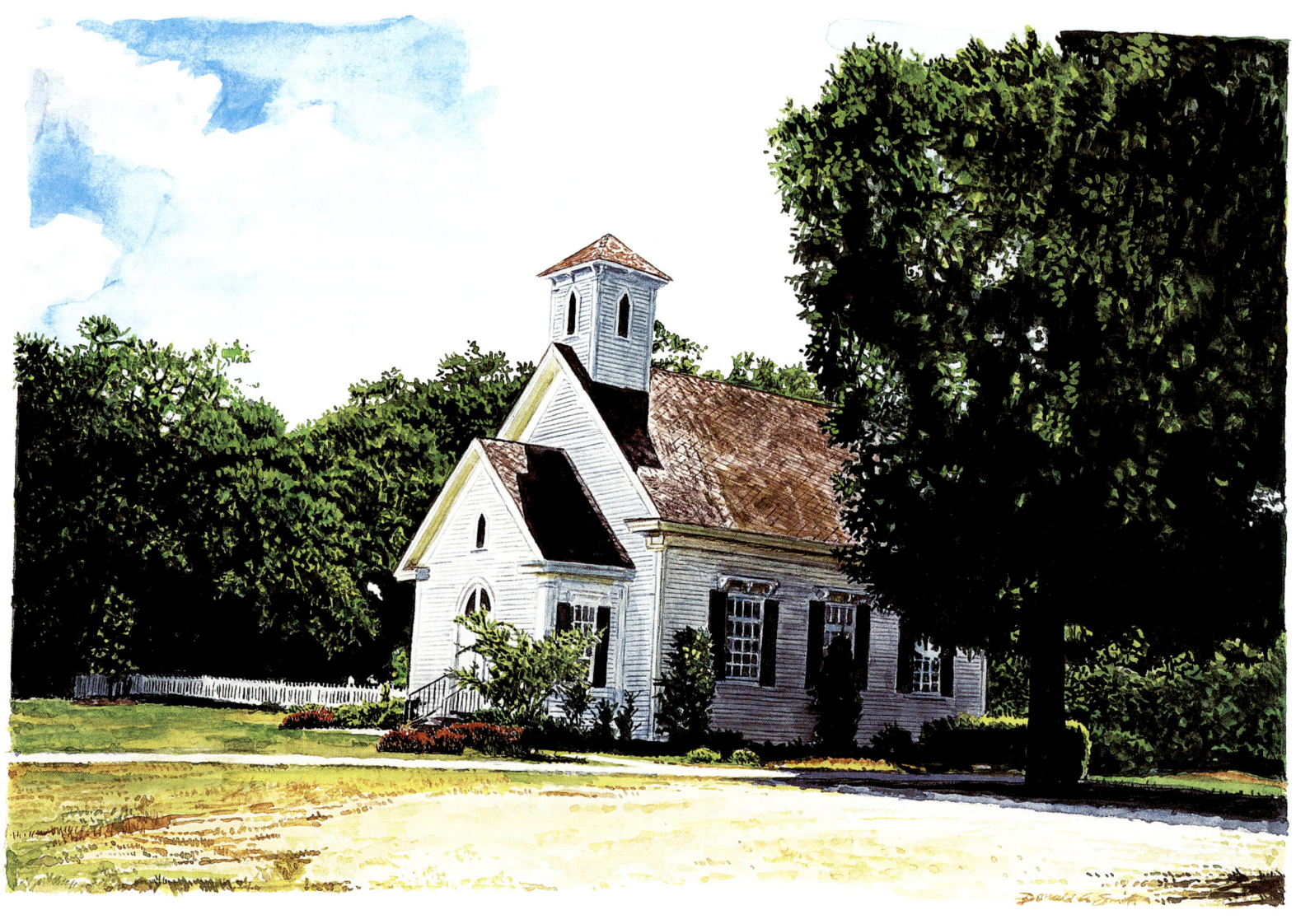

Centennial

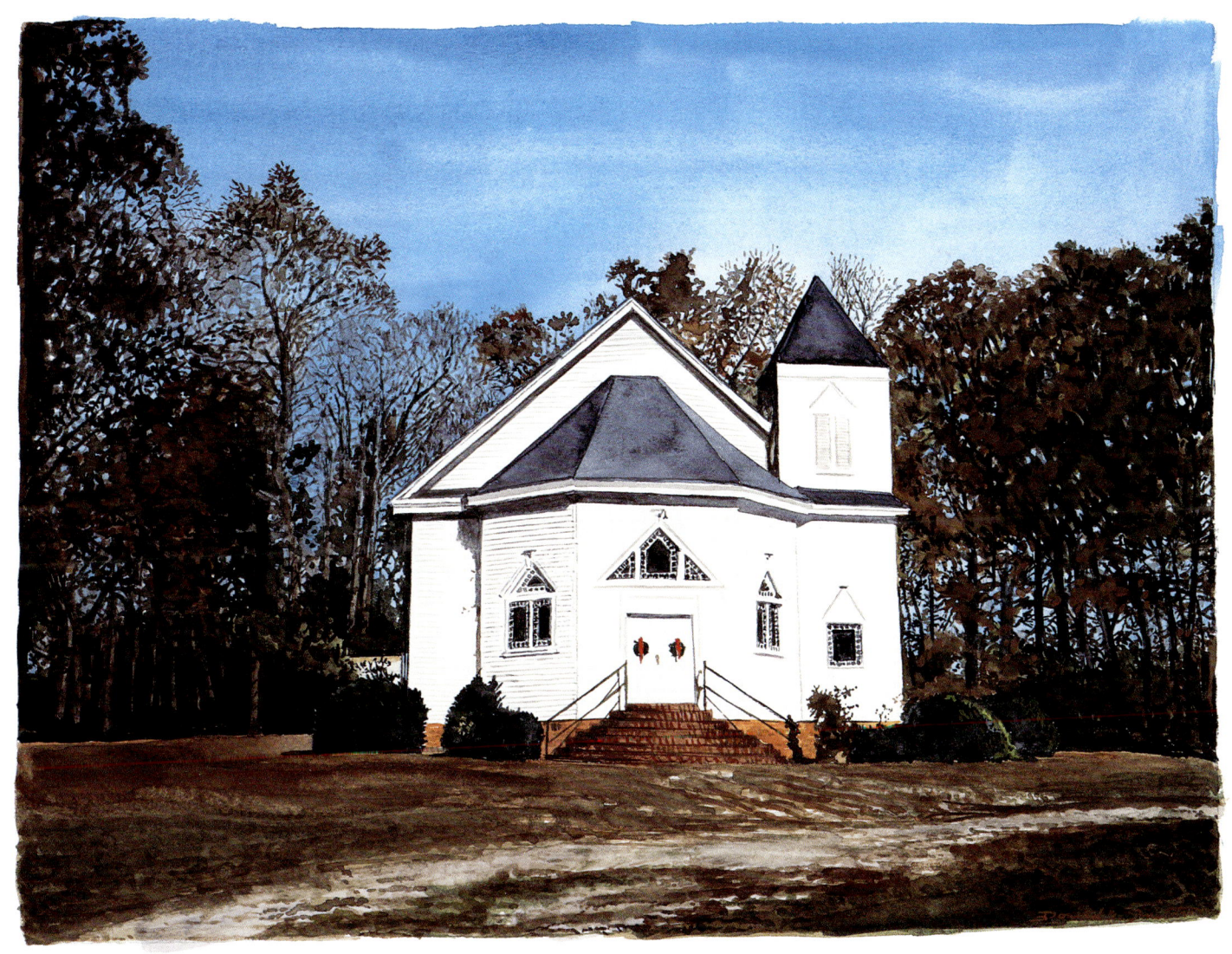

Shadydale

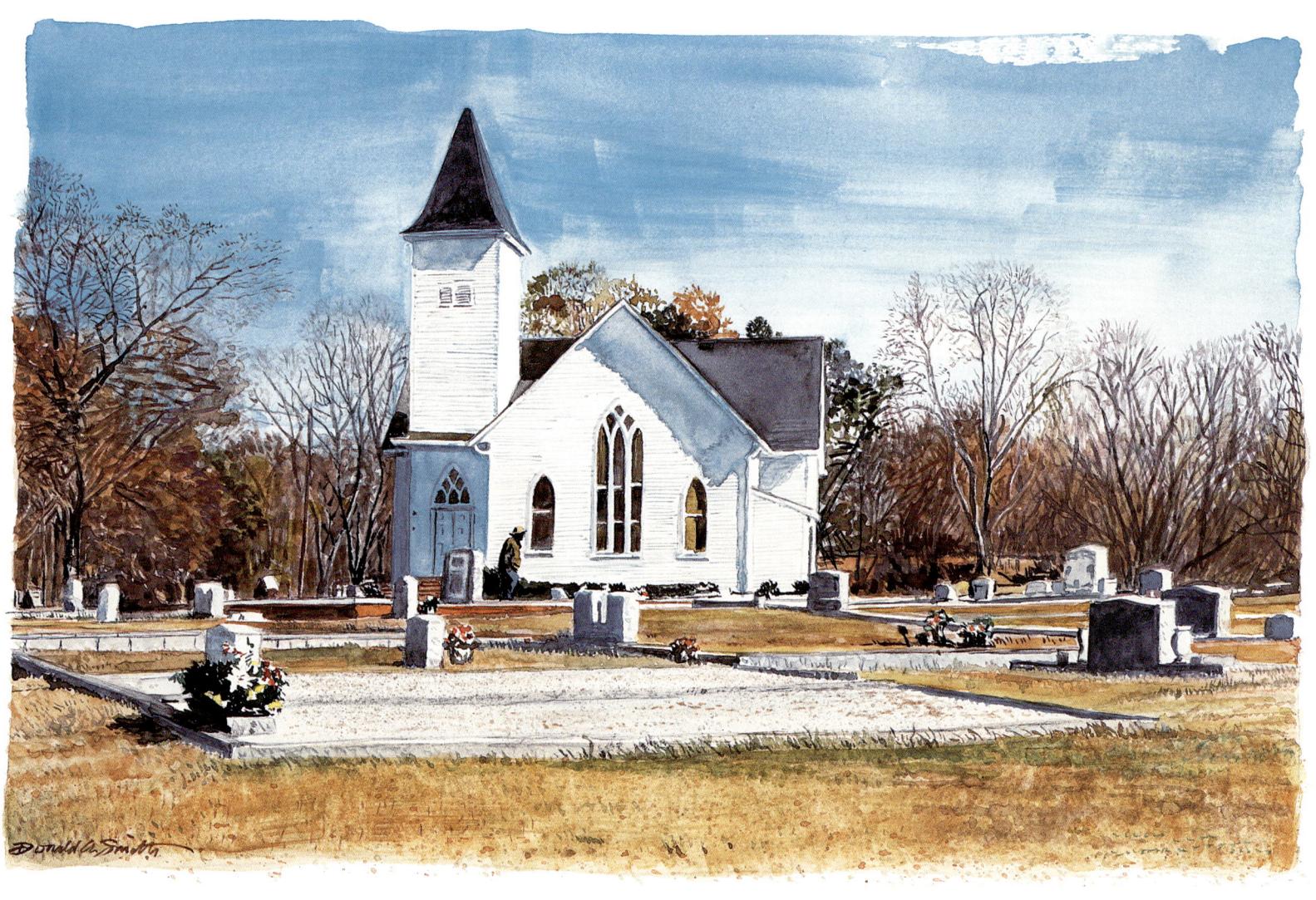

Shadydale

CHURCHES

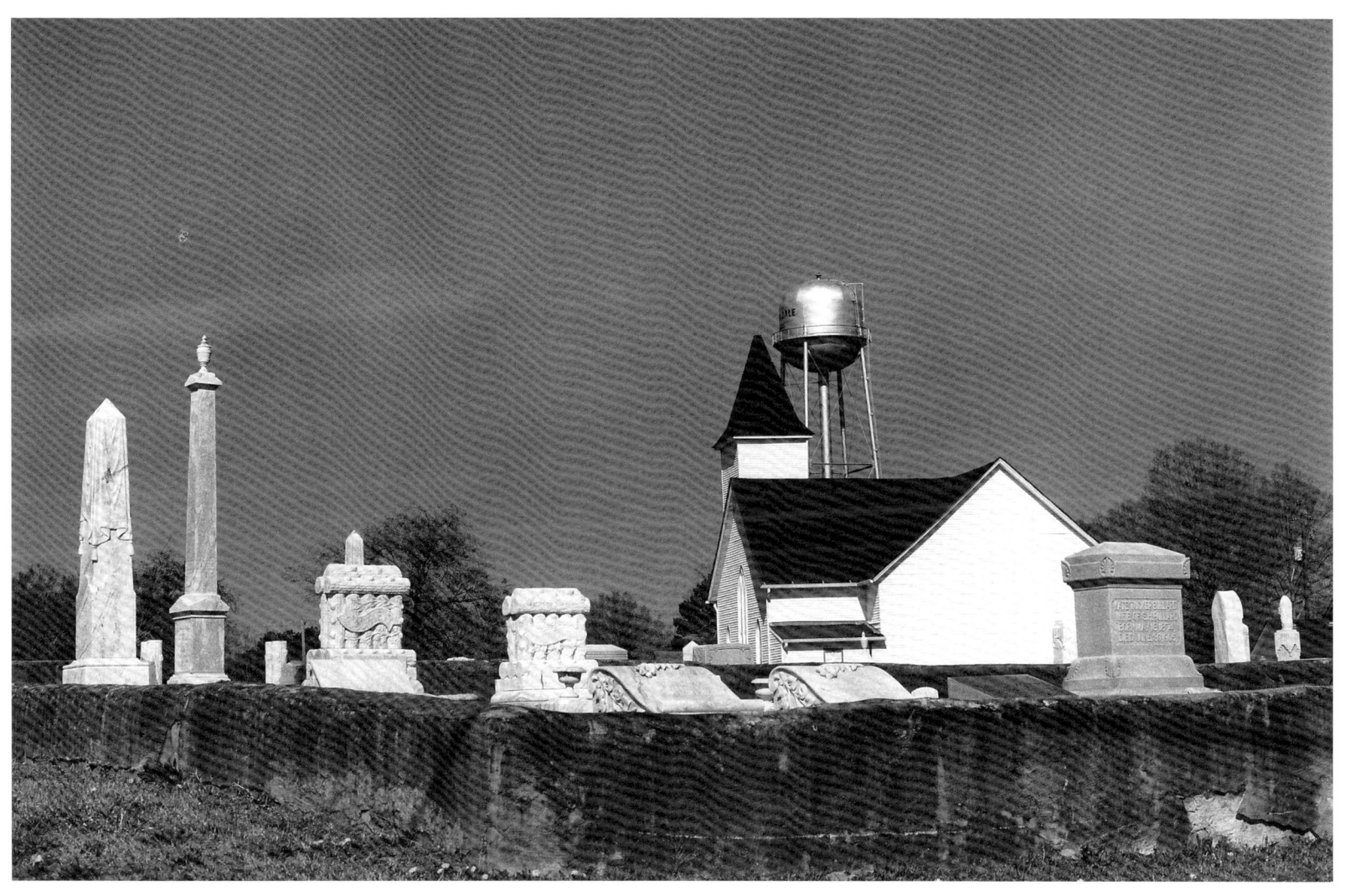

Shadydale

CHURCHES

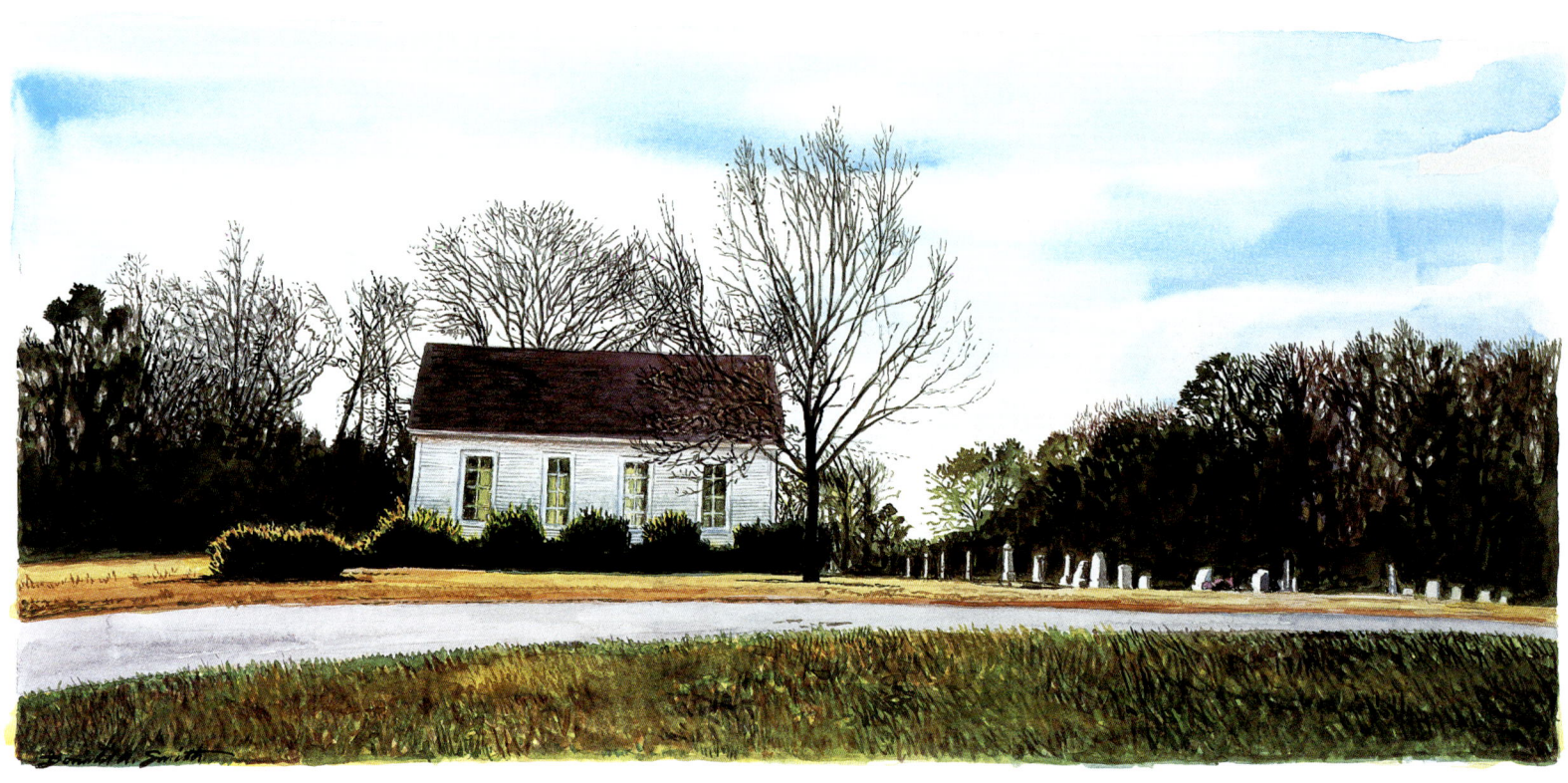

Pennington

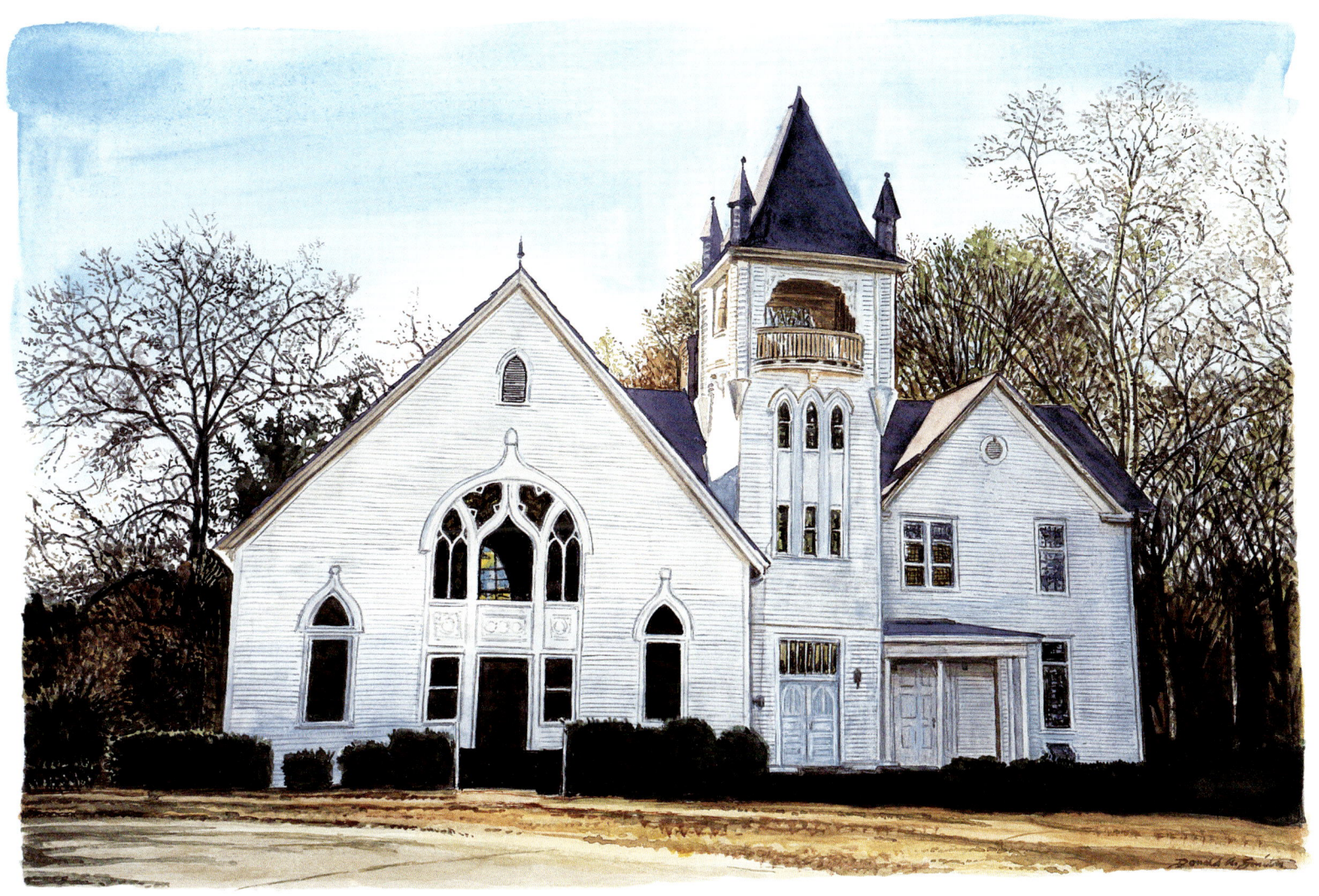

Monticello

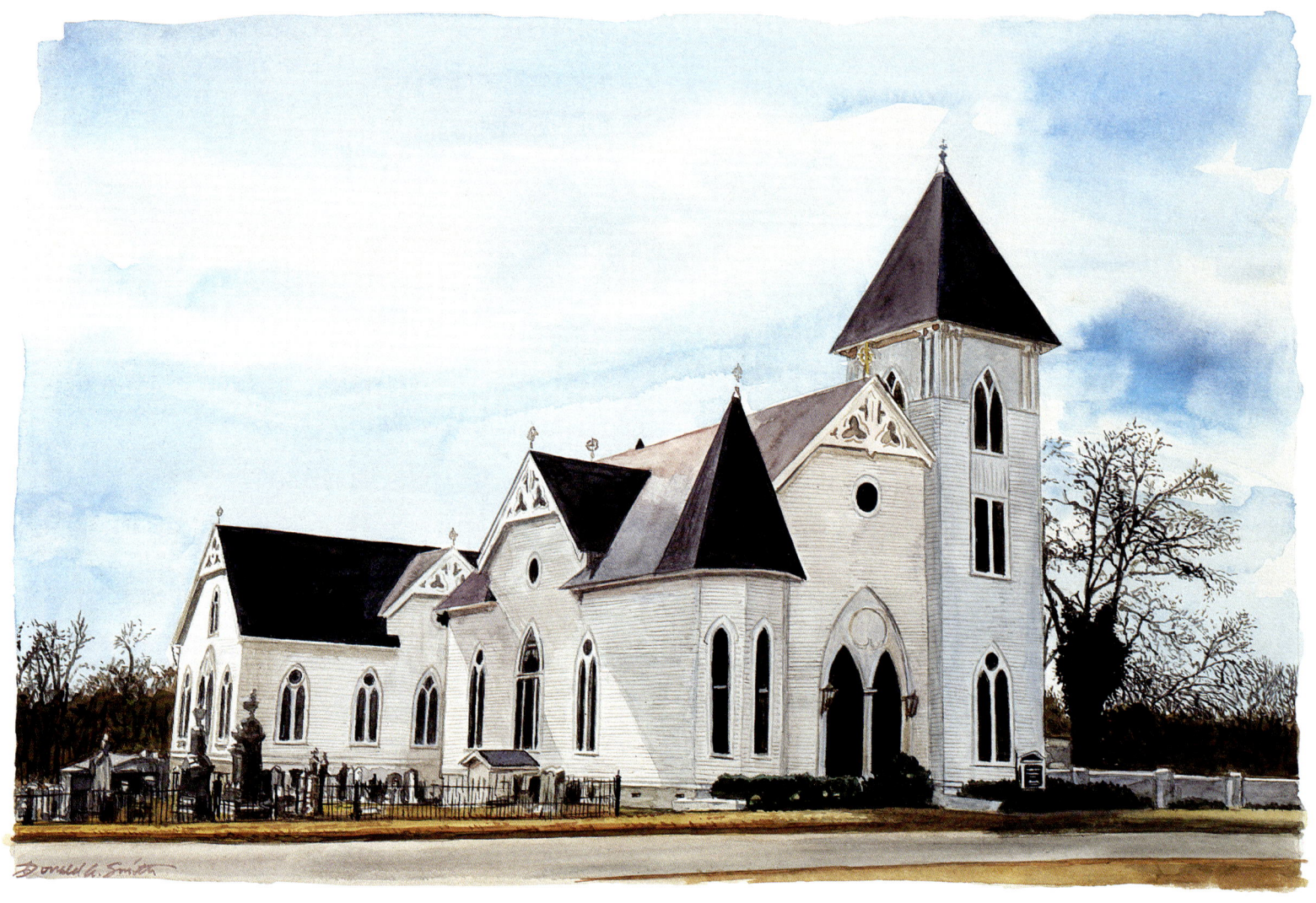

Monticello

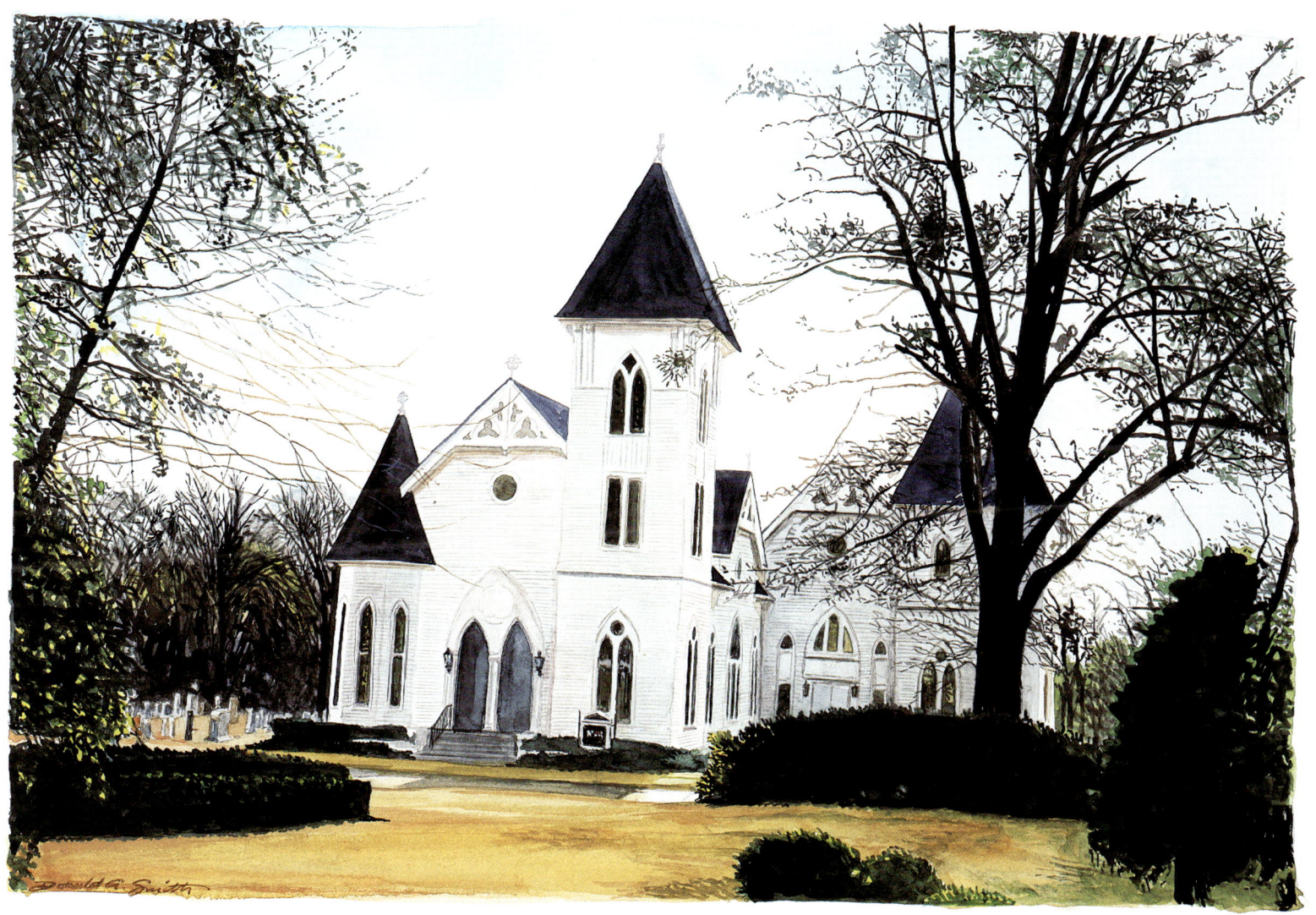

Monticello

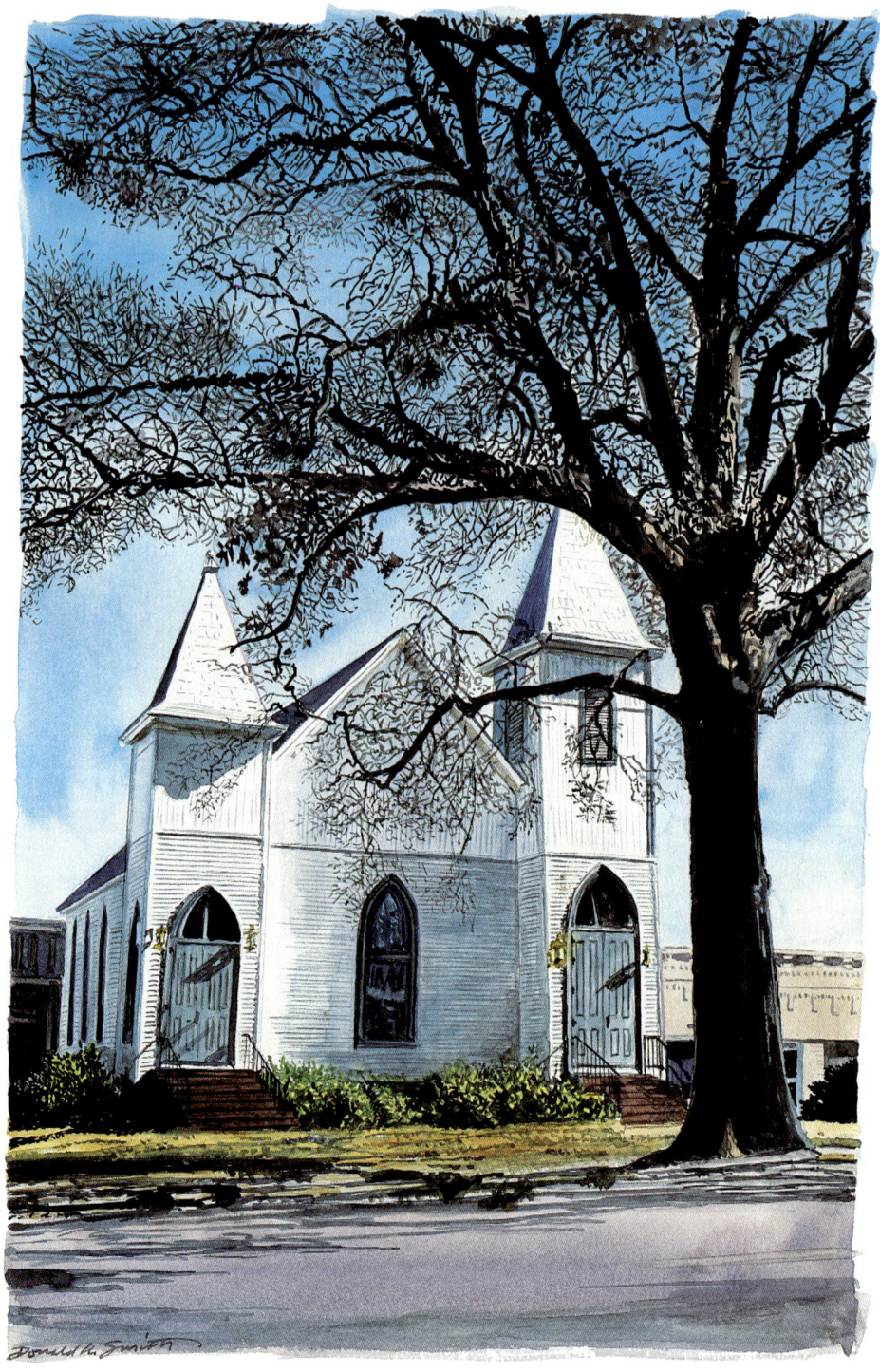

Forsyth

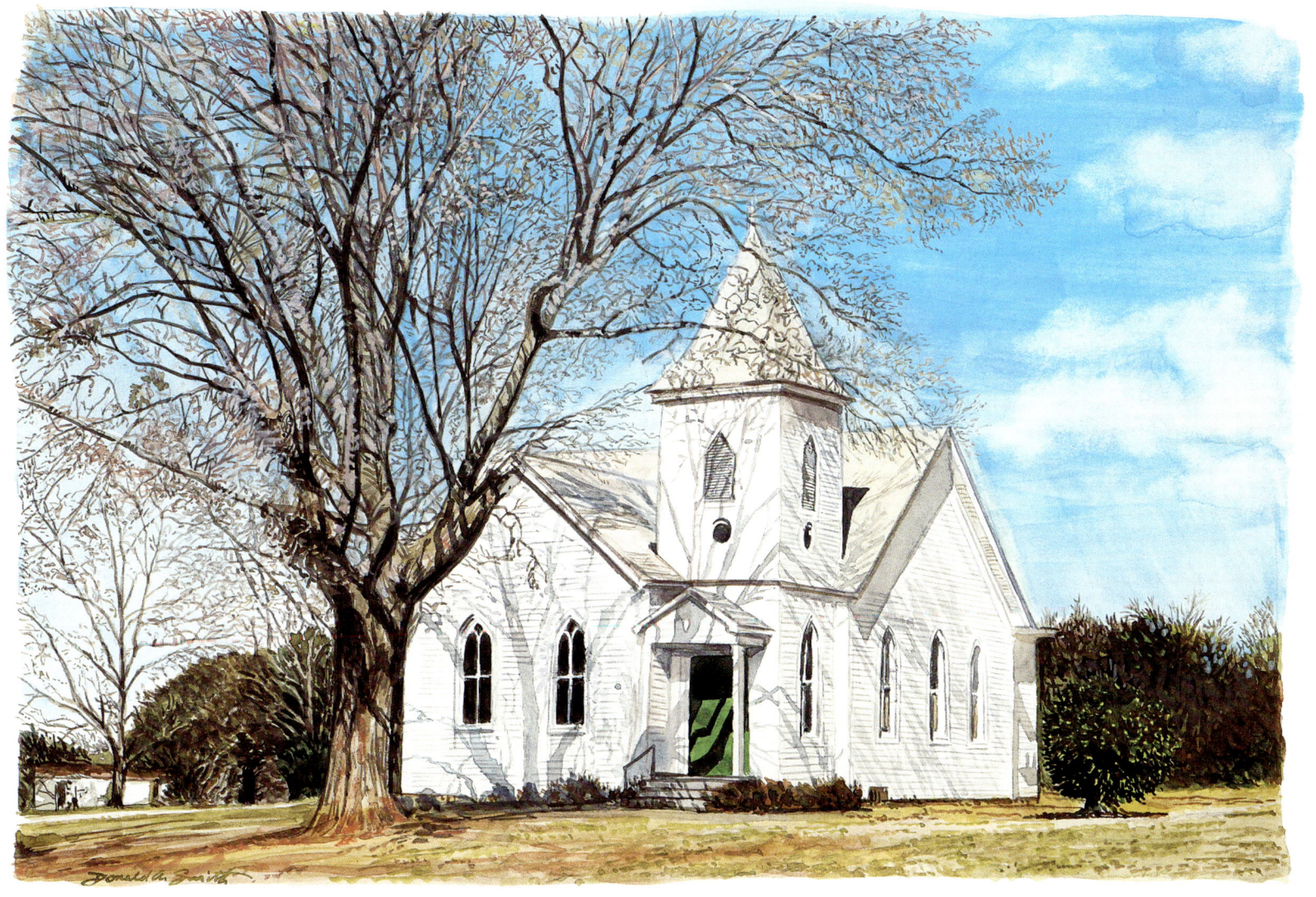

Smarr

CHURCHES

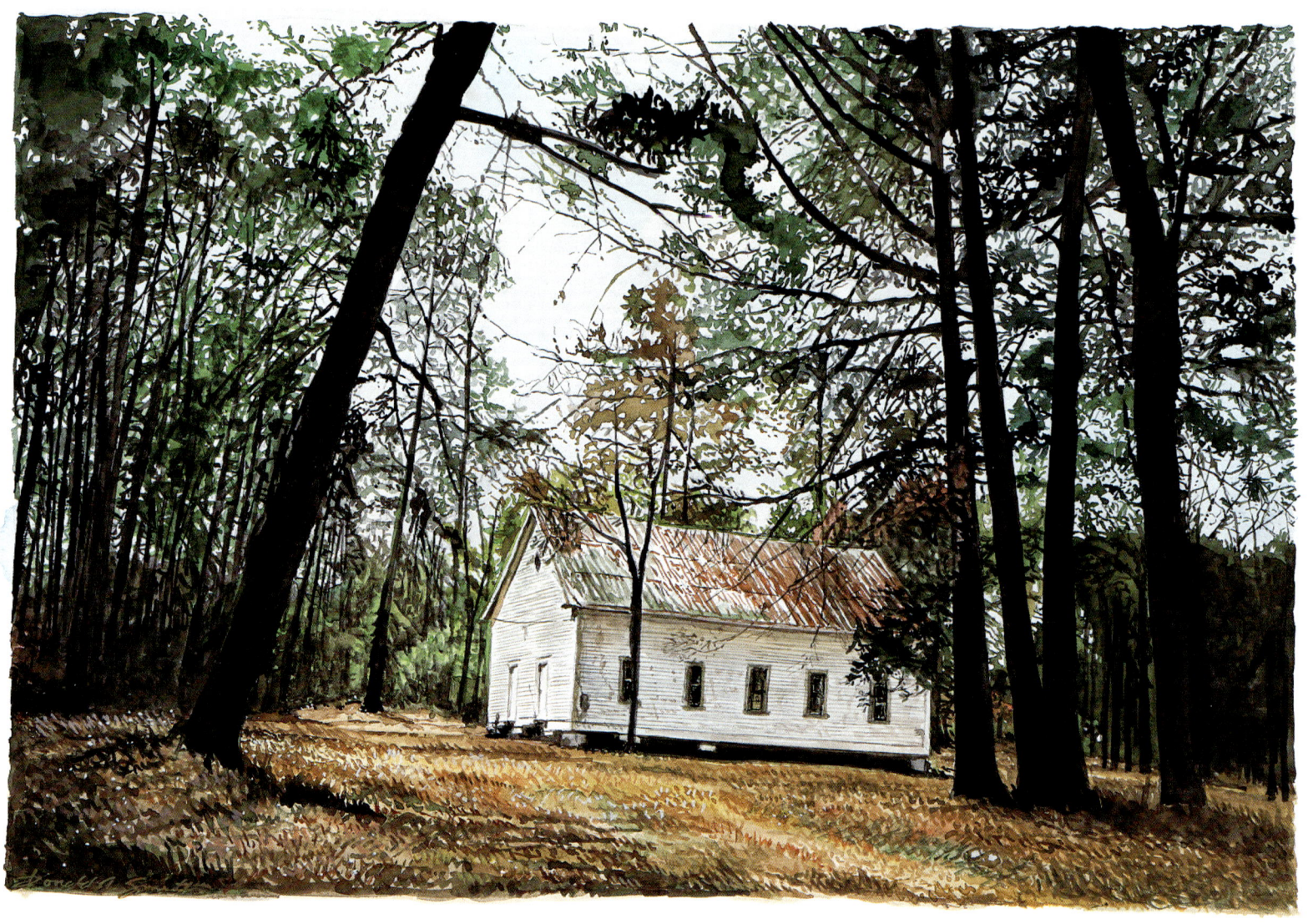

Jasper County

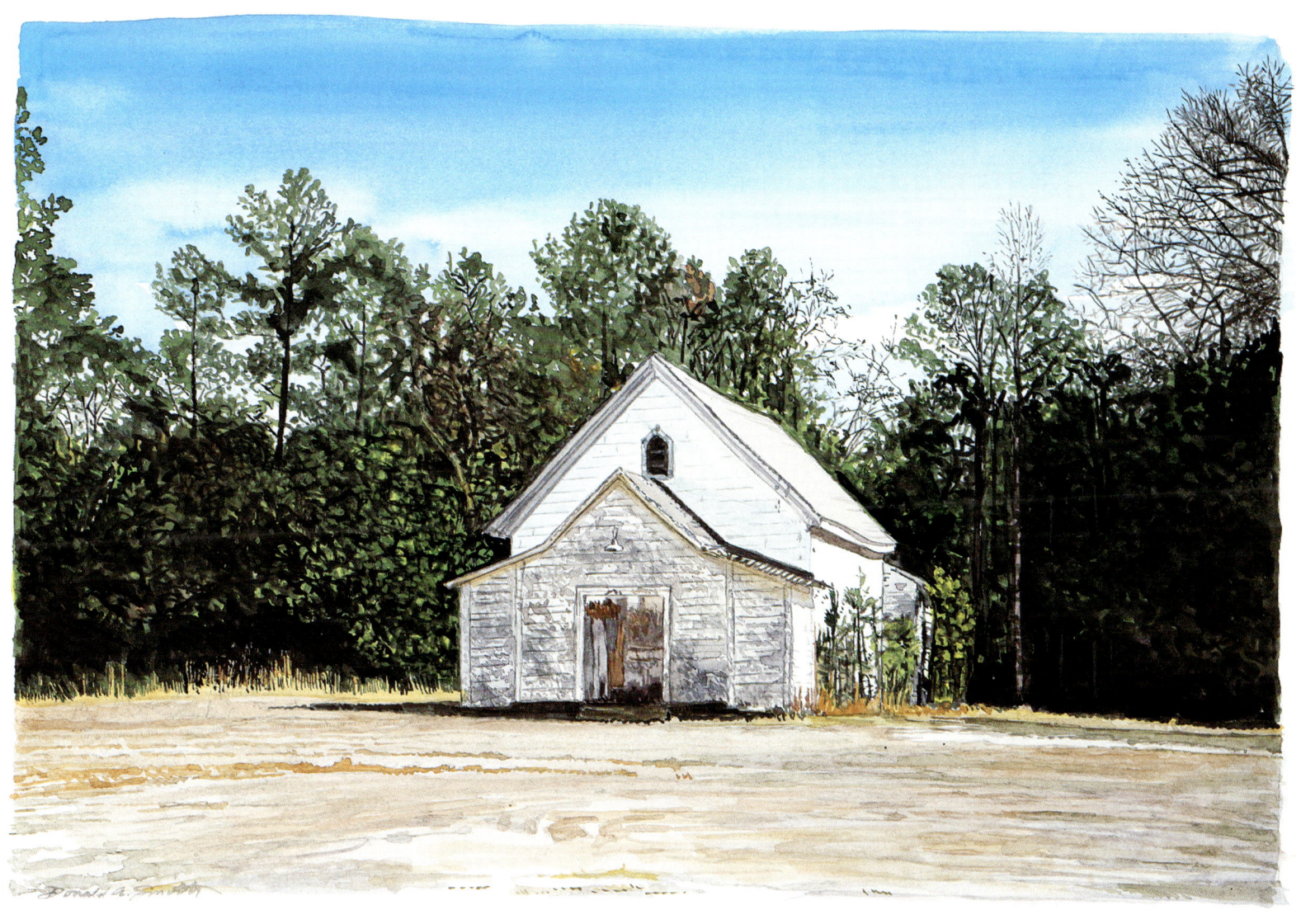

Butts County

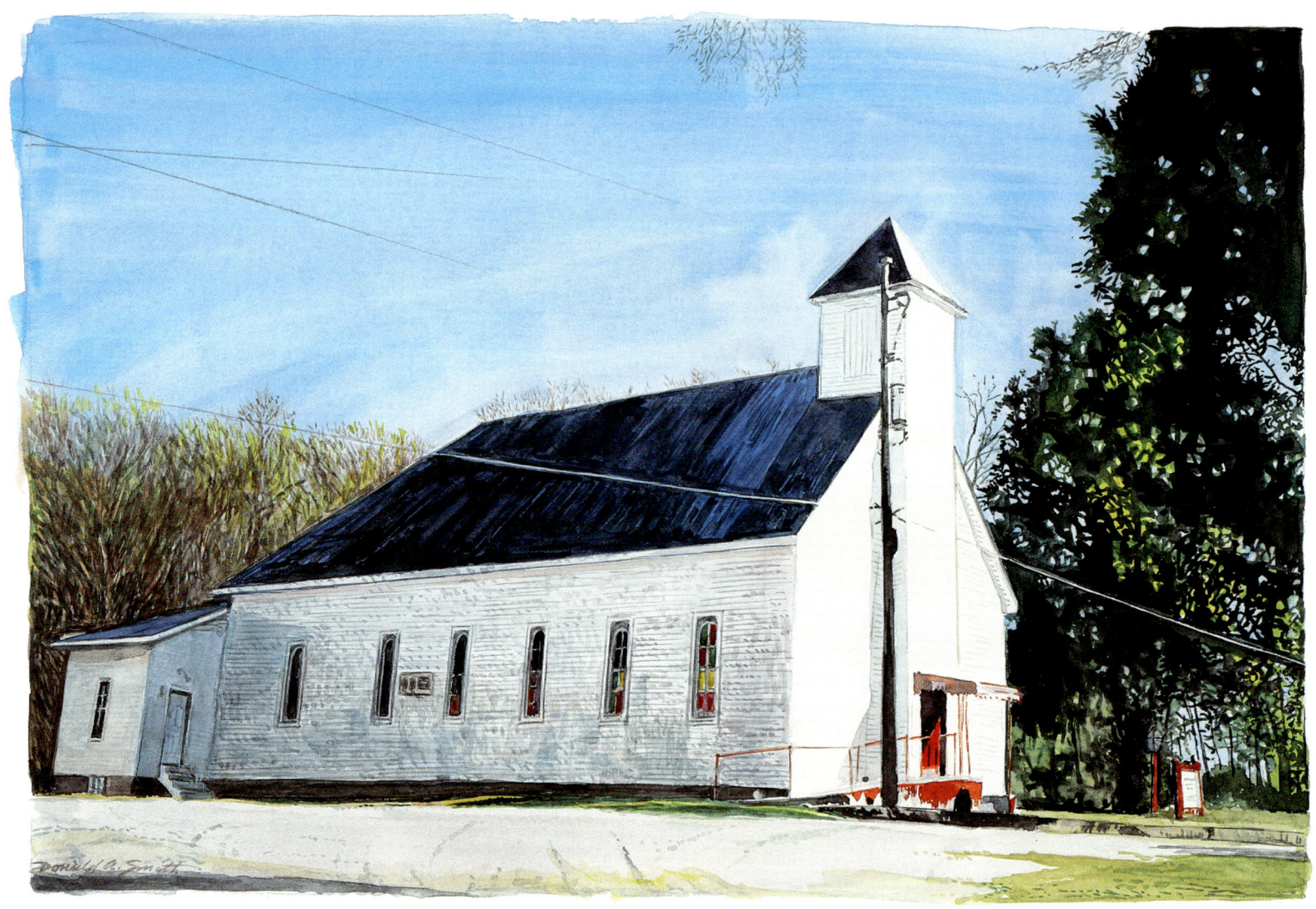

Jackson

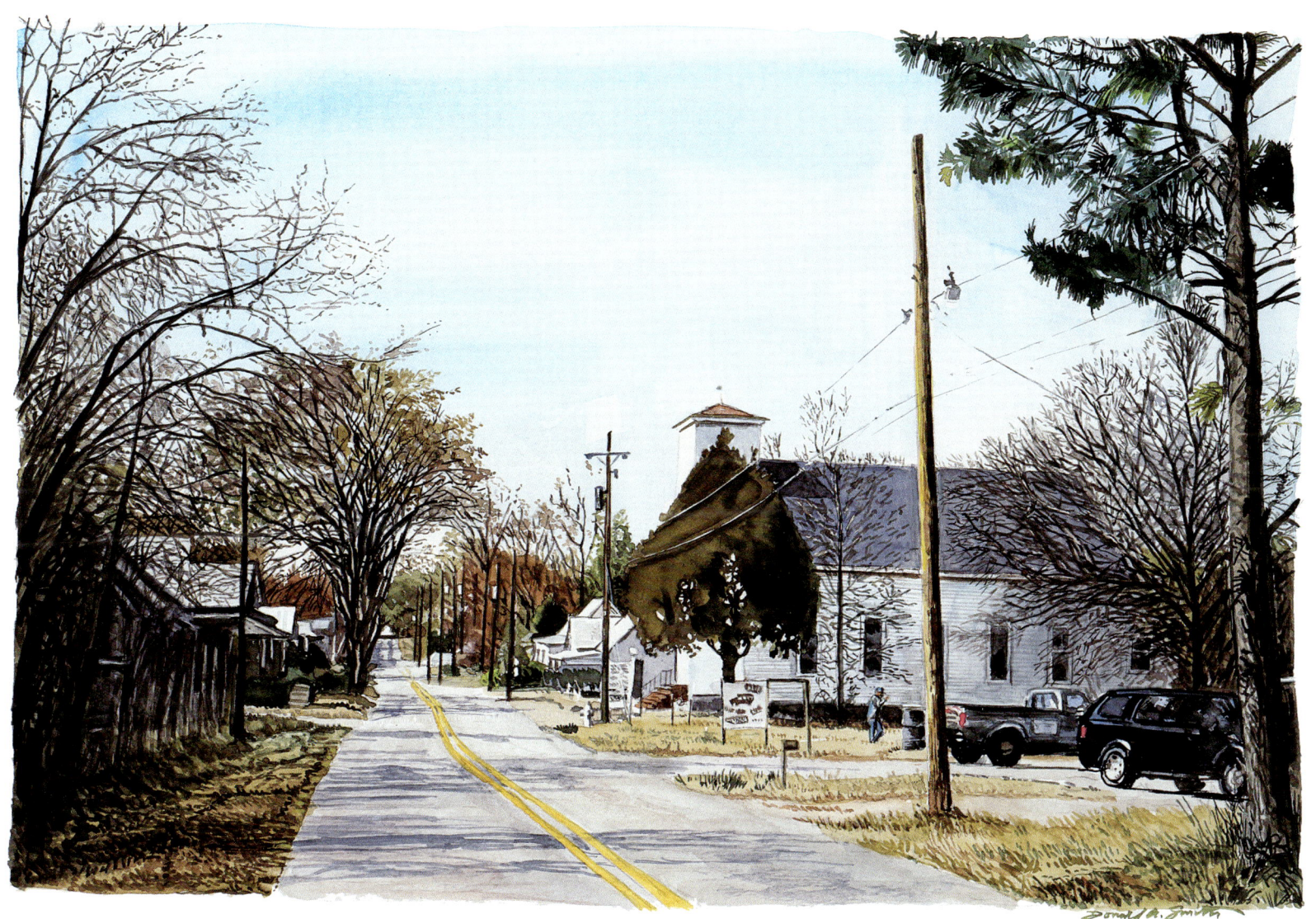

Jackson

CHURCHES

93

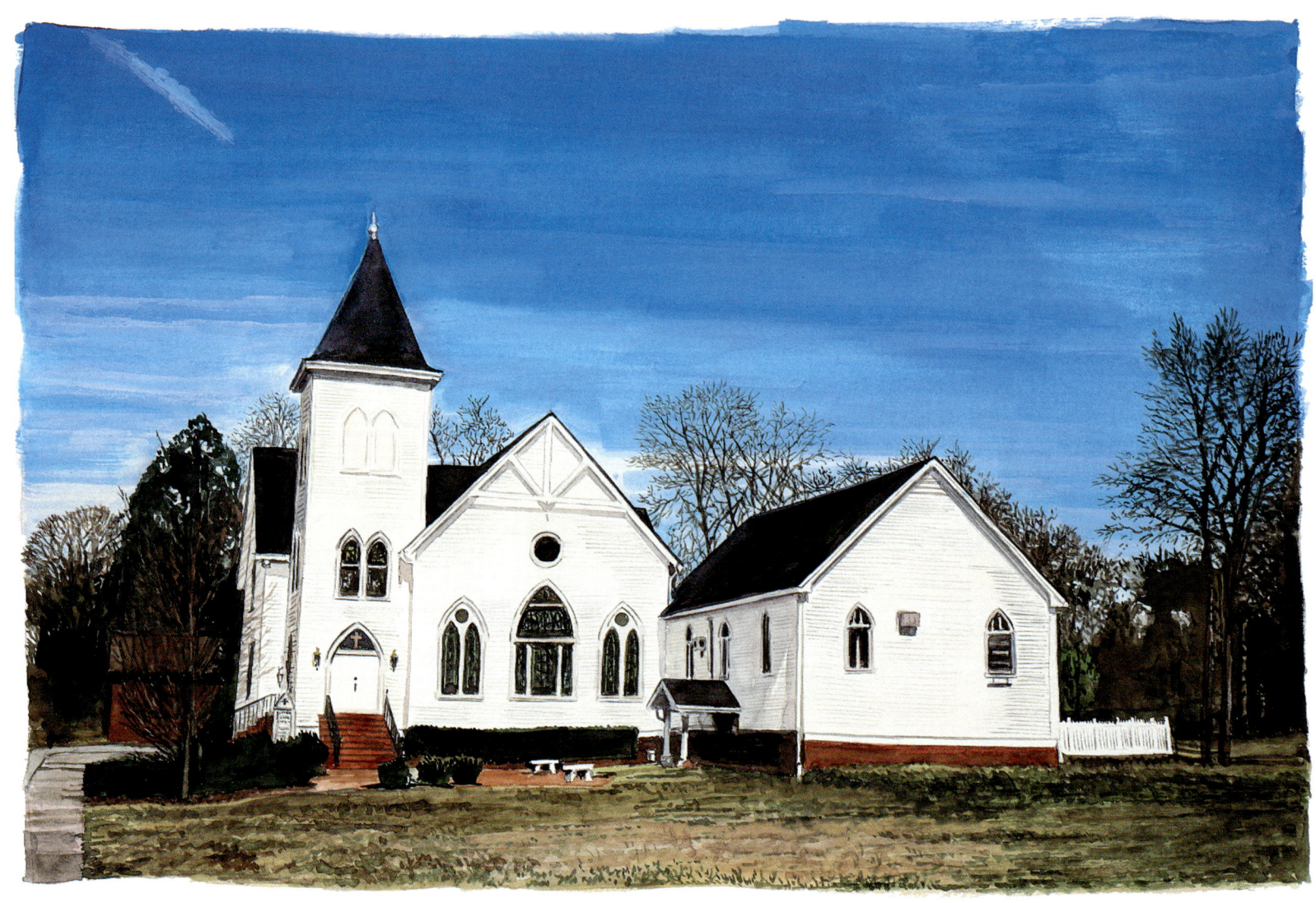

Jackson

CHURCHES

94

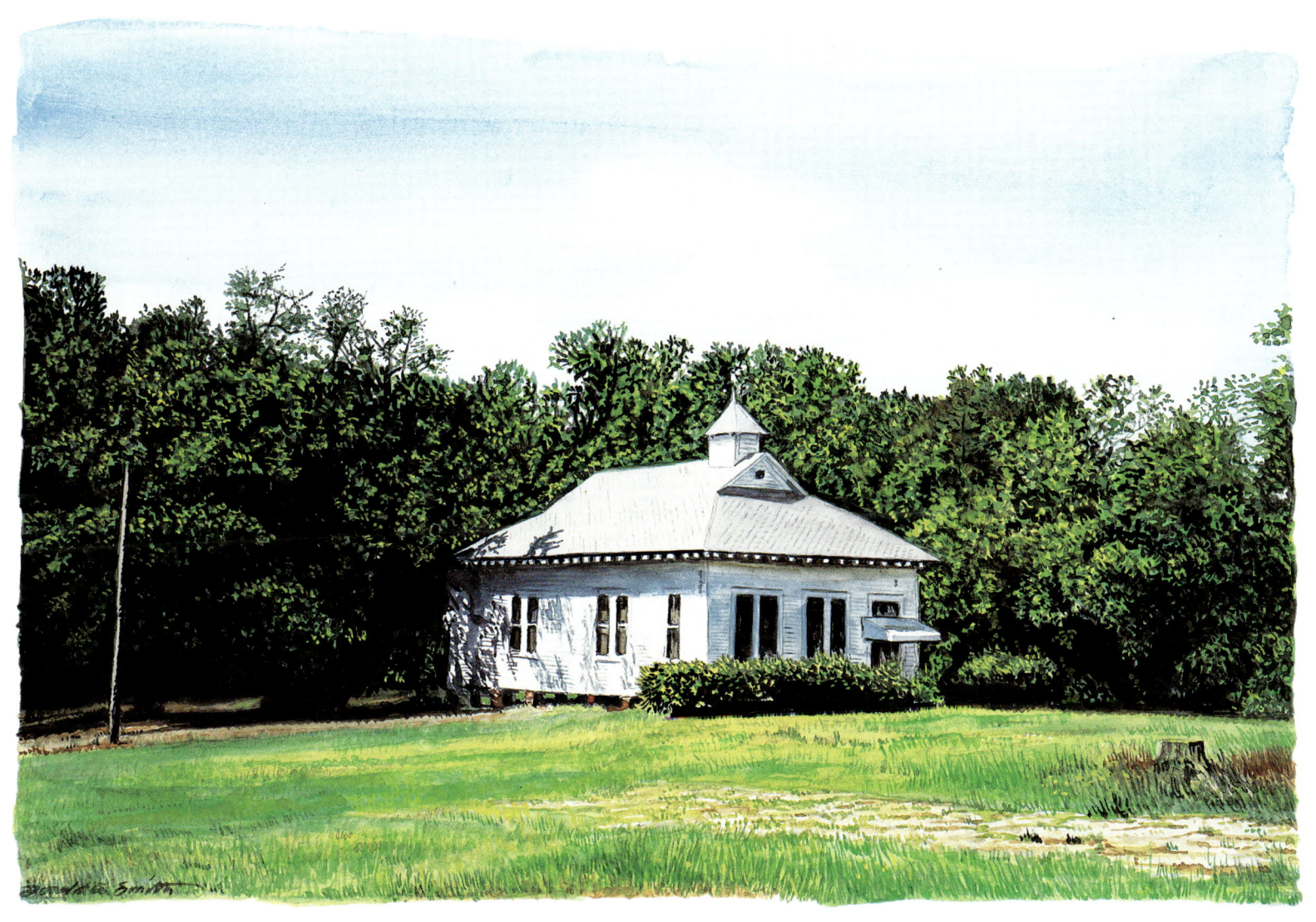

Morgan County

CHURCHES

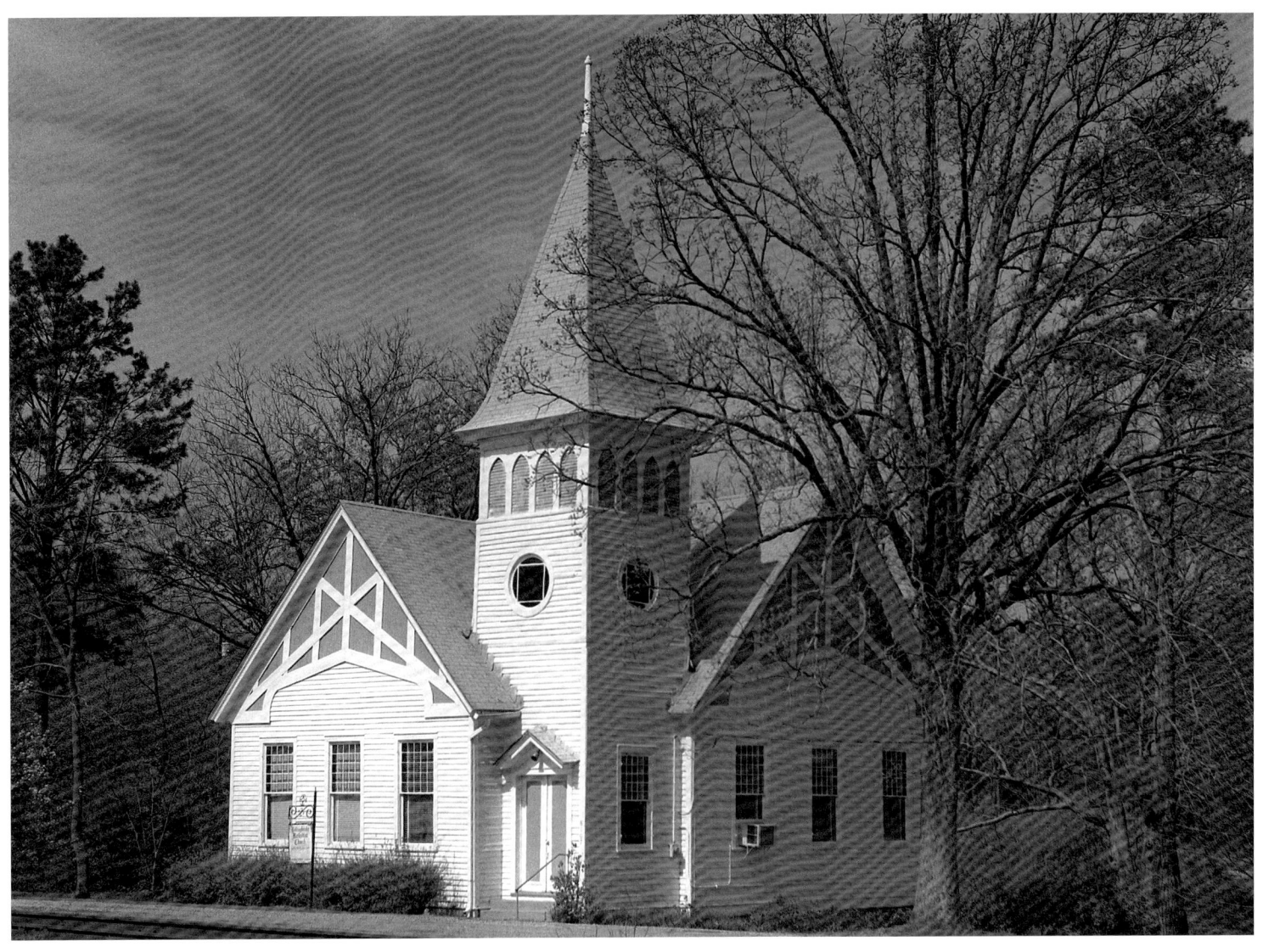

Bolingbroke

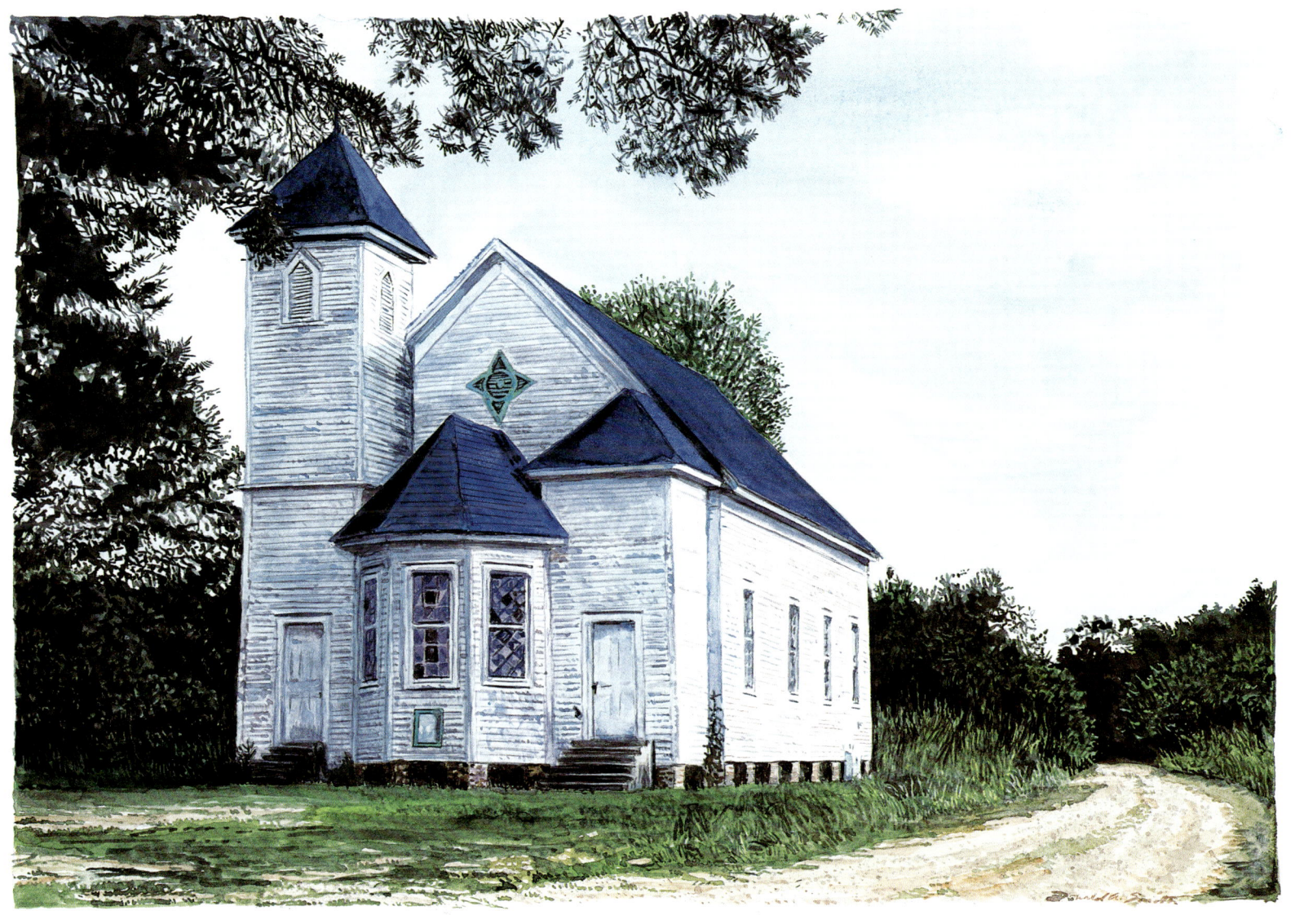

Newborn

CHURCHES

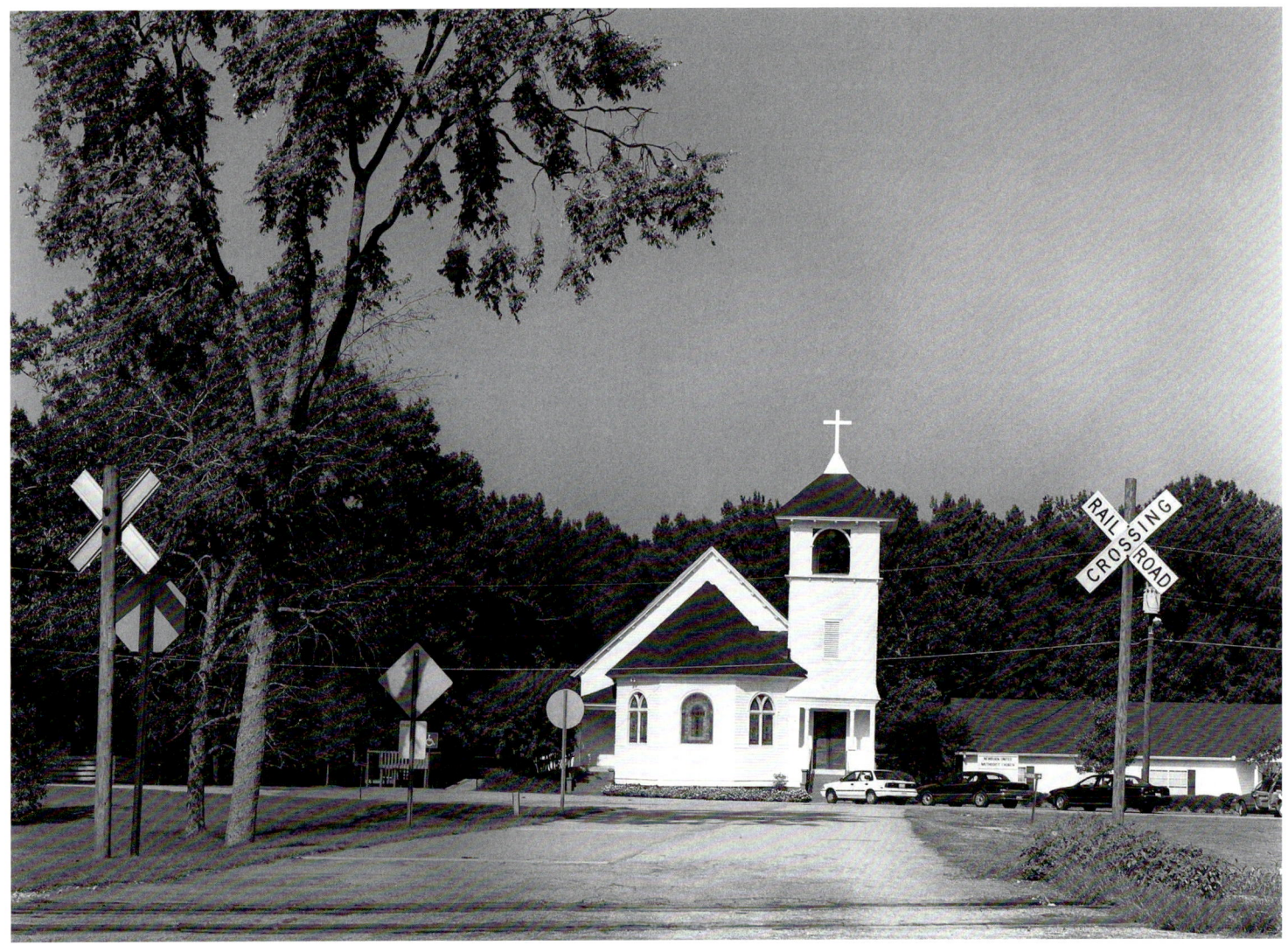

Newborn

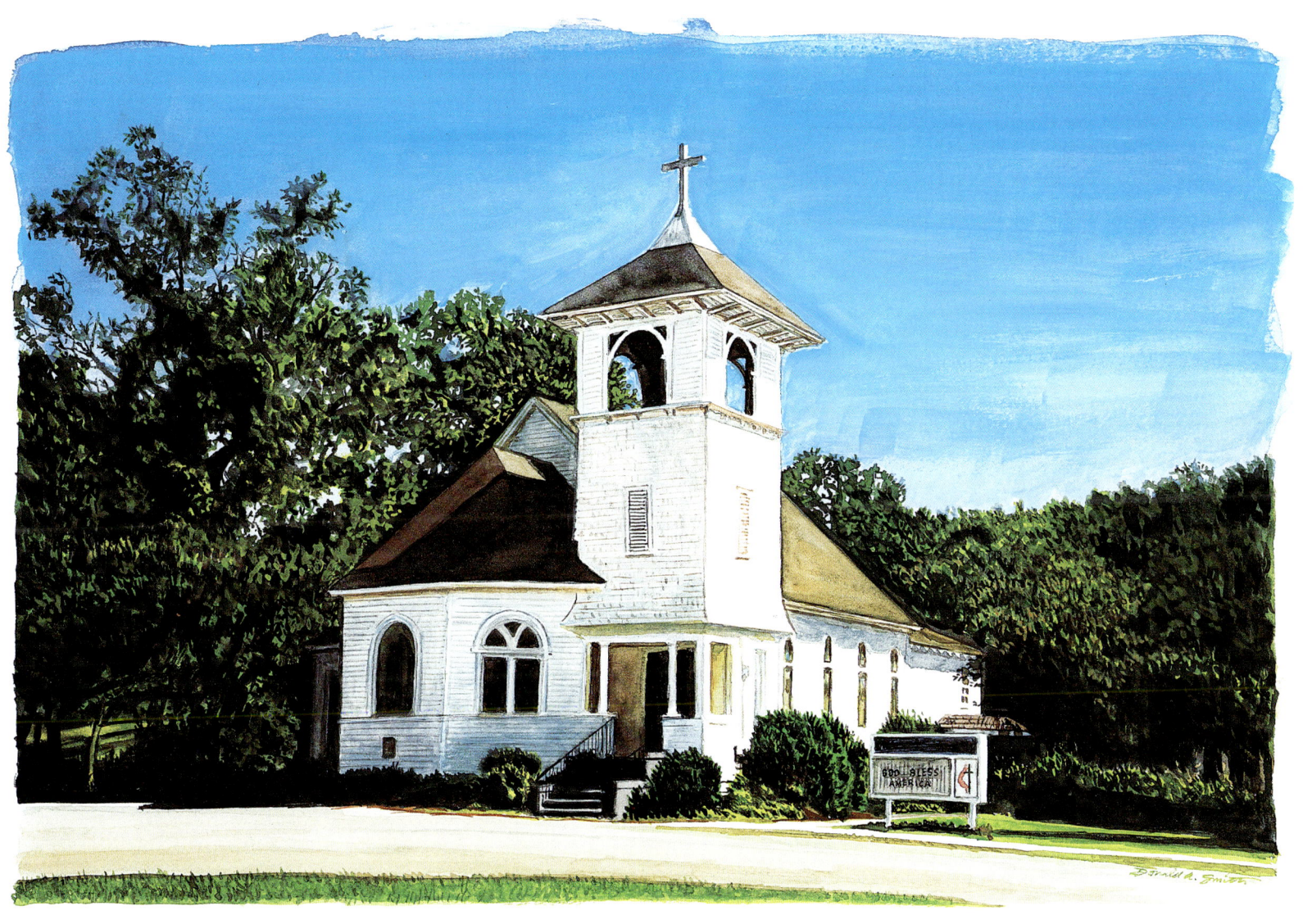

Newborn

CHURCHES

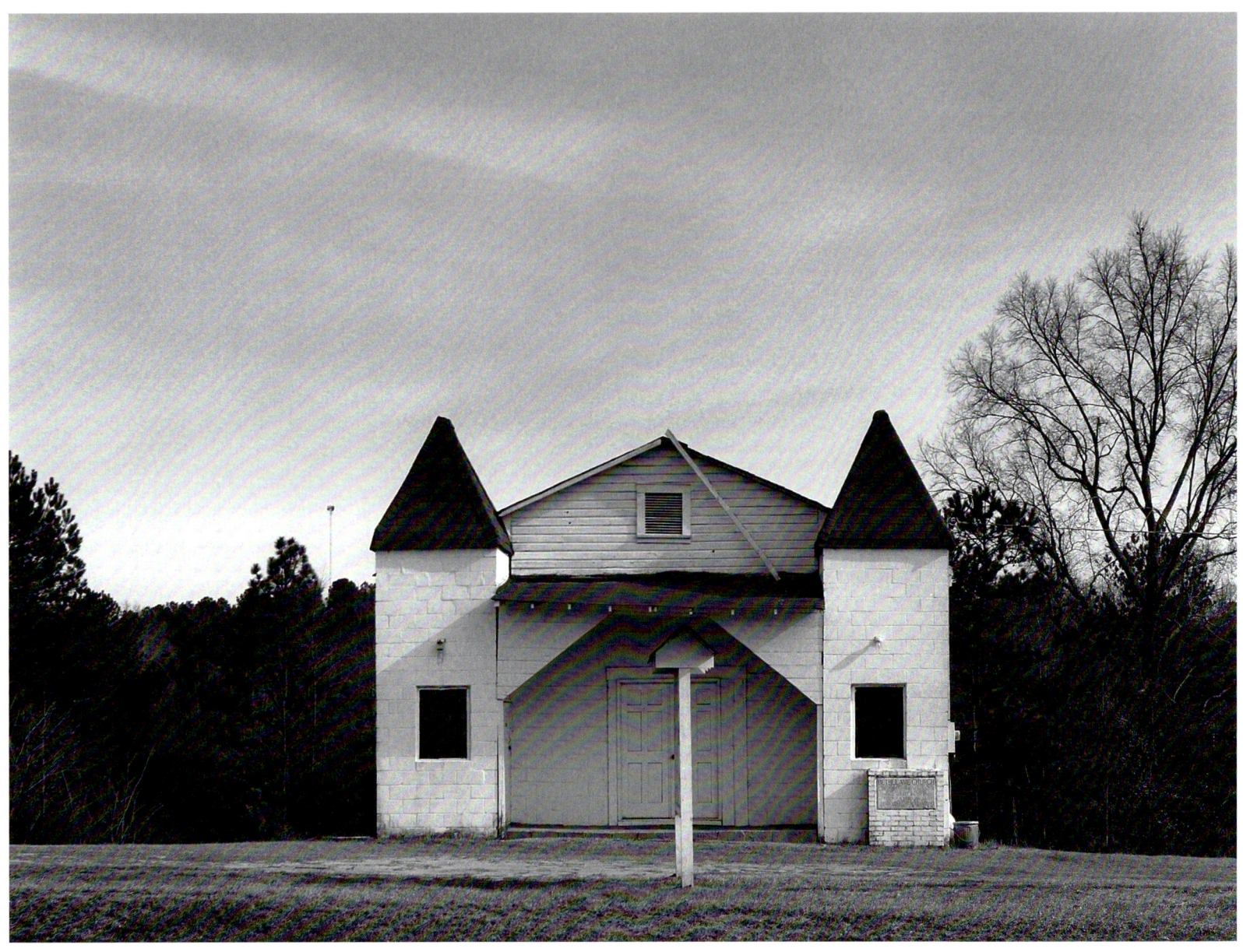

Byron

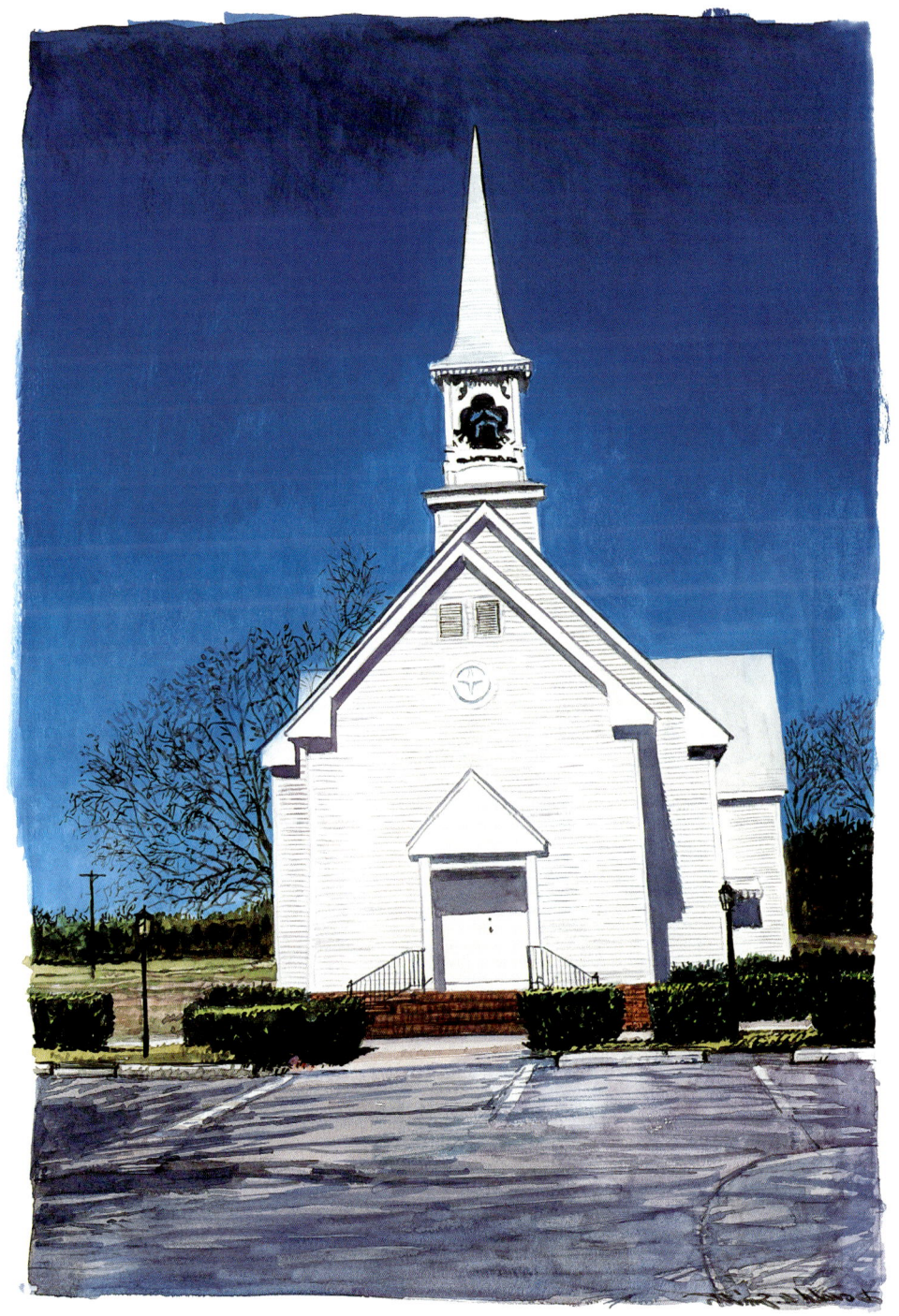

Byron

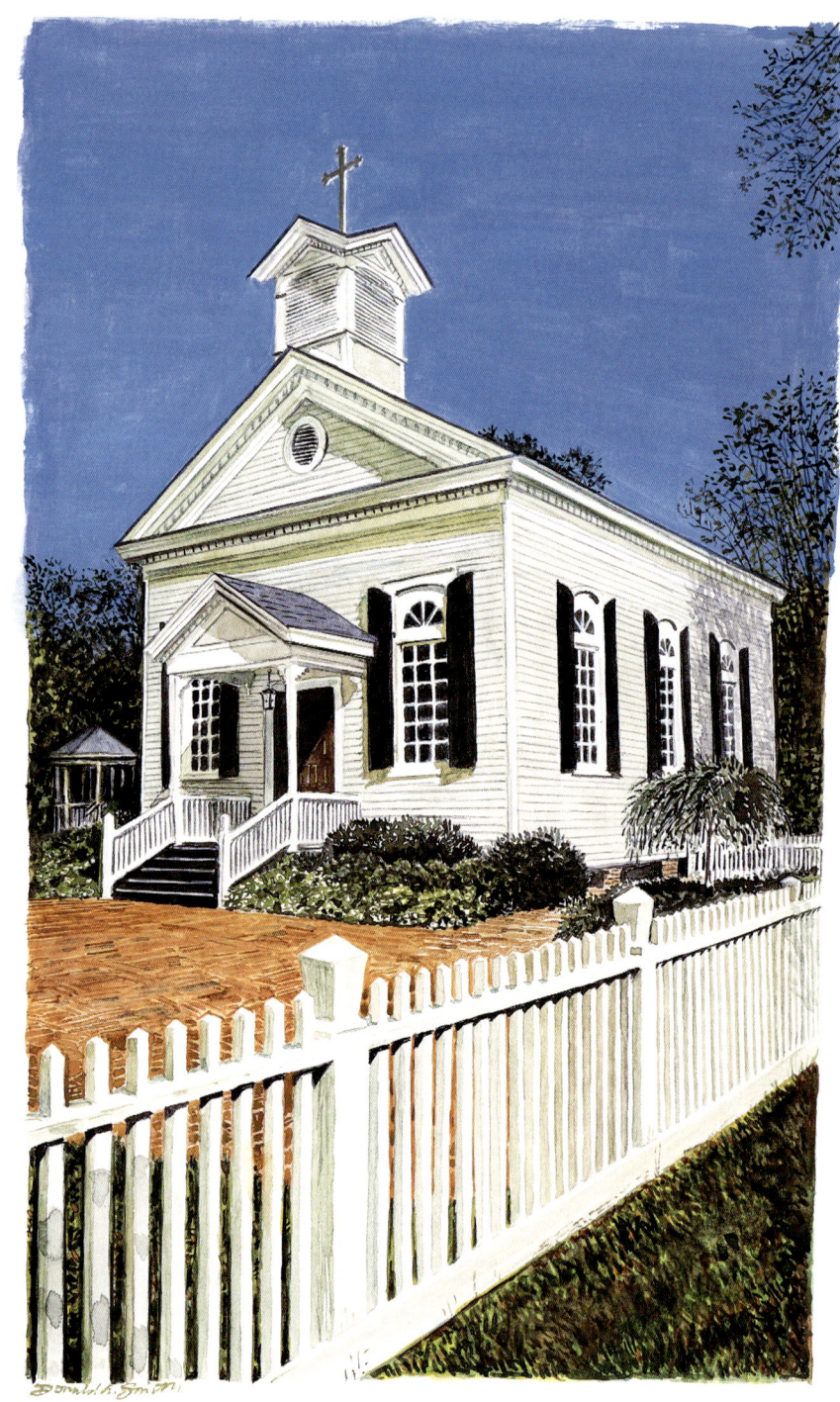

Thomasville

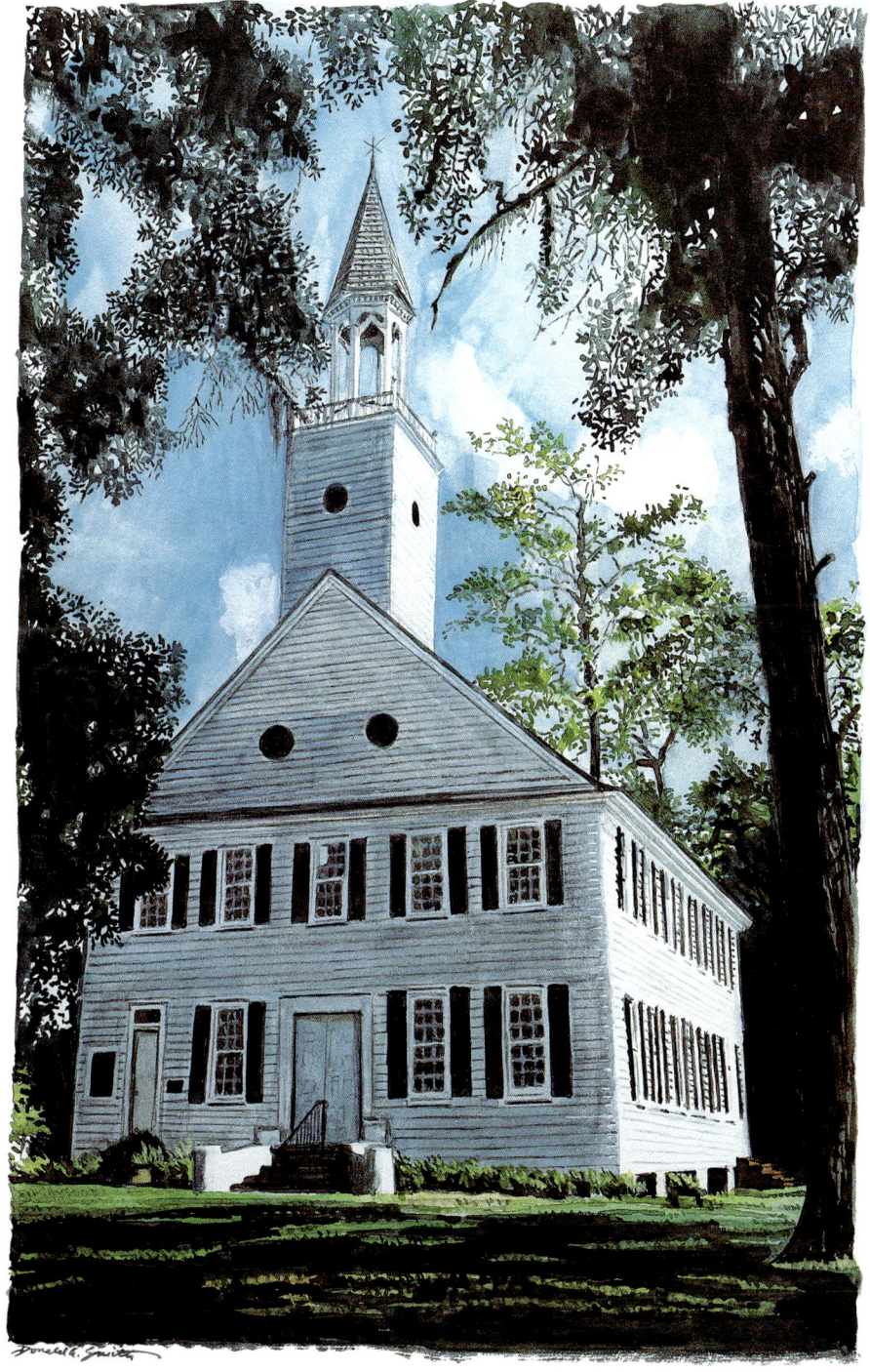

Midway

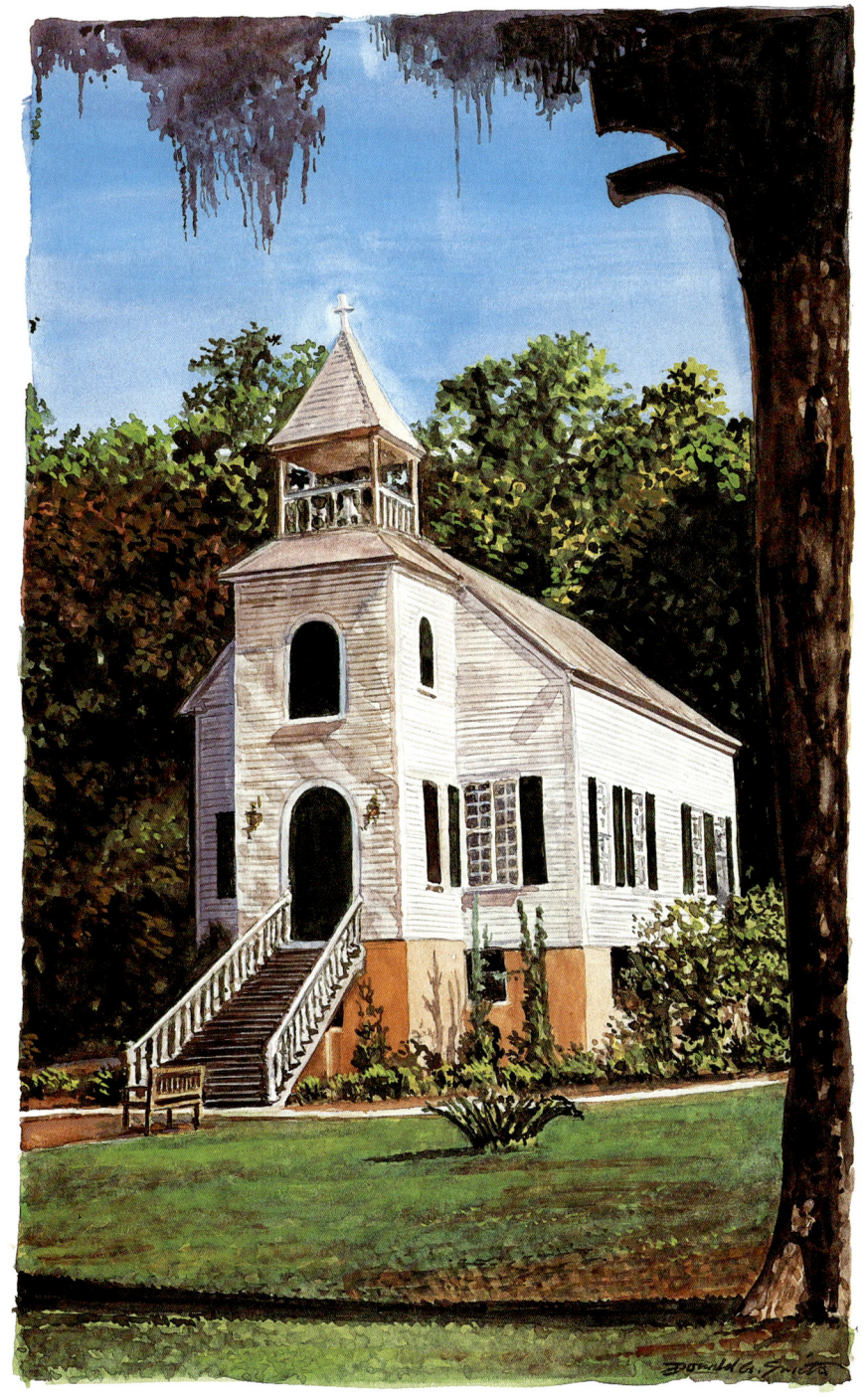

St. Marys

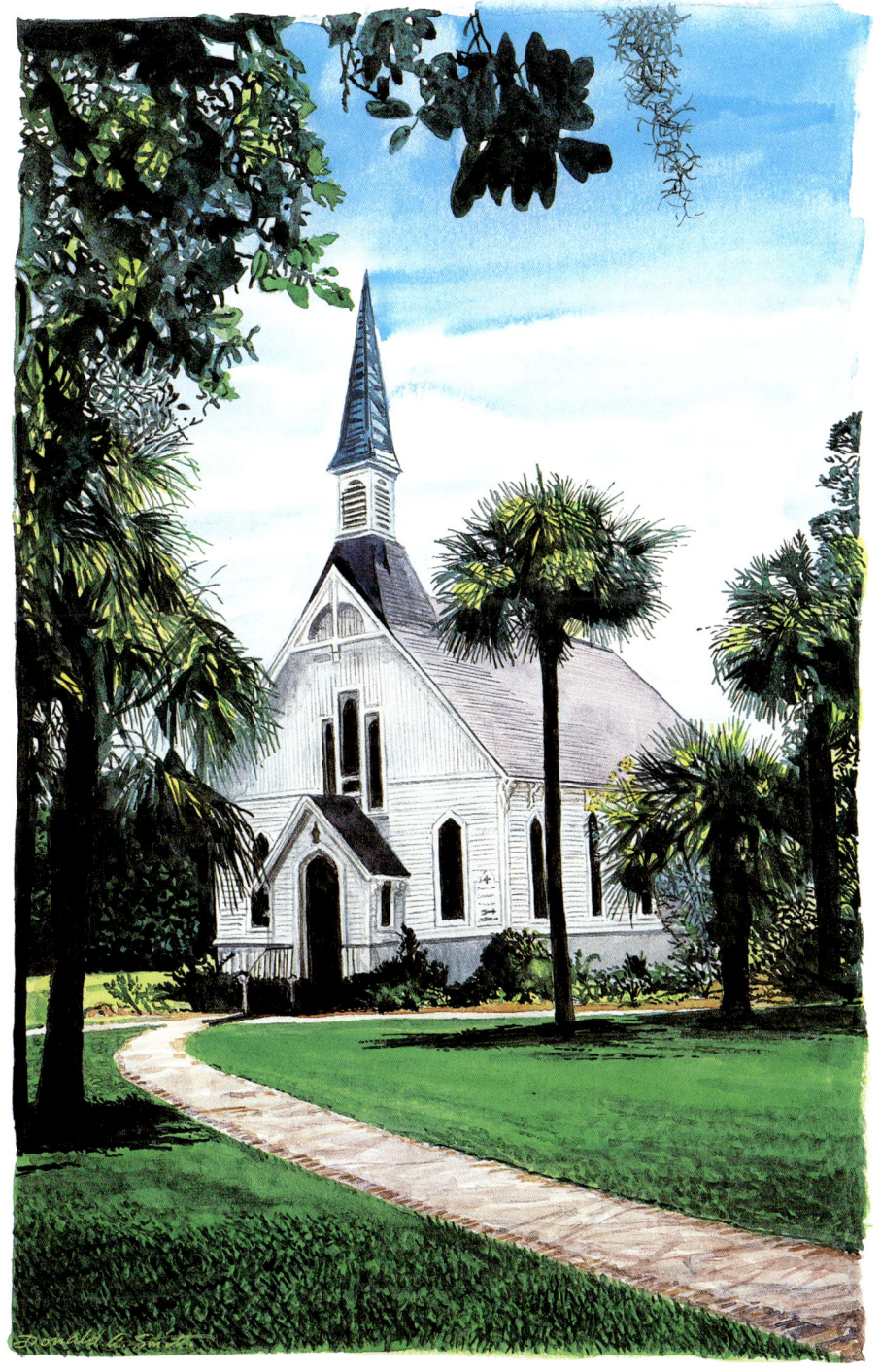

St. Simons

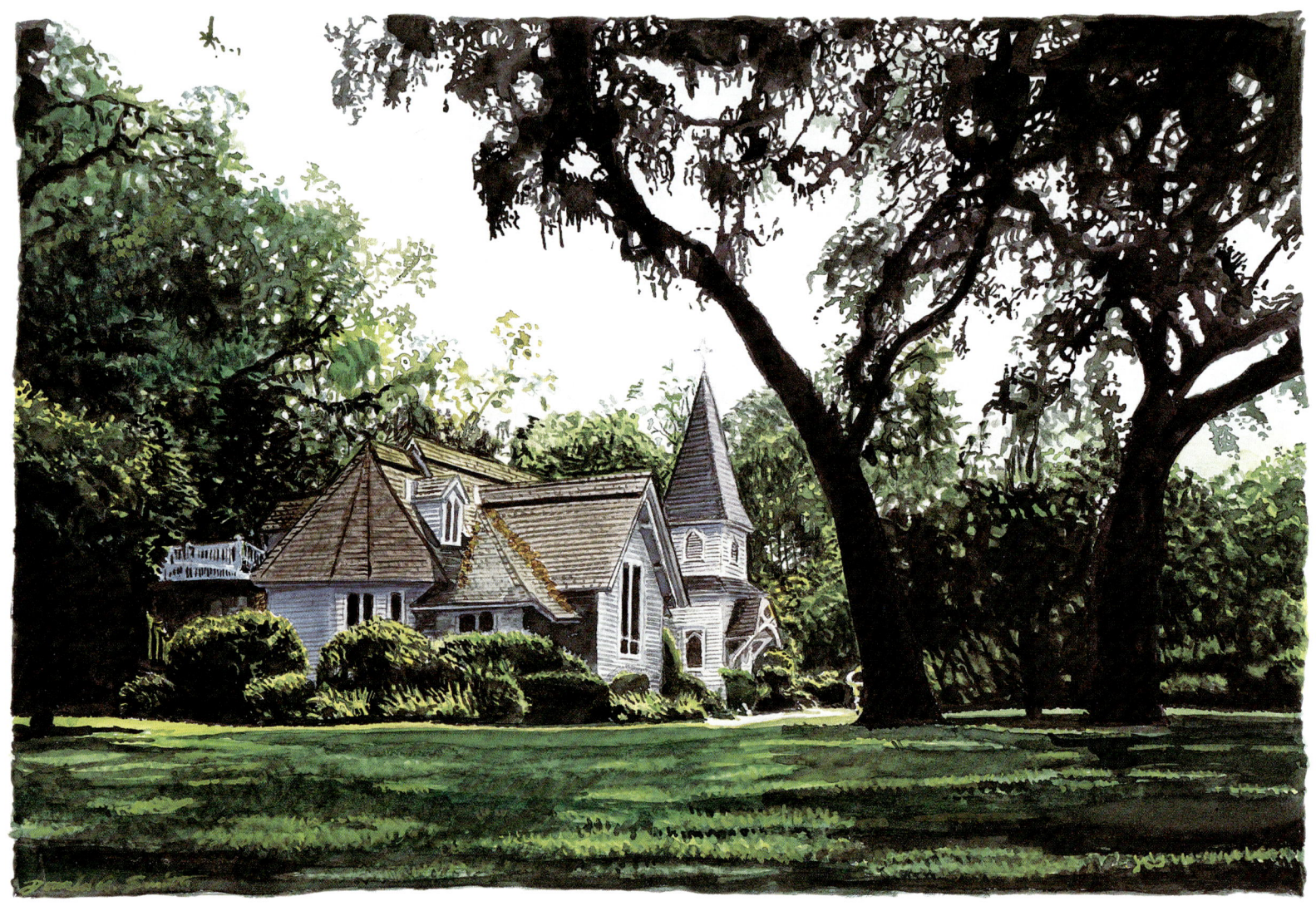

St. Simons

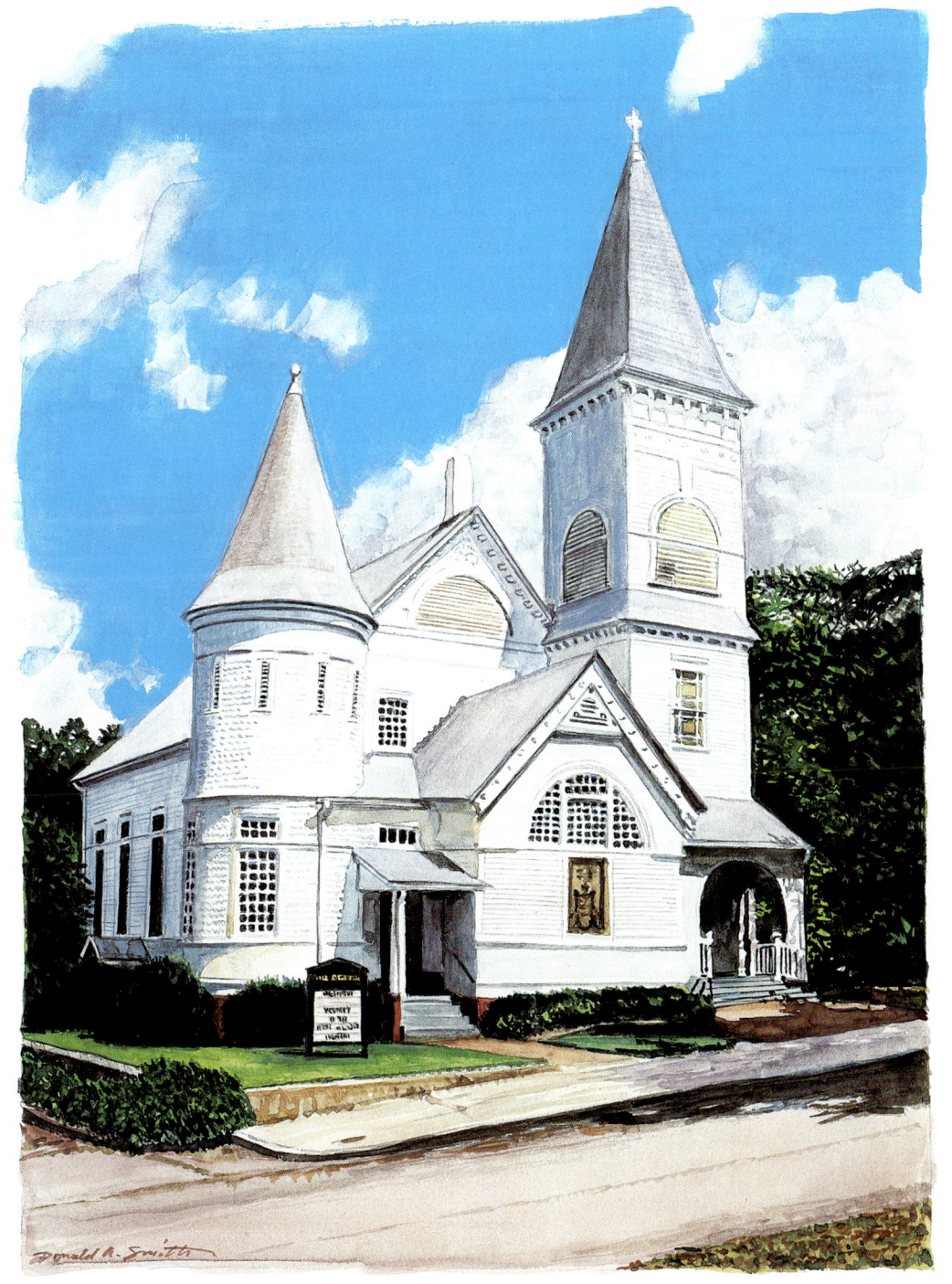

Senoa

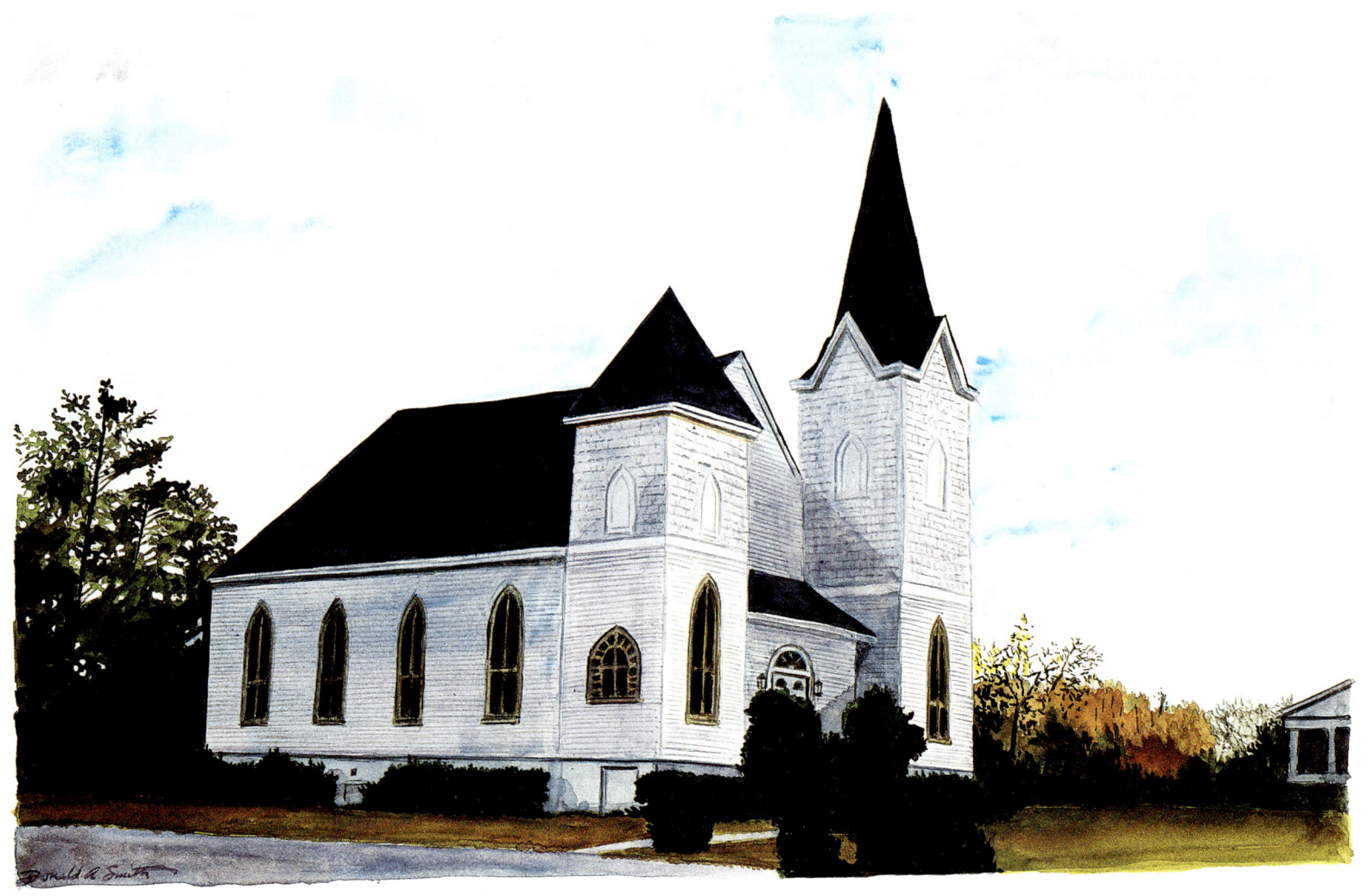

Williamson

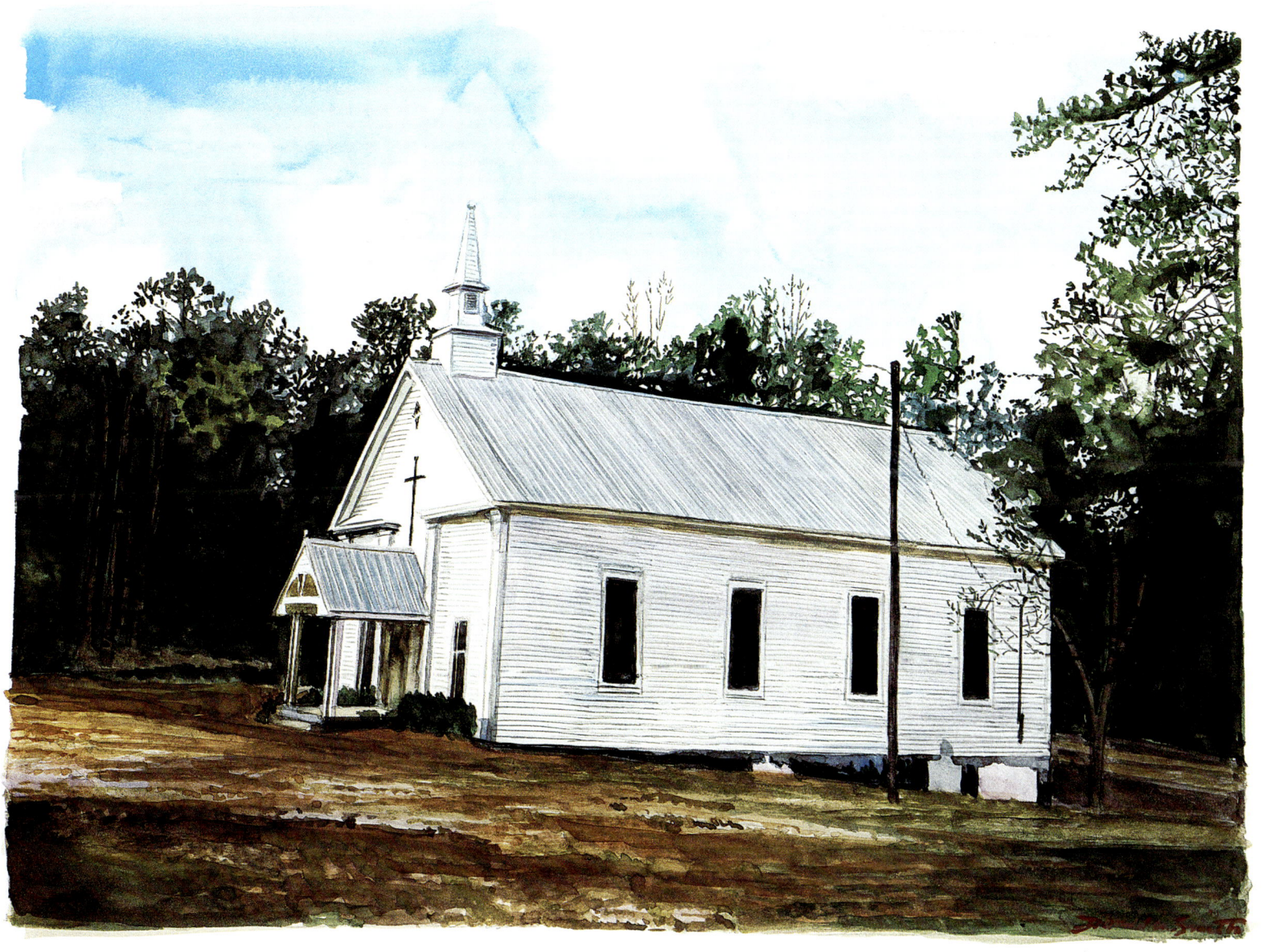

Harris City

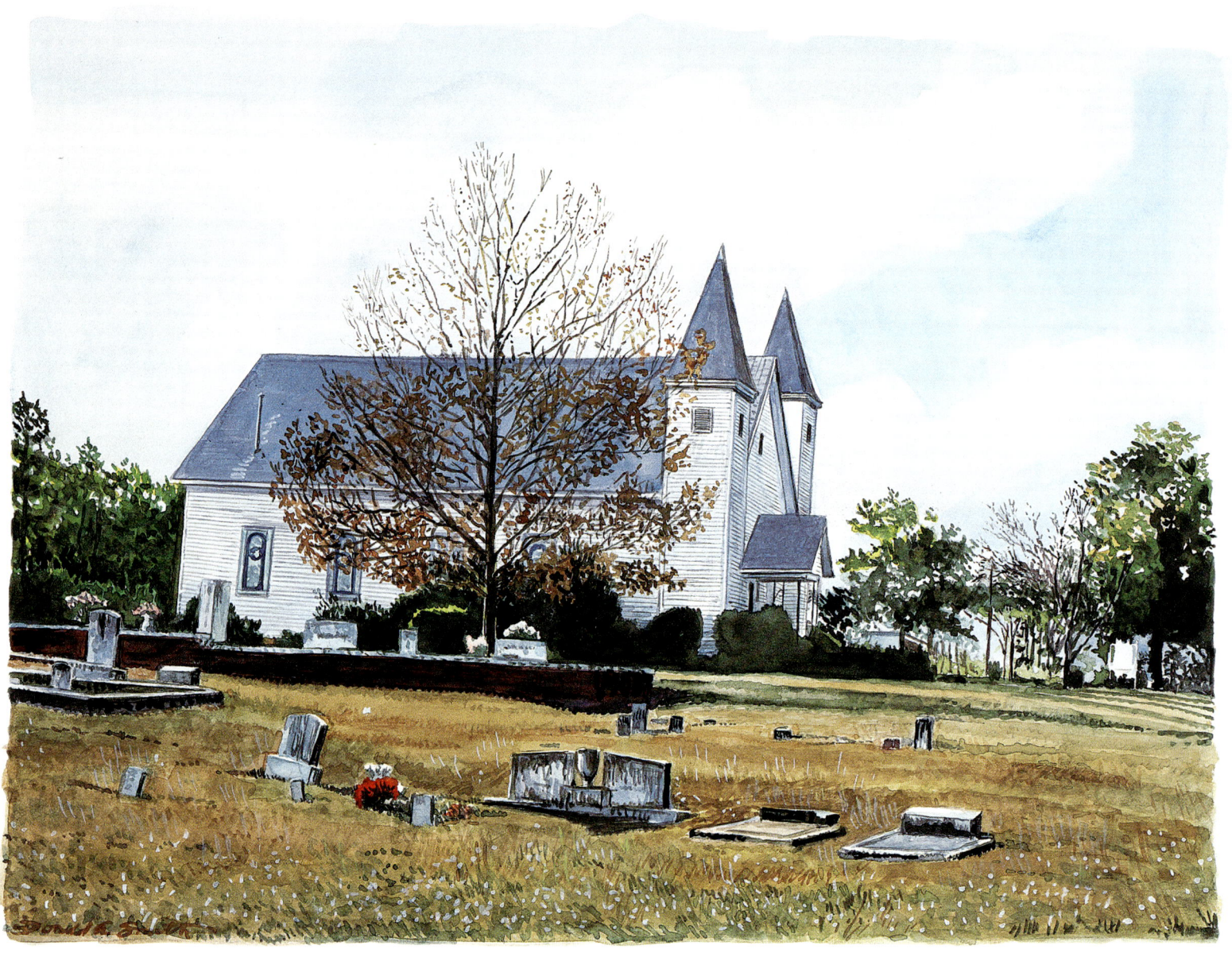

Woodbury

CHURCHES

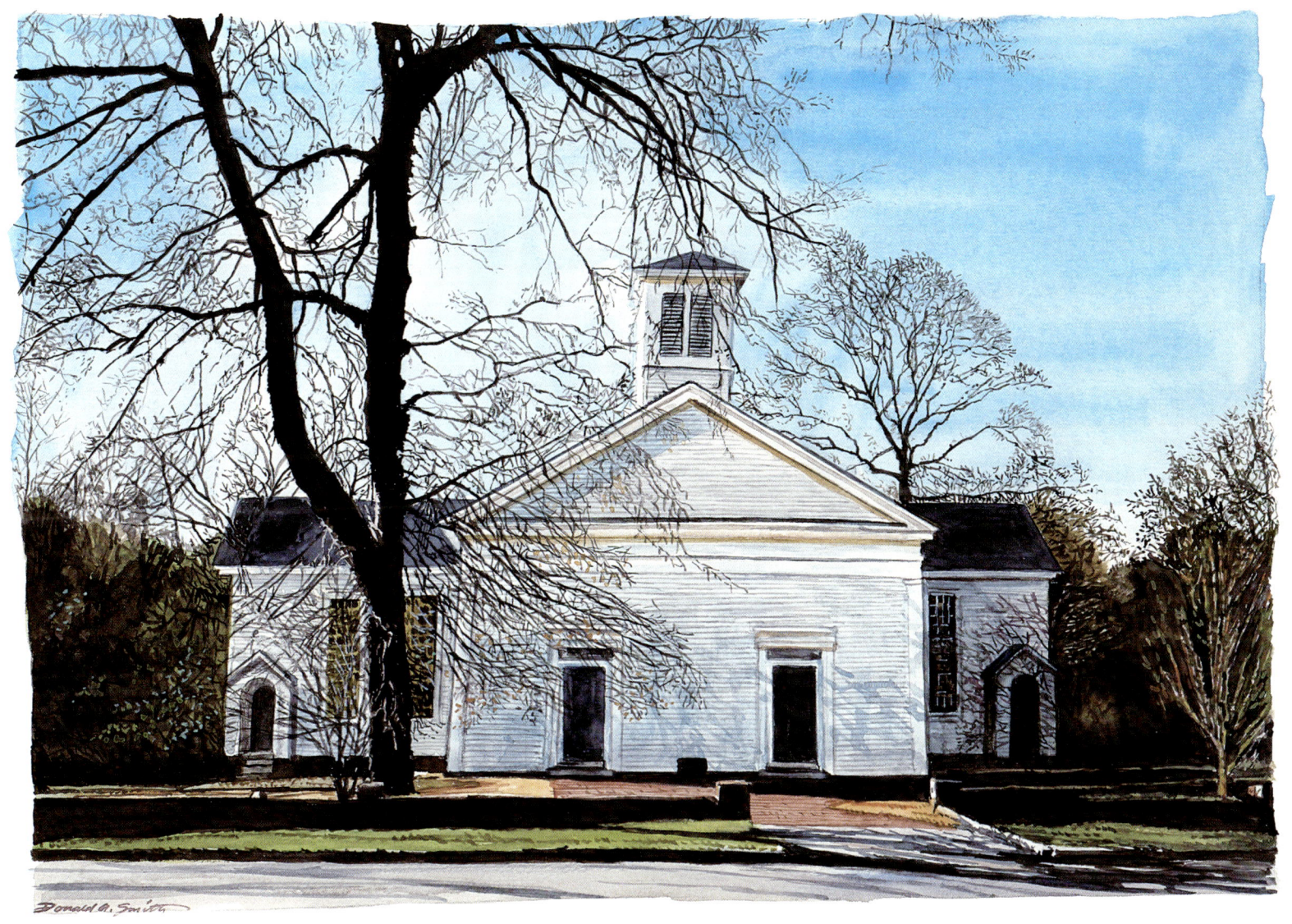

Oxford

CHURCHES

III

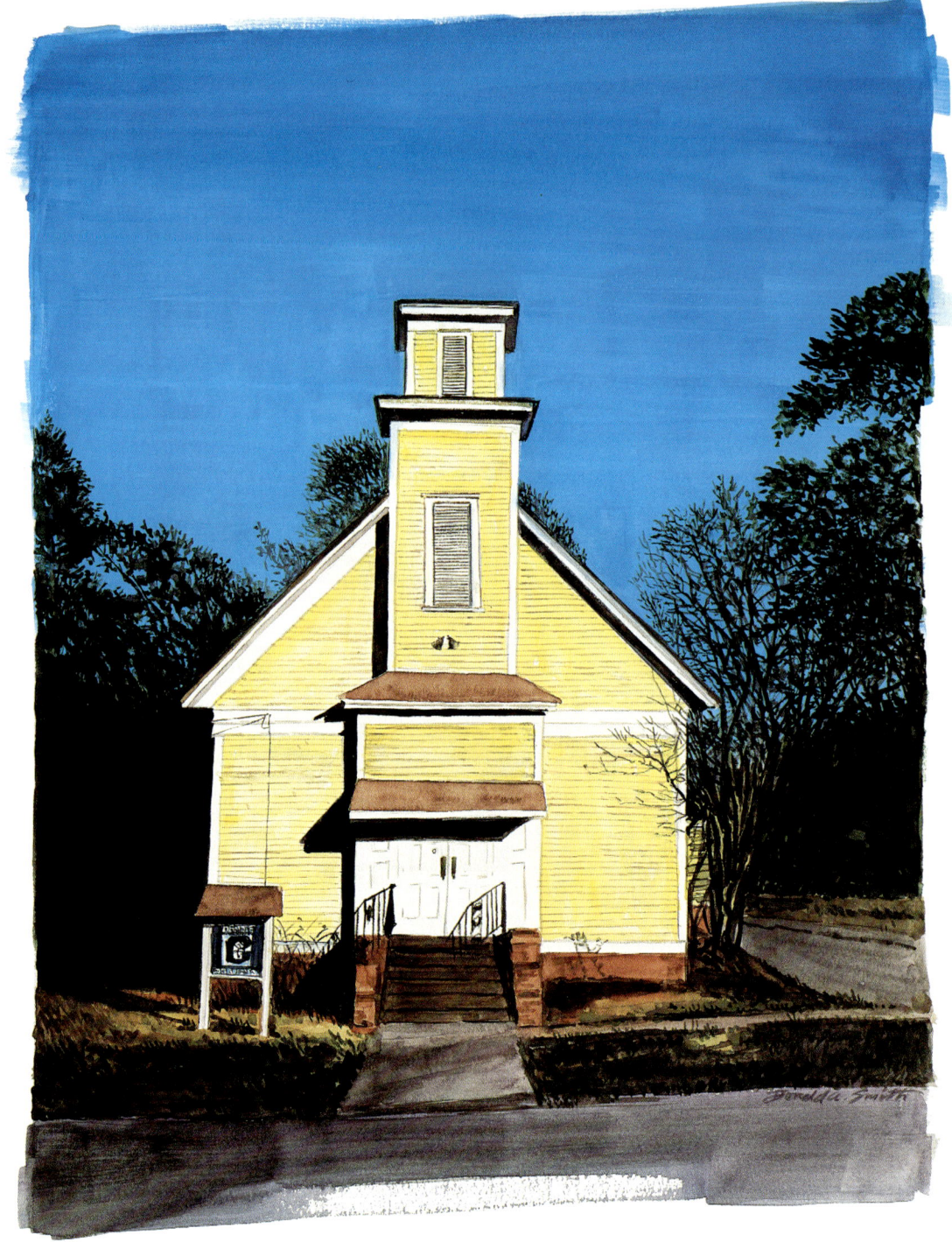

Monroe

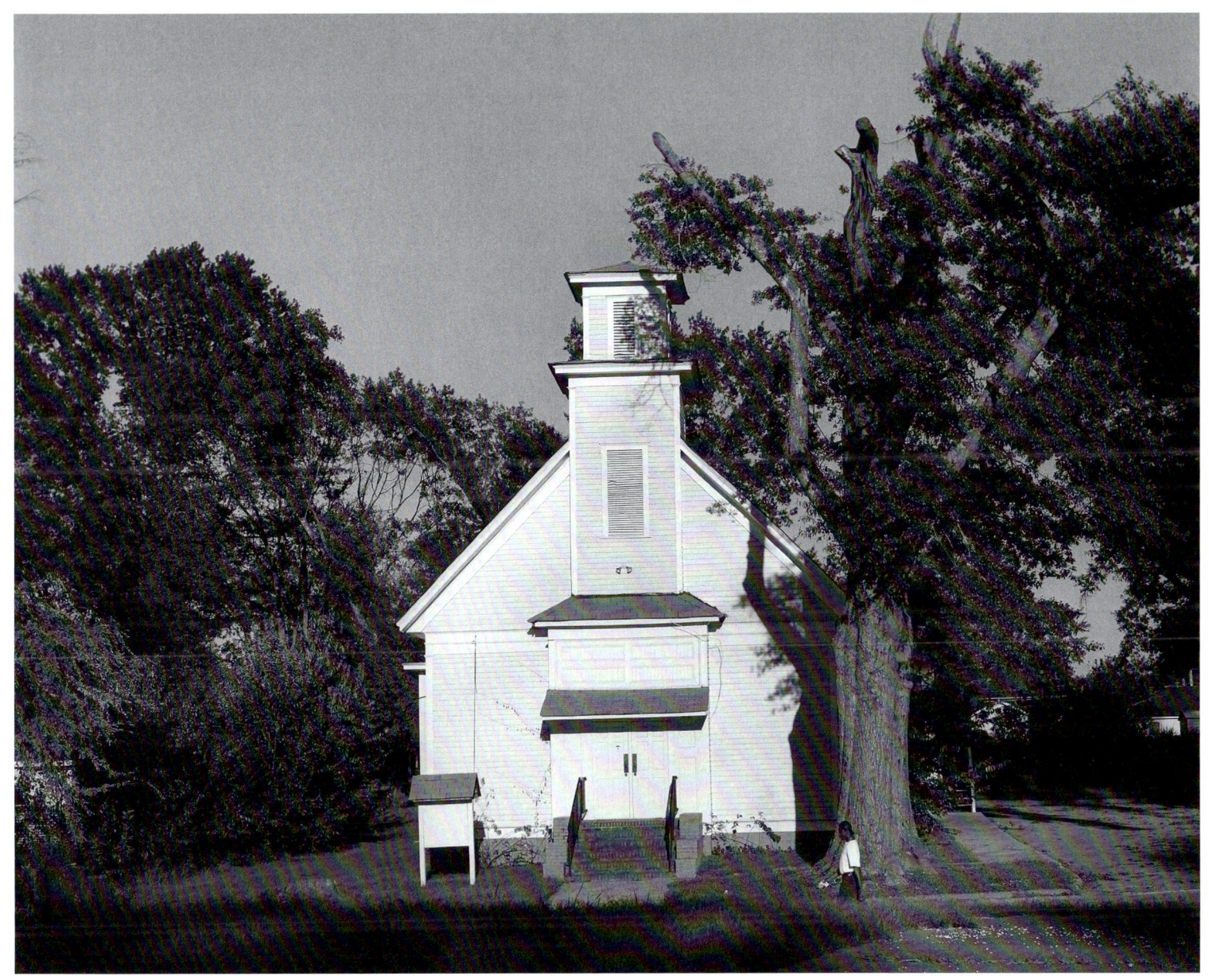

Monroe

CHURCHES

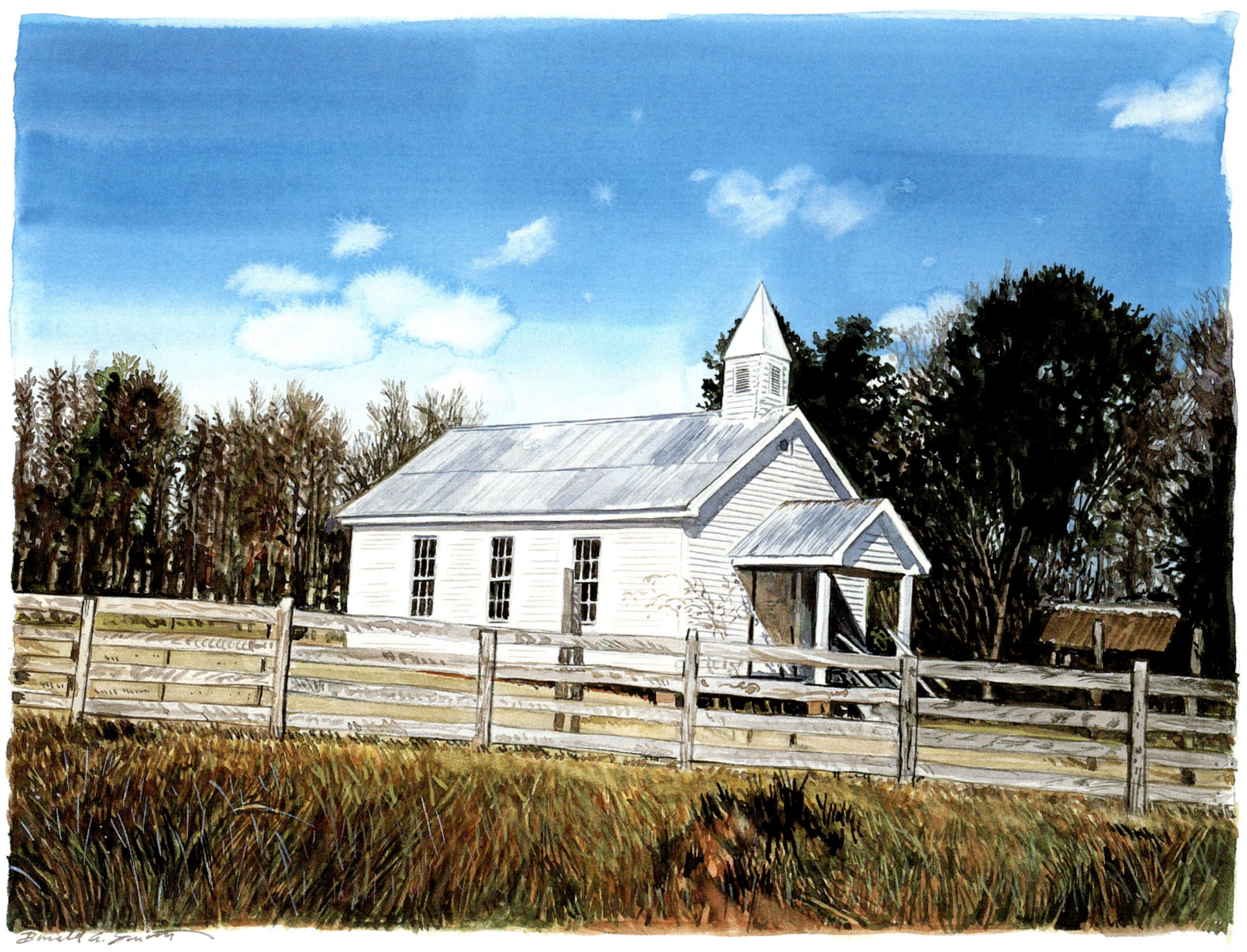

Oconee County

CHURCHES

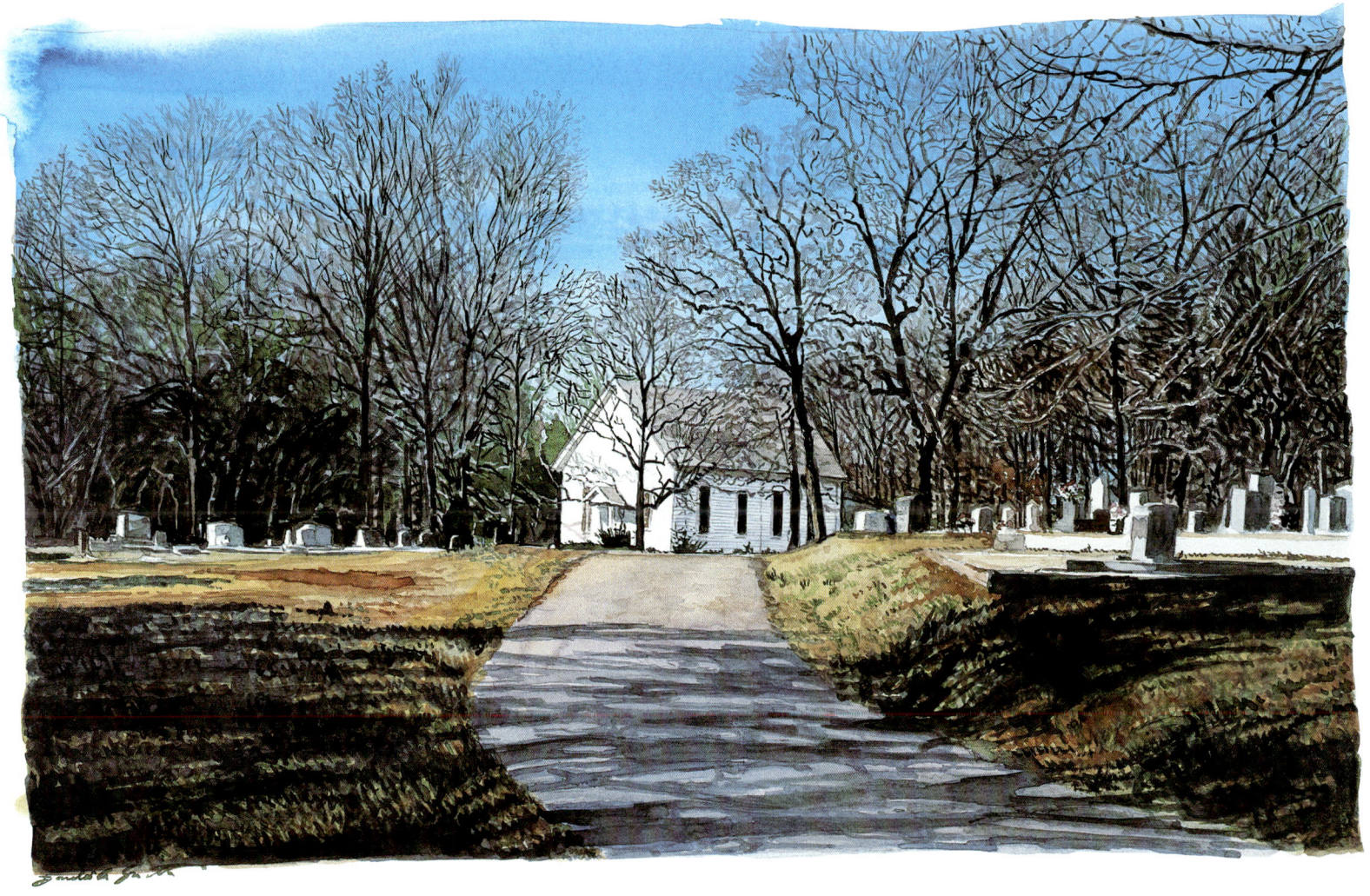

Athens

CHURCHES

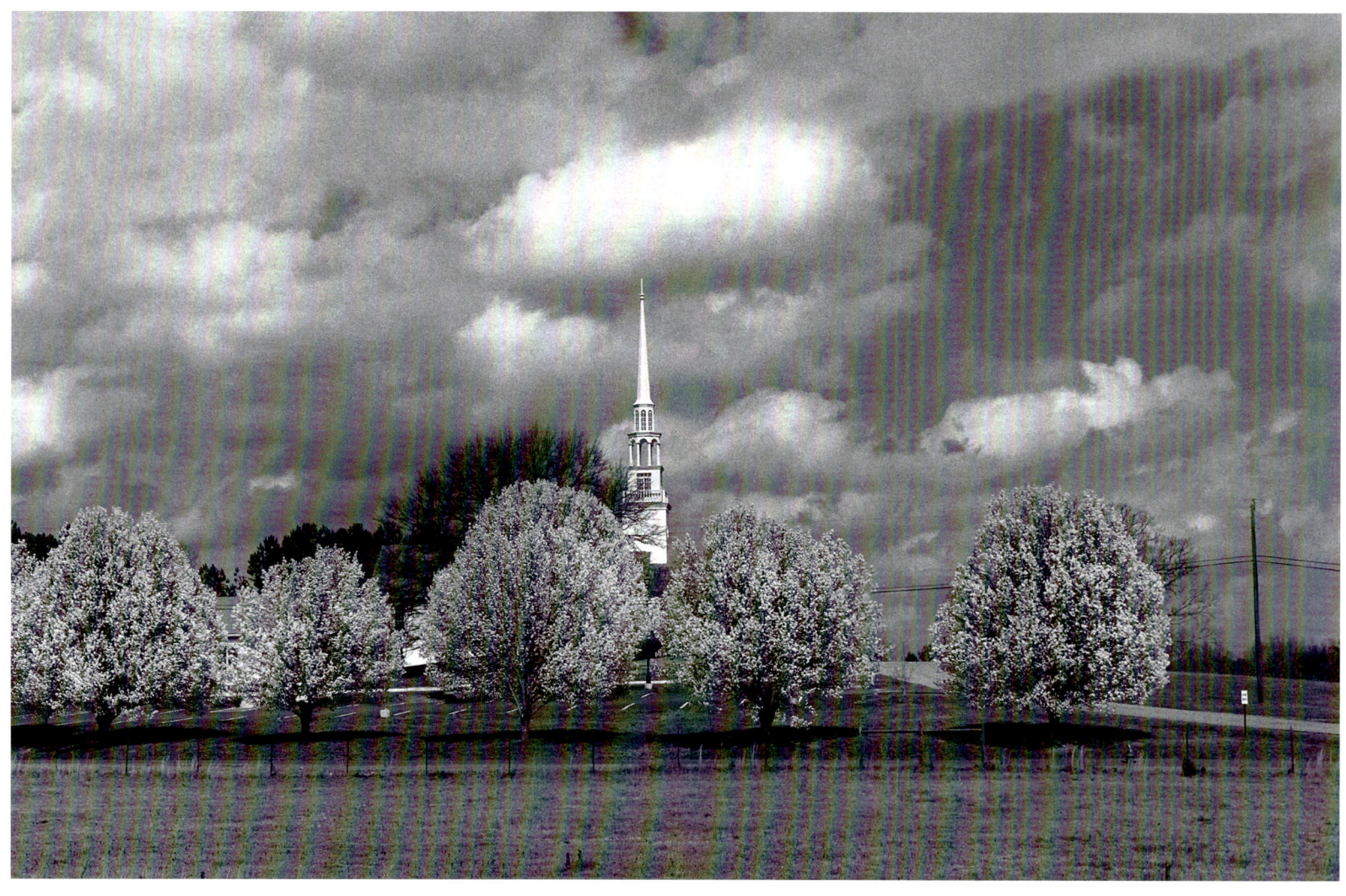

Oconee County

CHURCHES

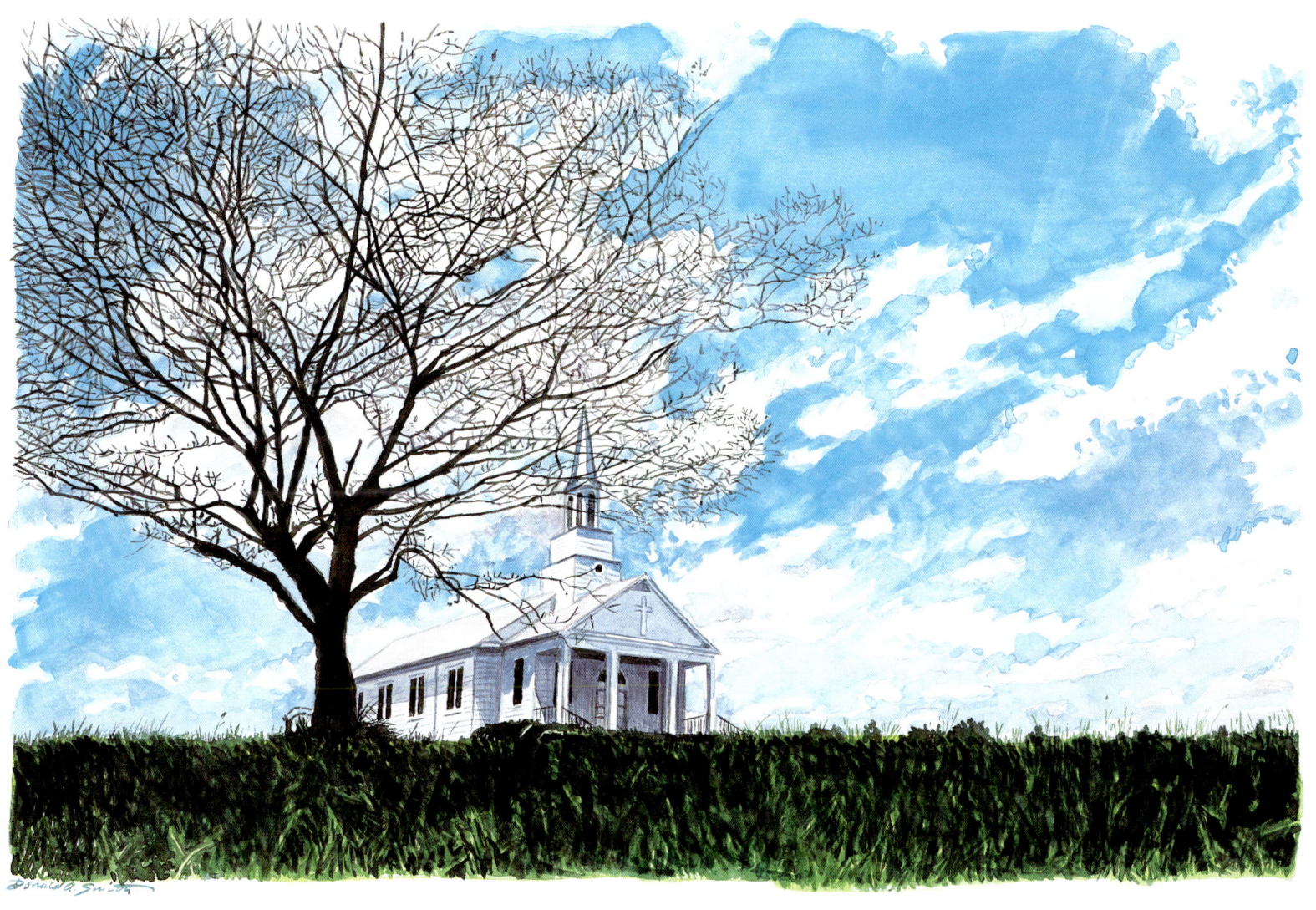

Oconee County

CHURCHES

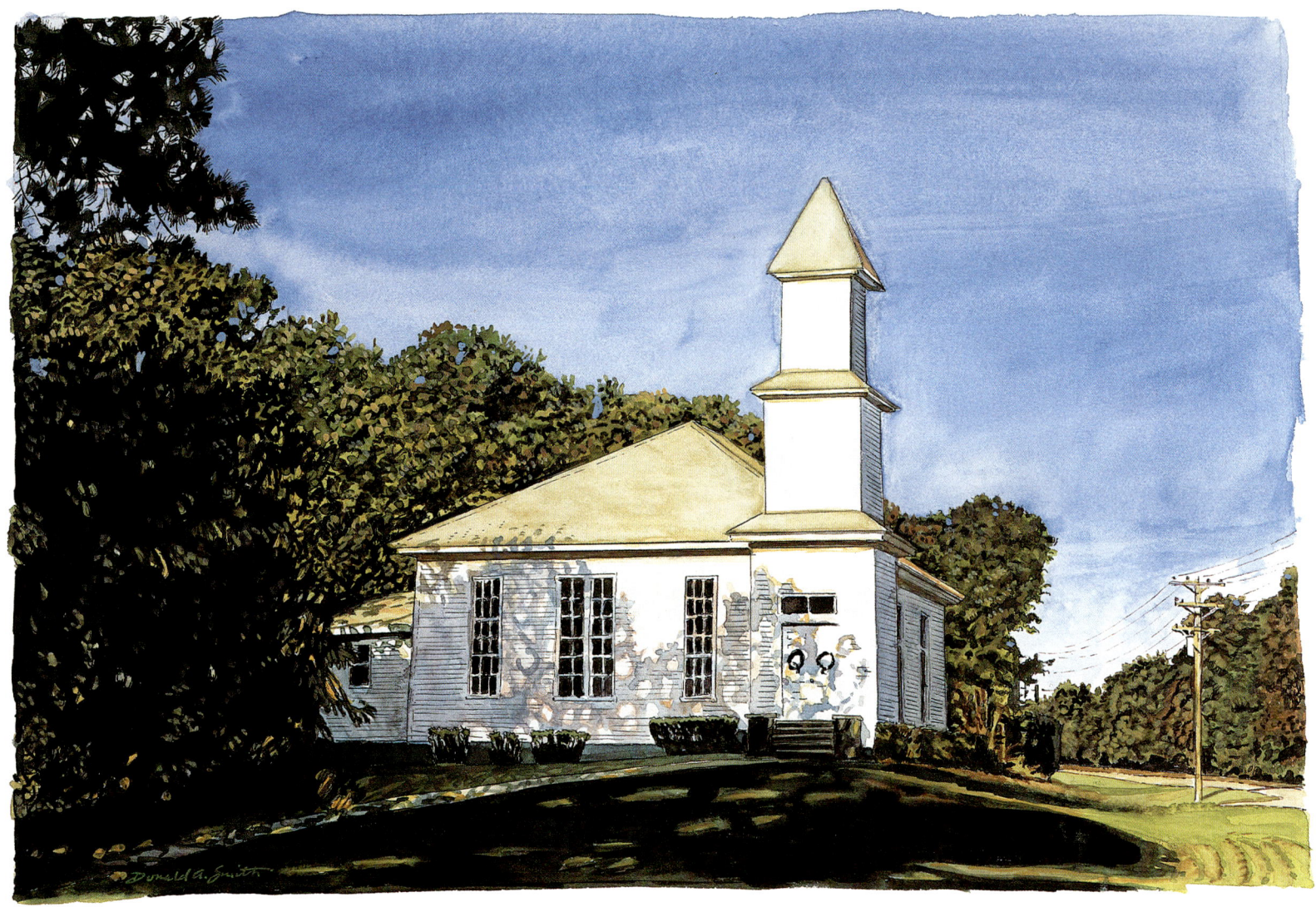

Attica (near Athens)

CHURCHES

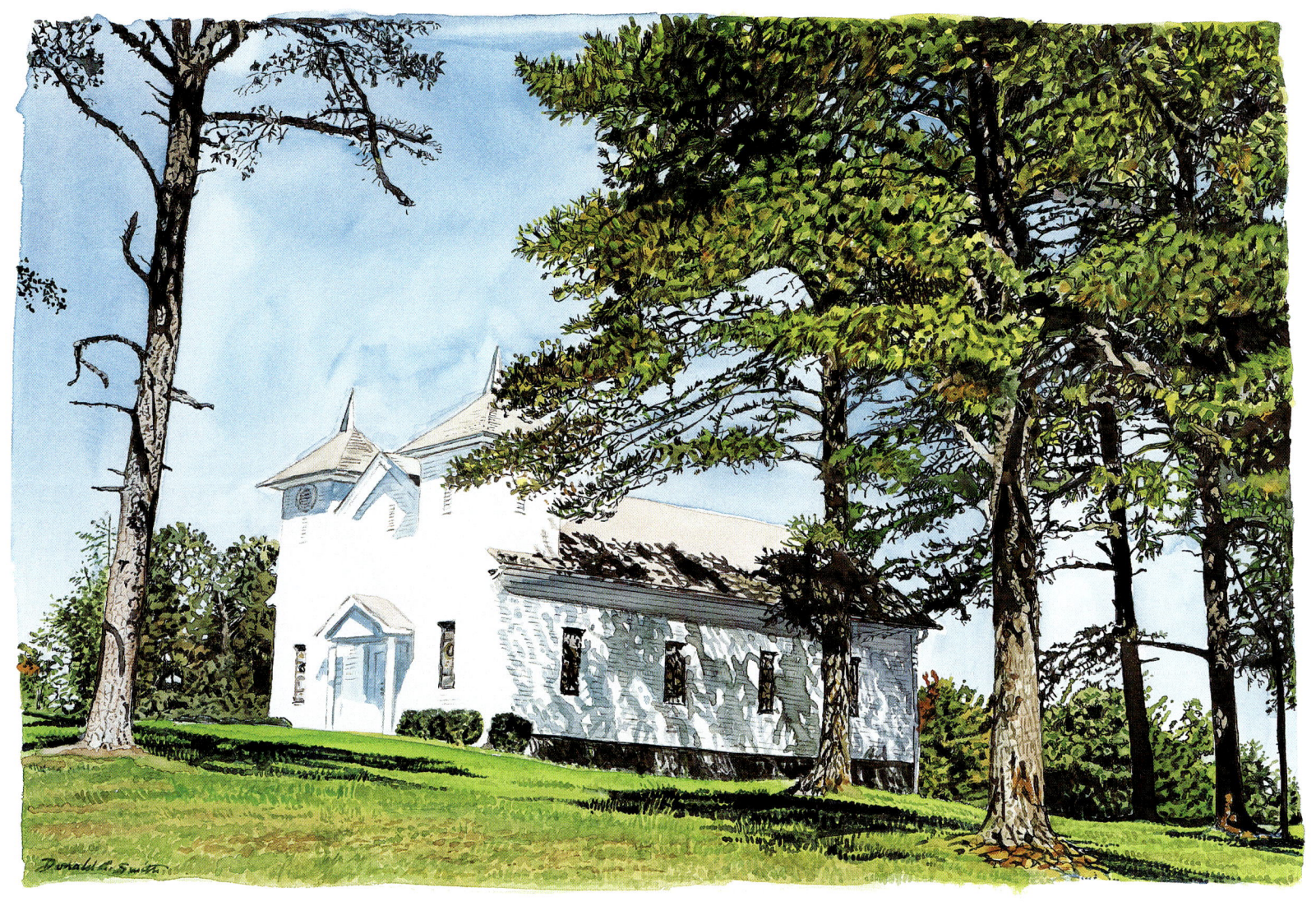

Jackson County

CHURCHES

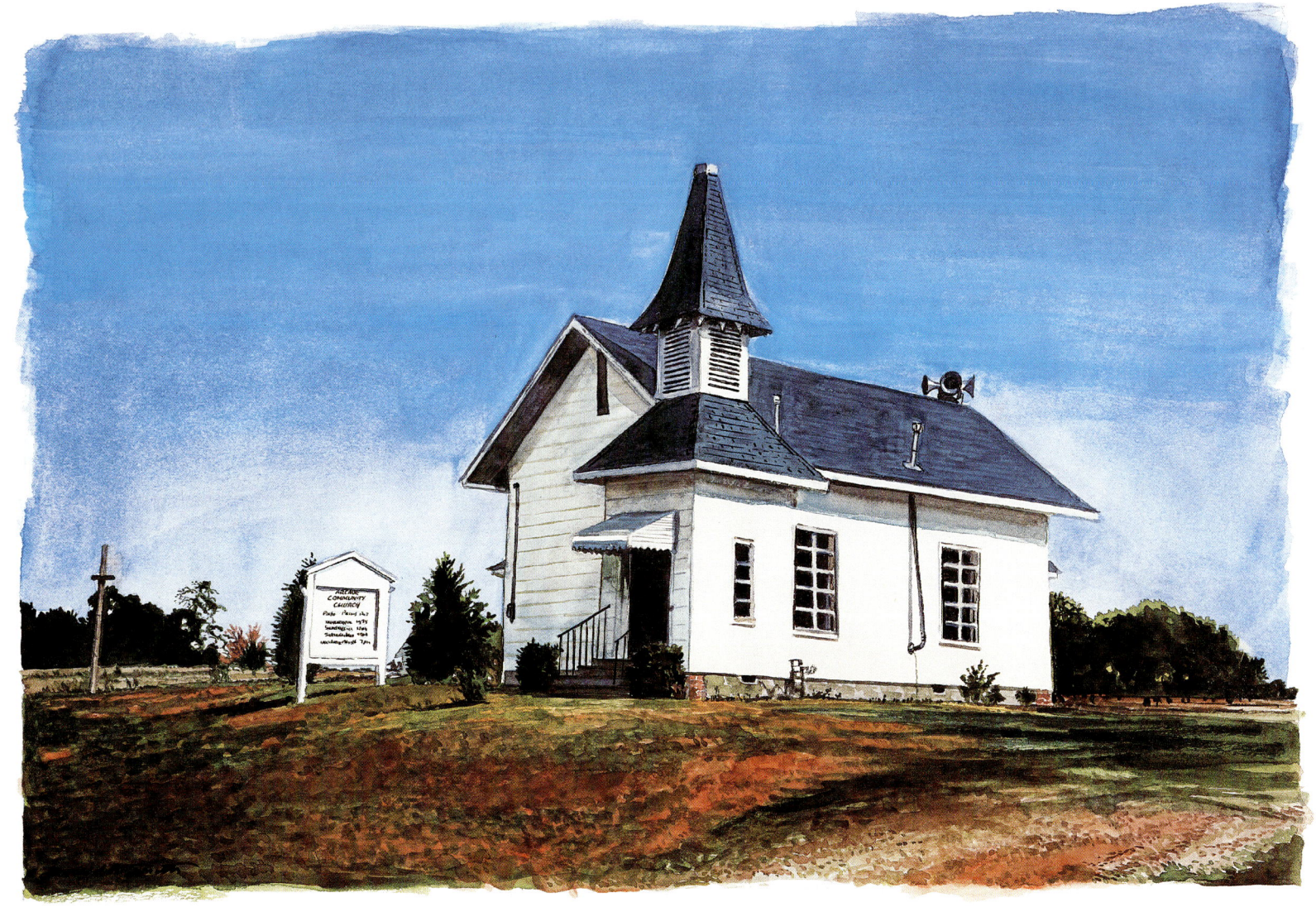

Arcade

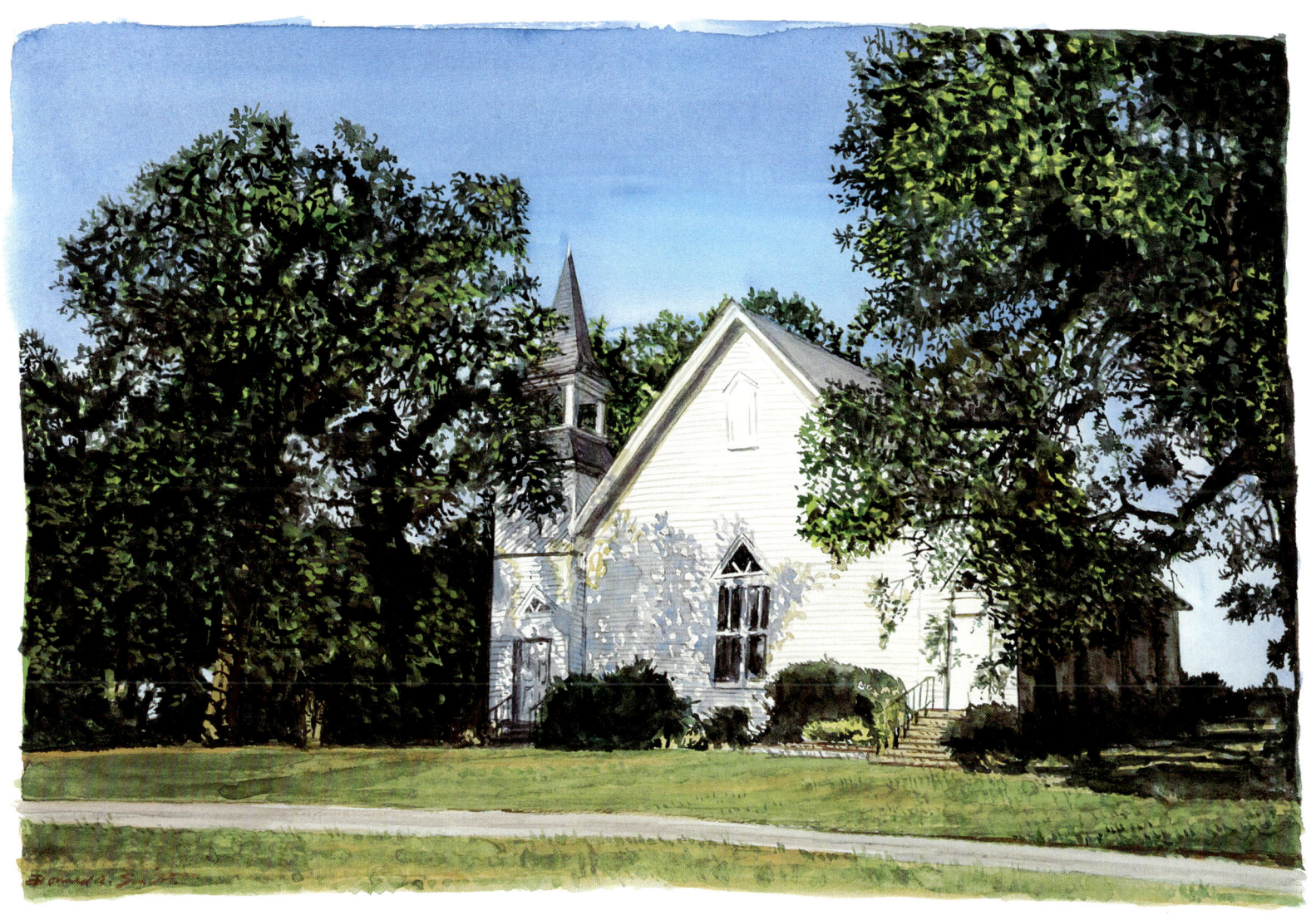

Dry Pond

CHURCHES

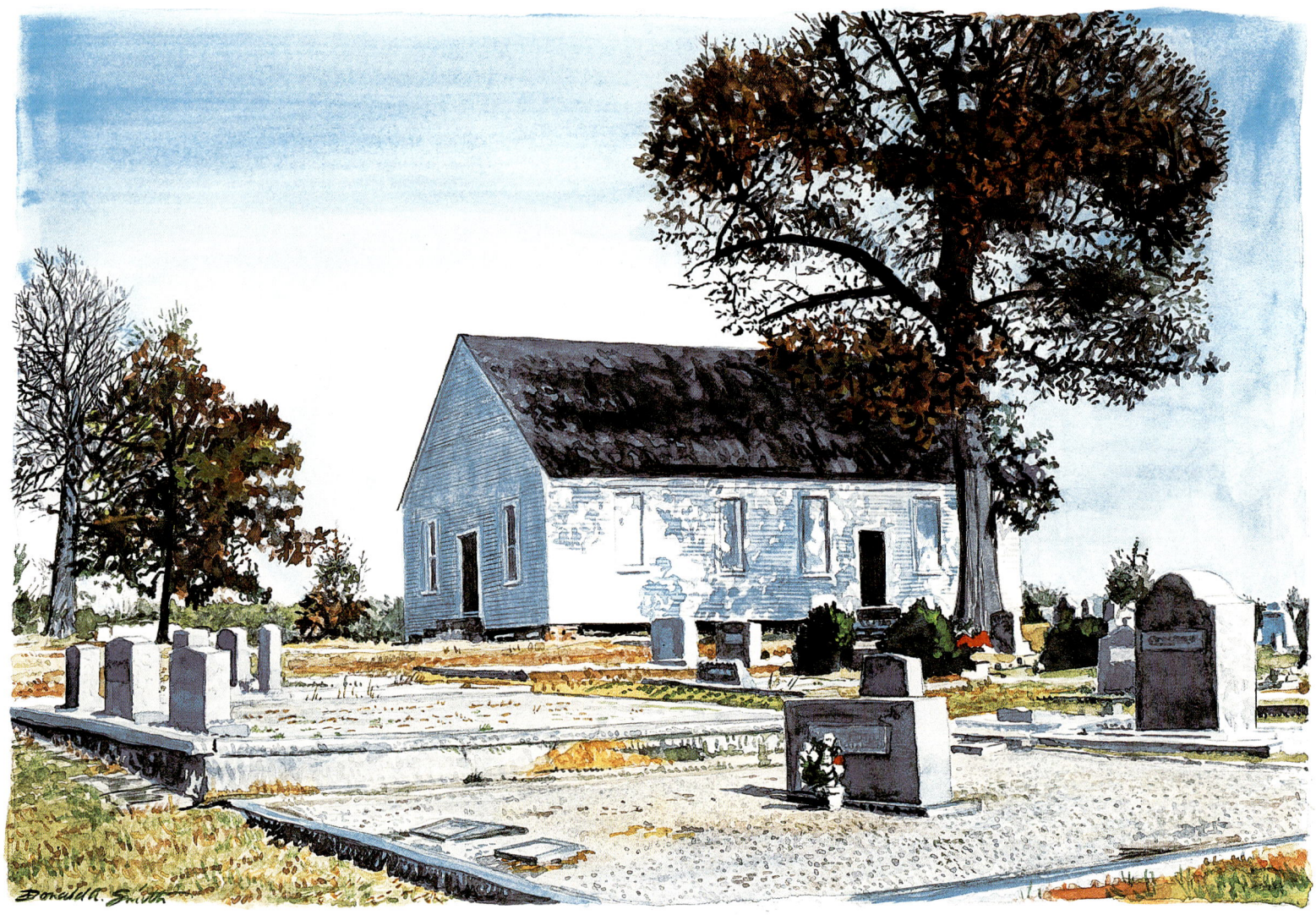

Ila

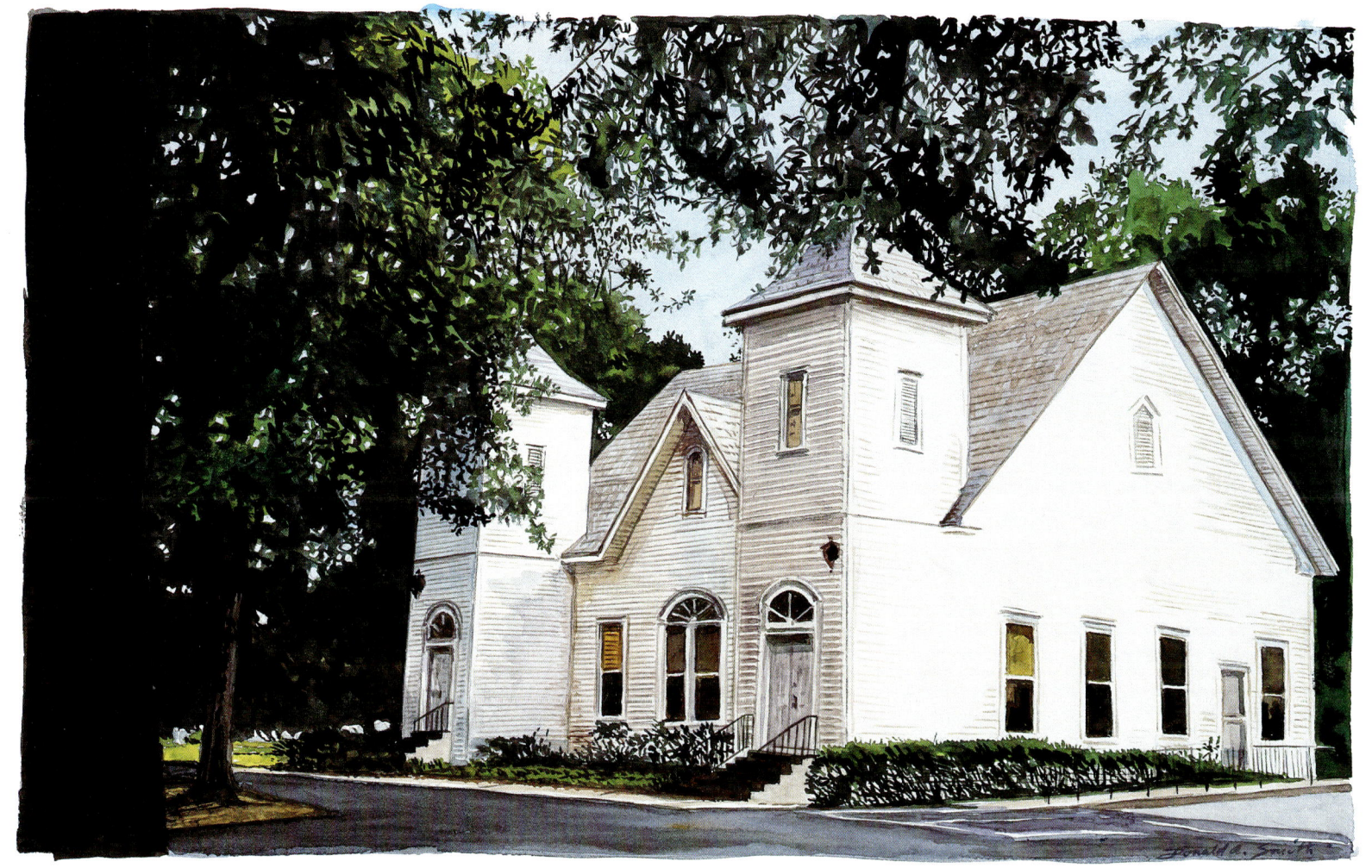

Neese

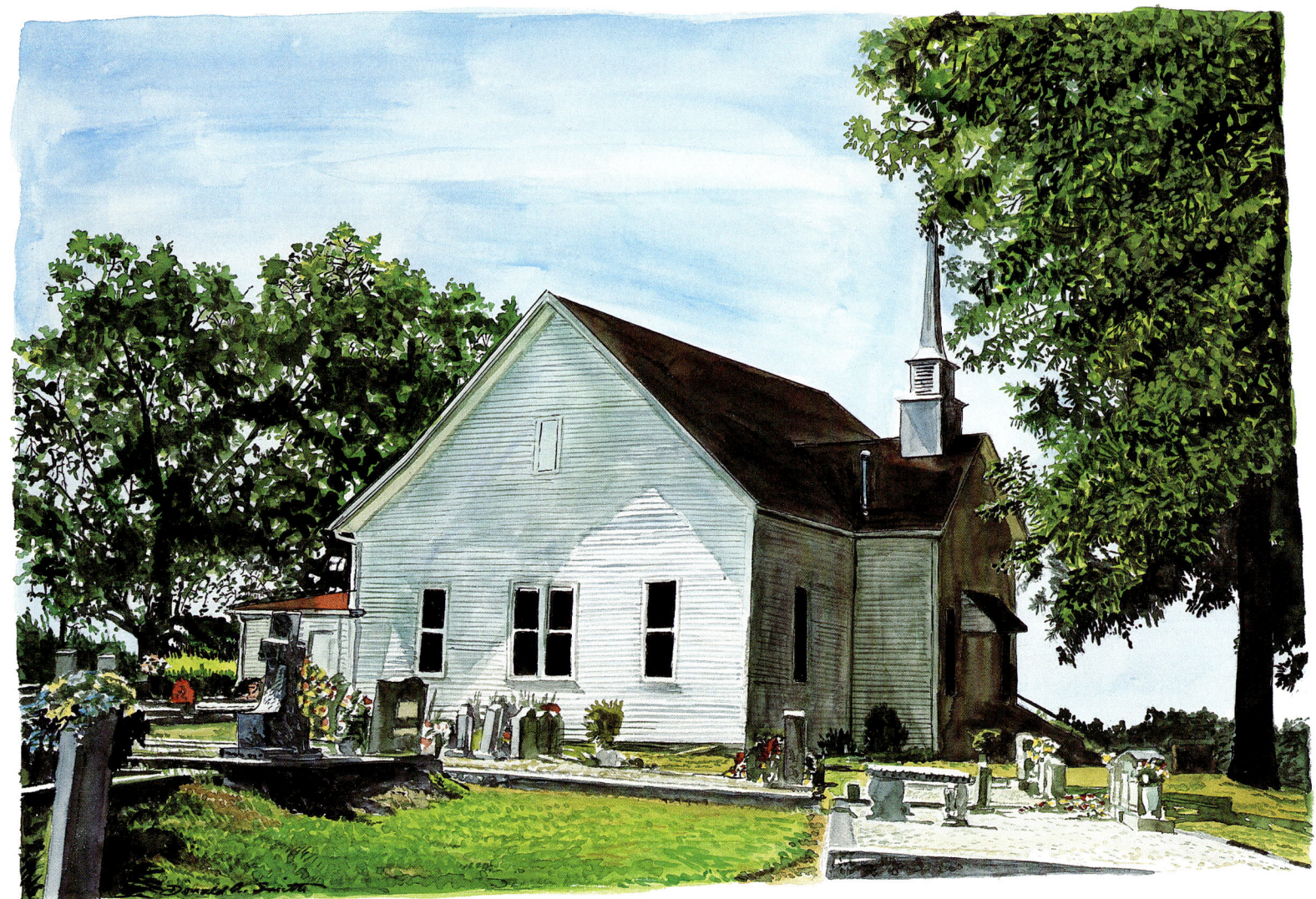

Nicholson

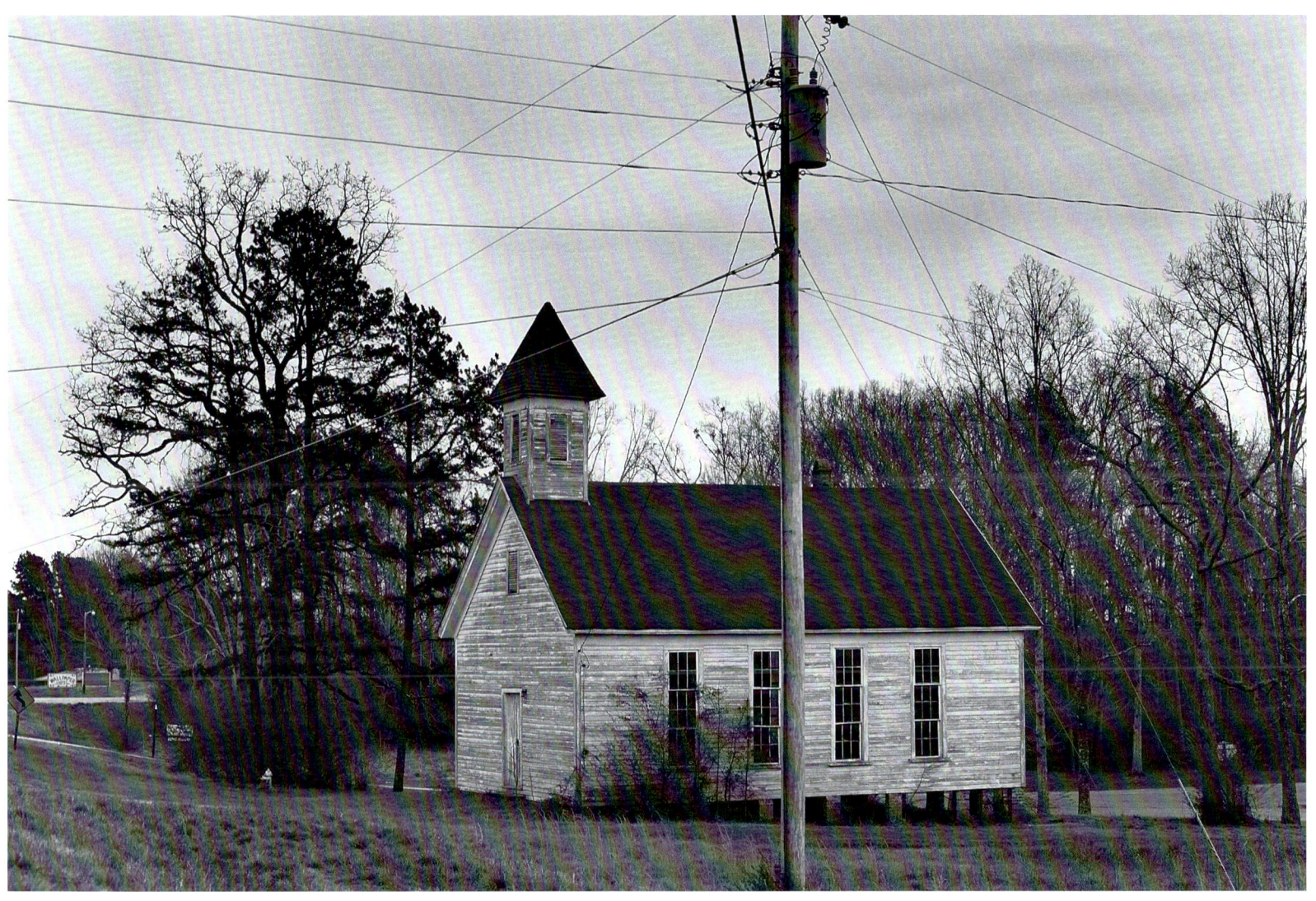

Center

CHURCHES

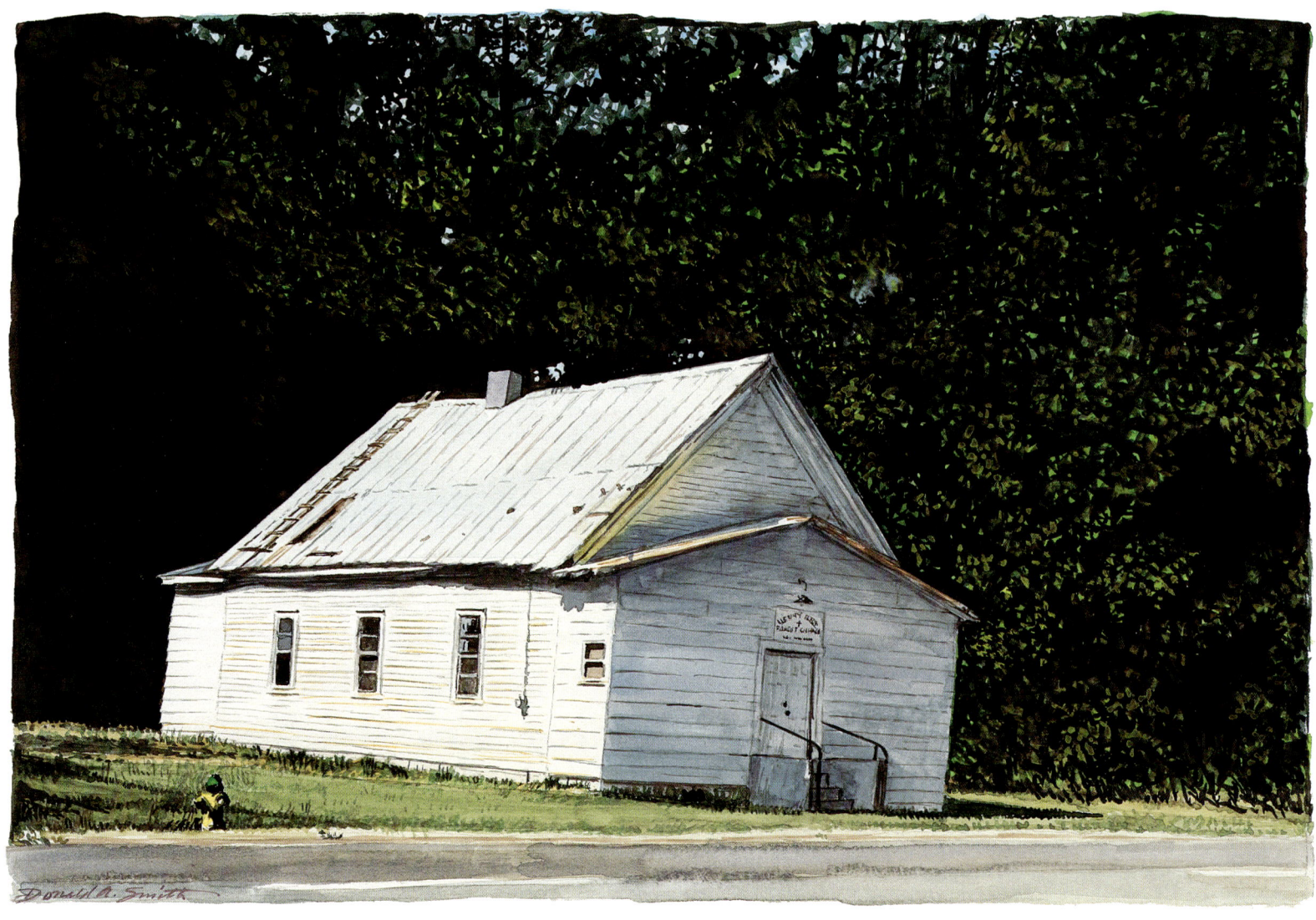

Comer

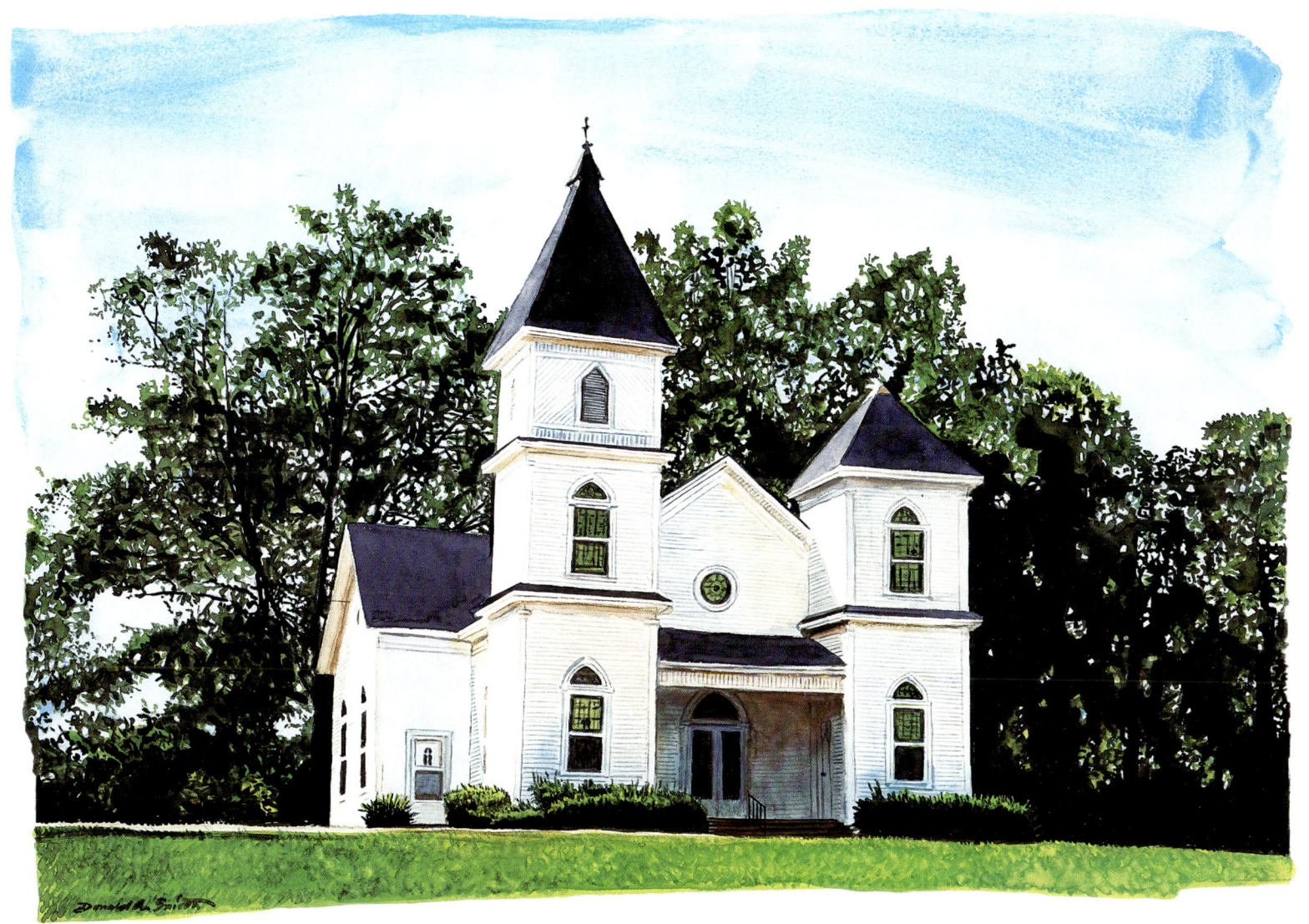

Braselton

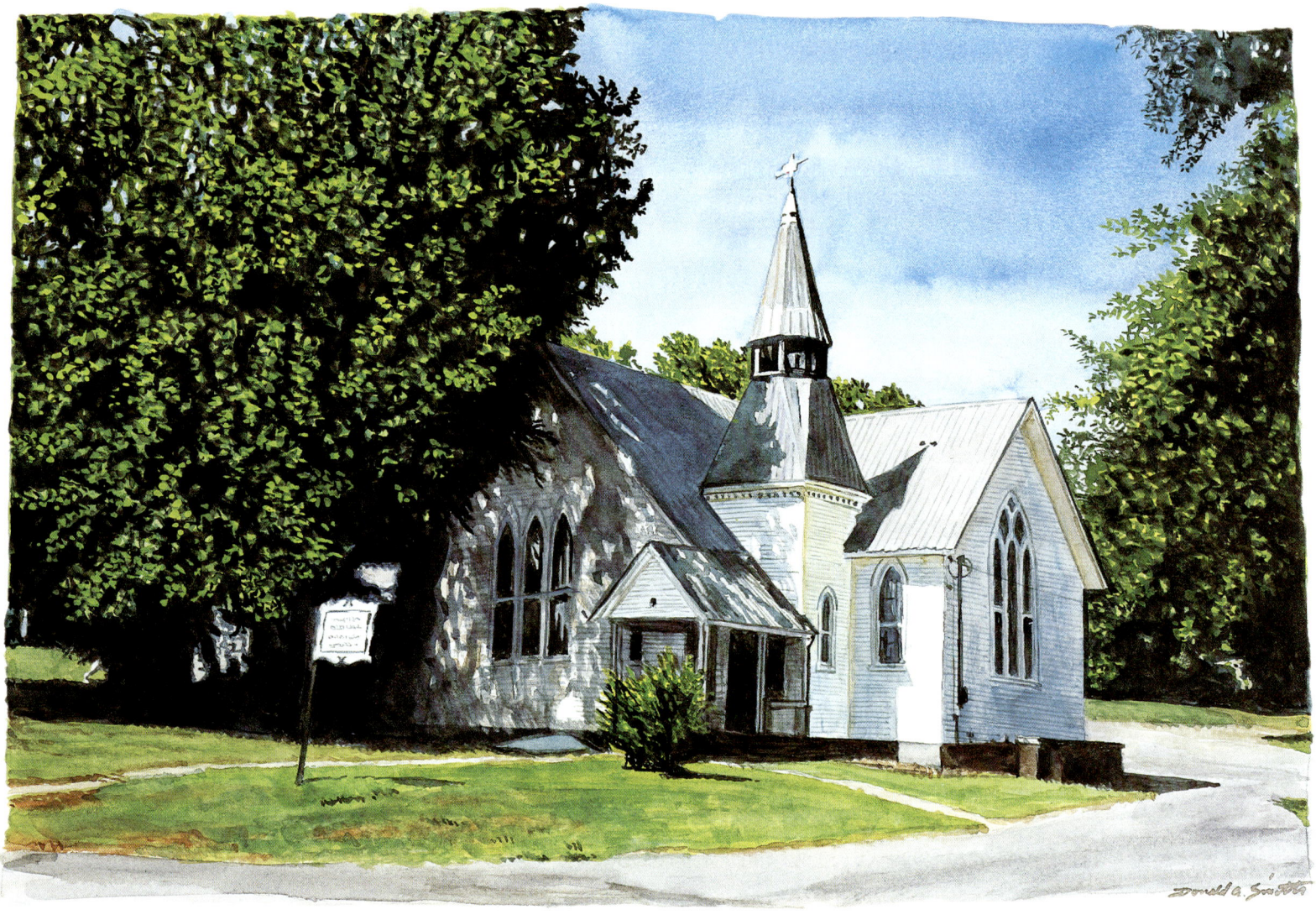

Hoschton

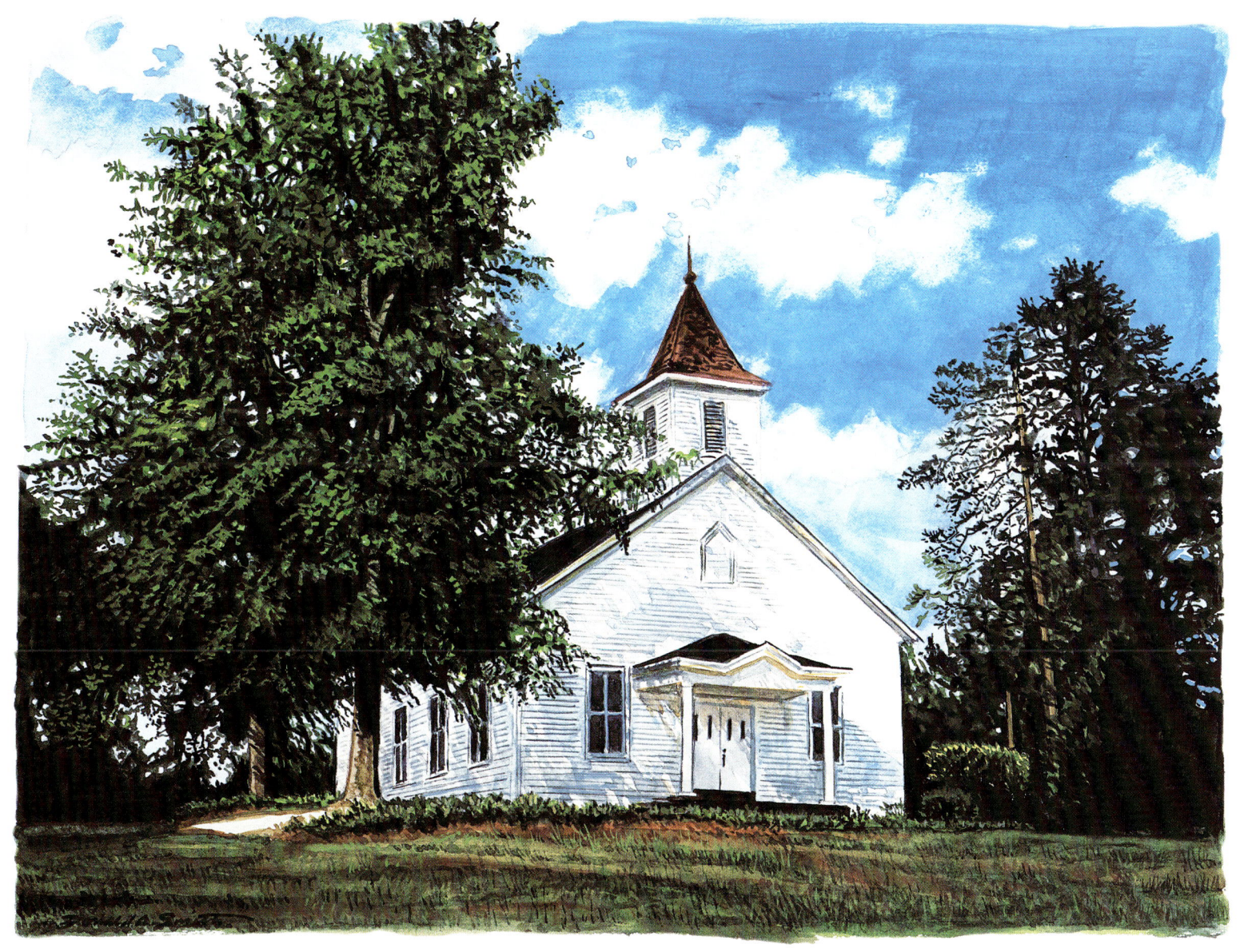

Near Maysville

CHURCHES

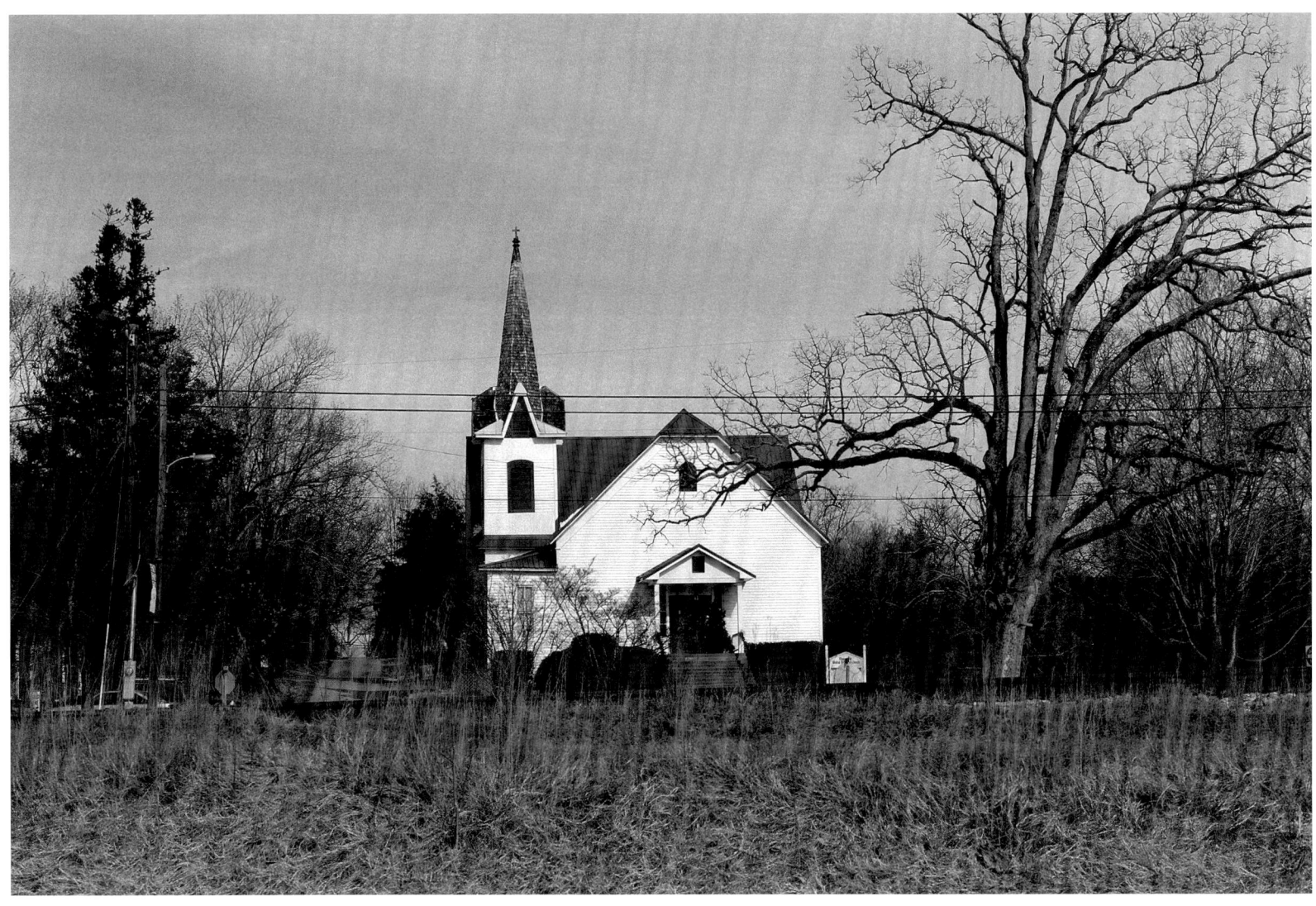

Maysville

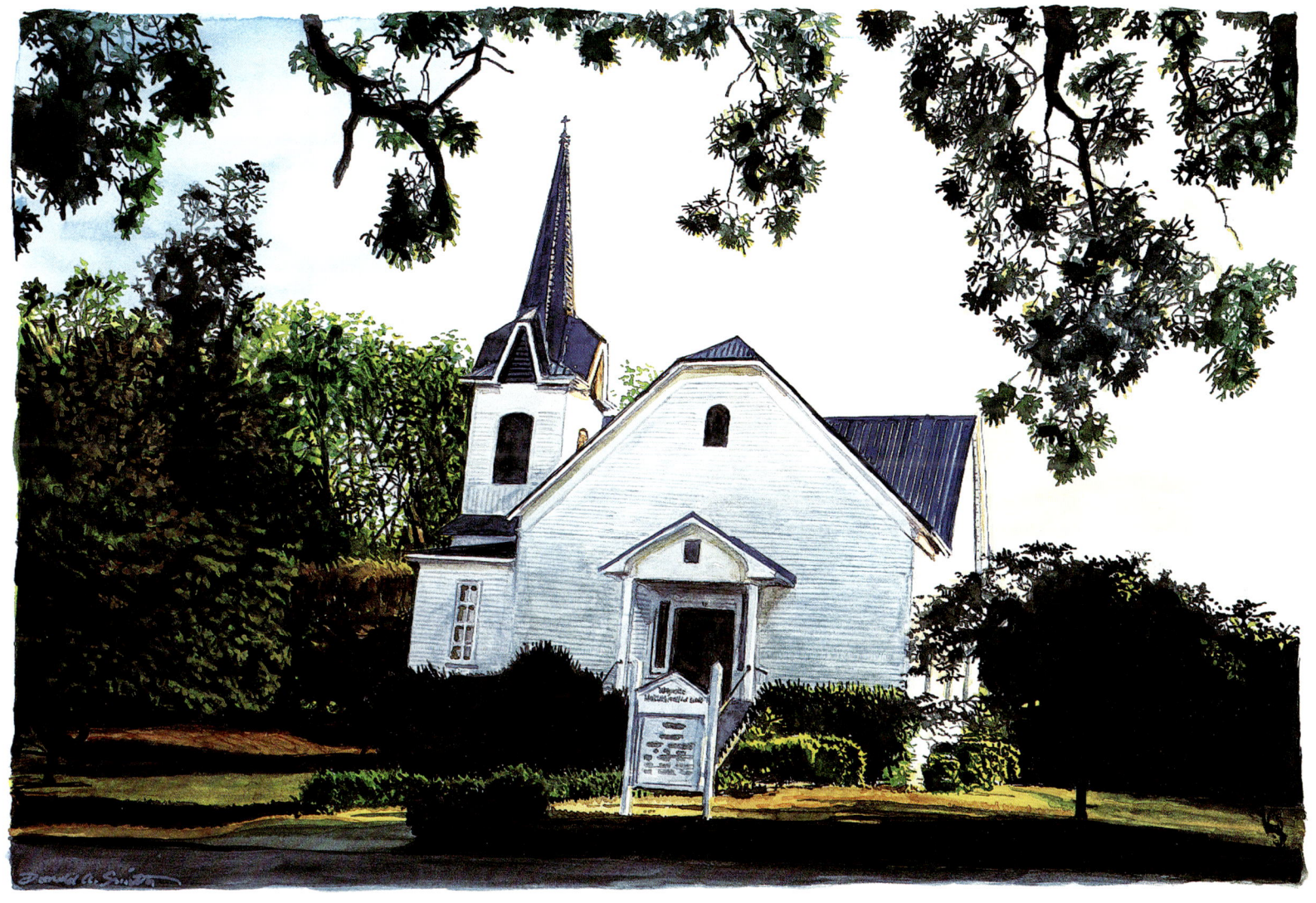

Maysville

CHURCHES

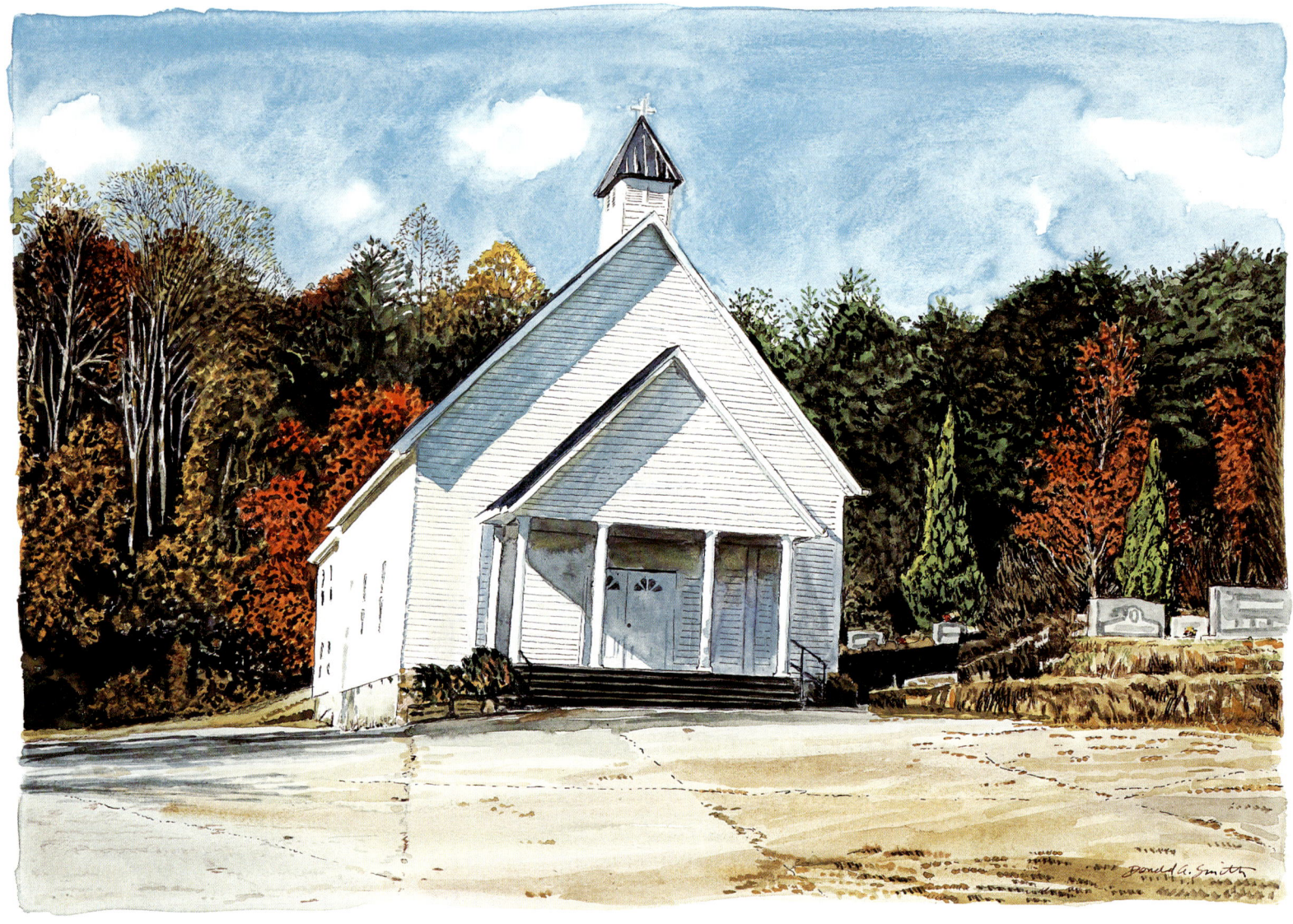

Helen

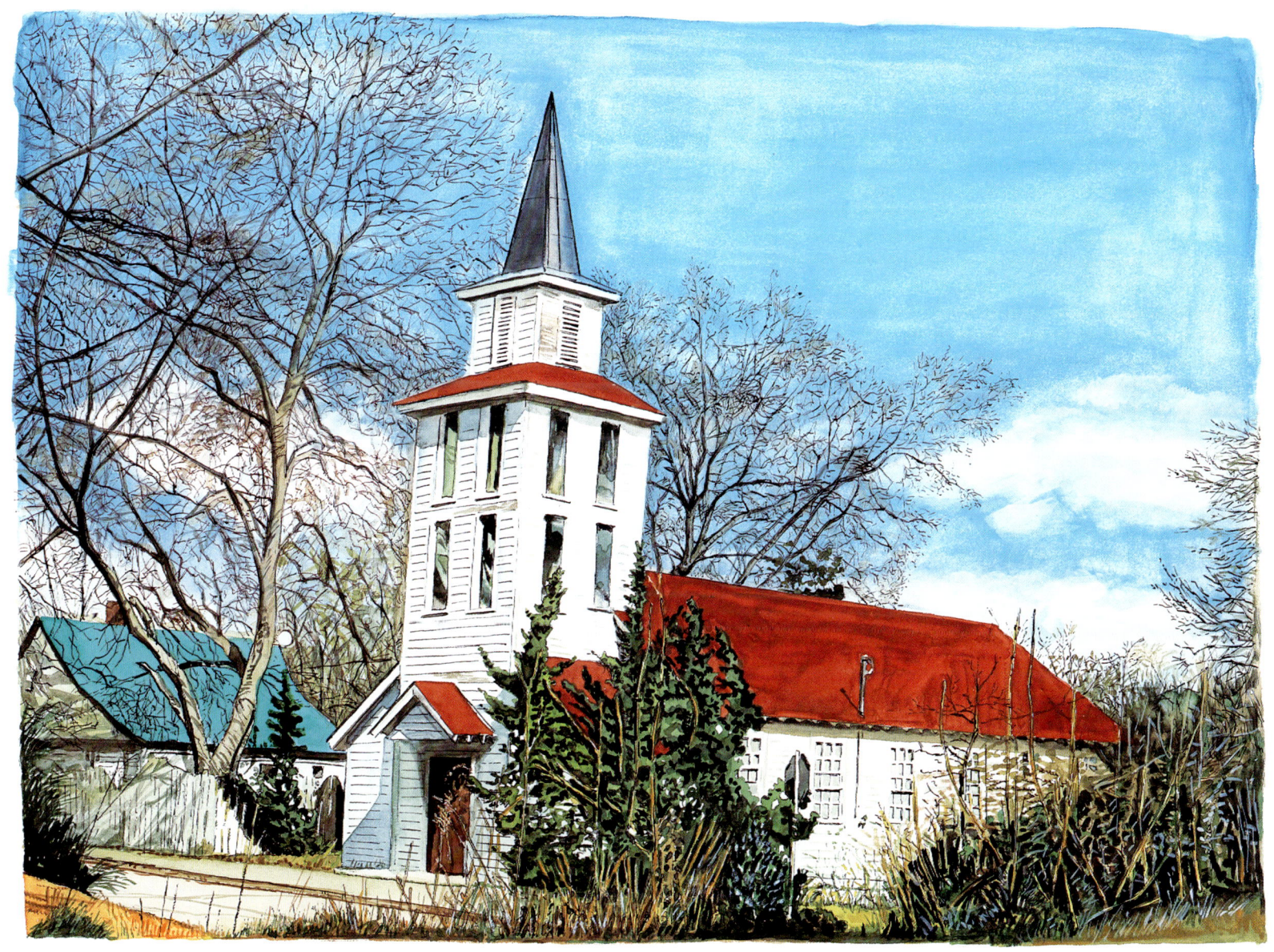

Gainesville

CHURCHES

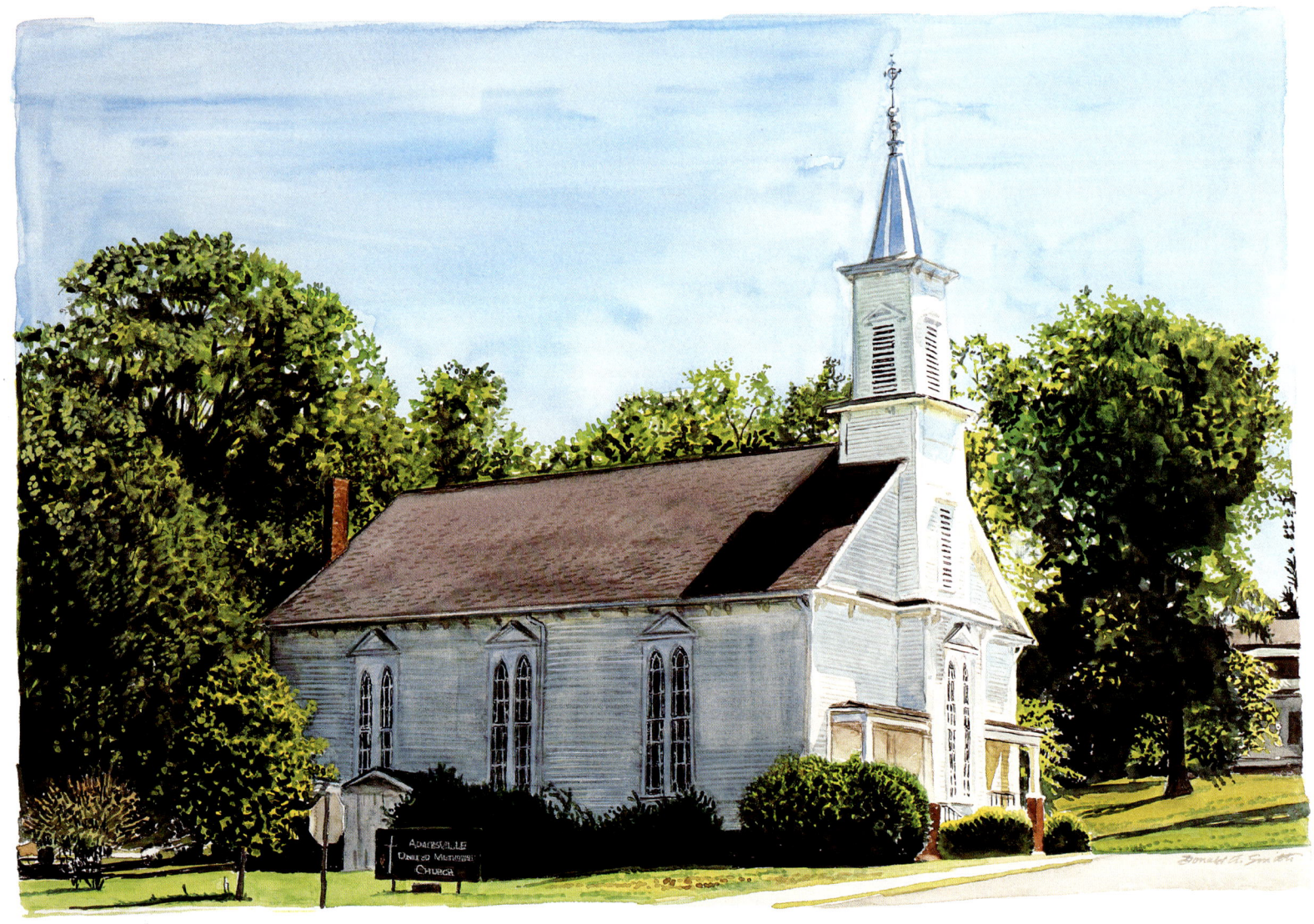

Adairsville

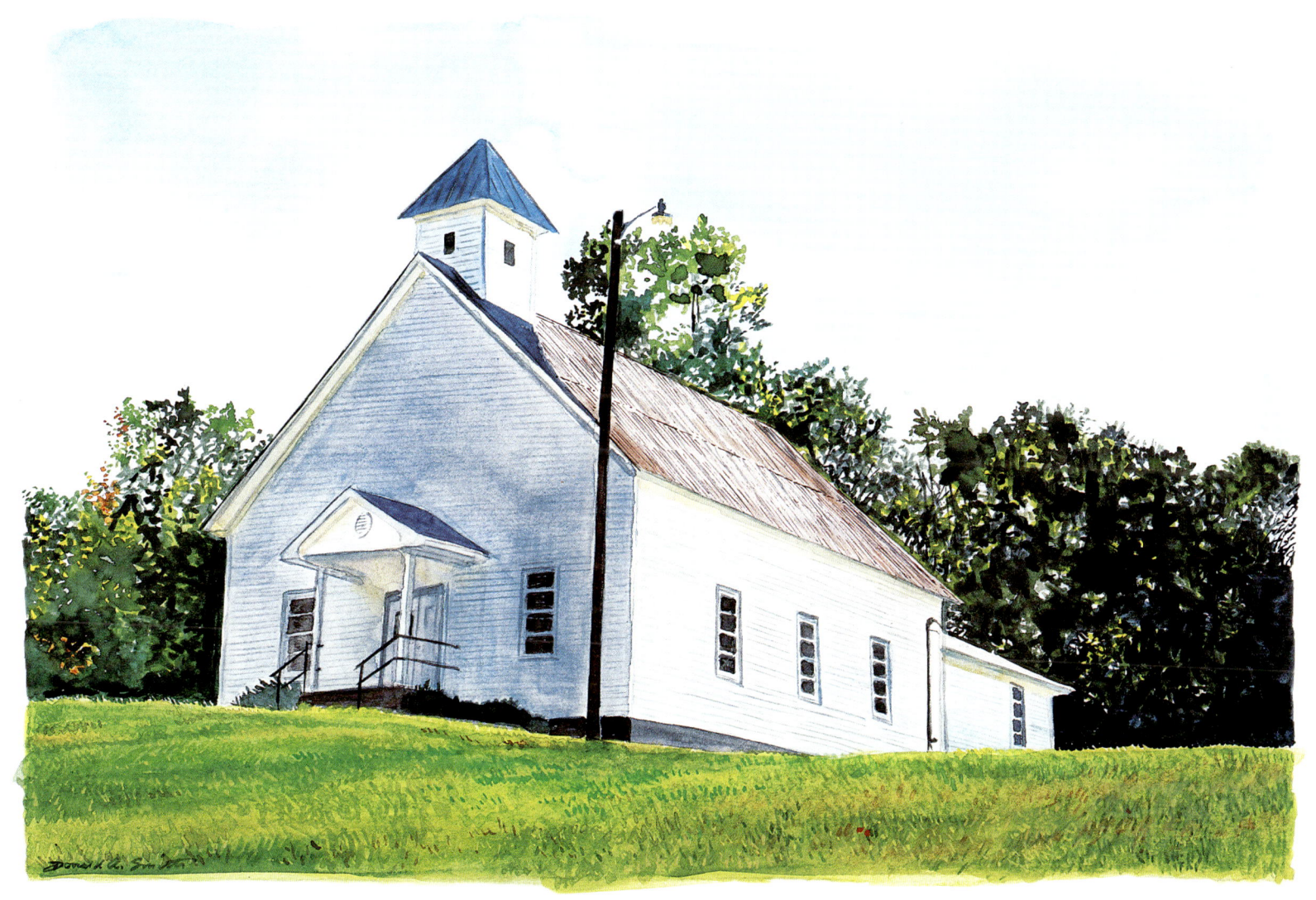

Cleveland

CHURCHES

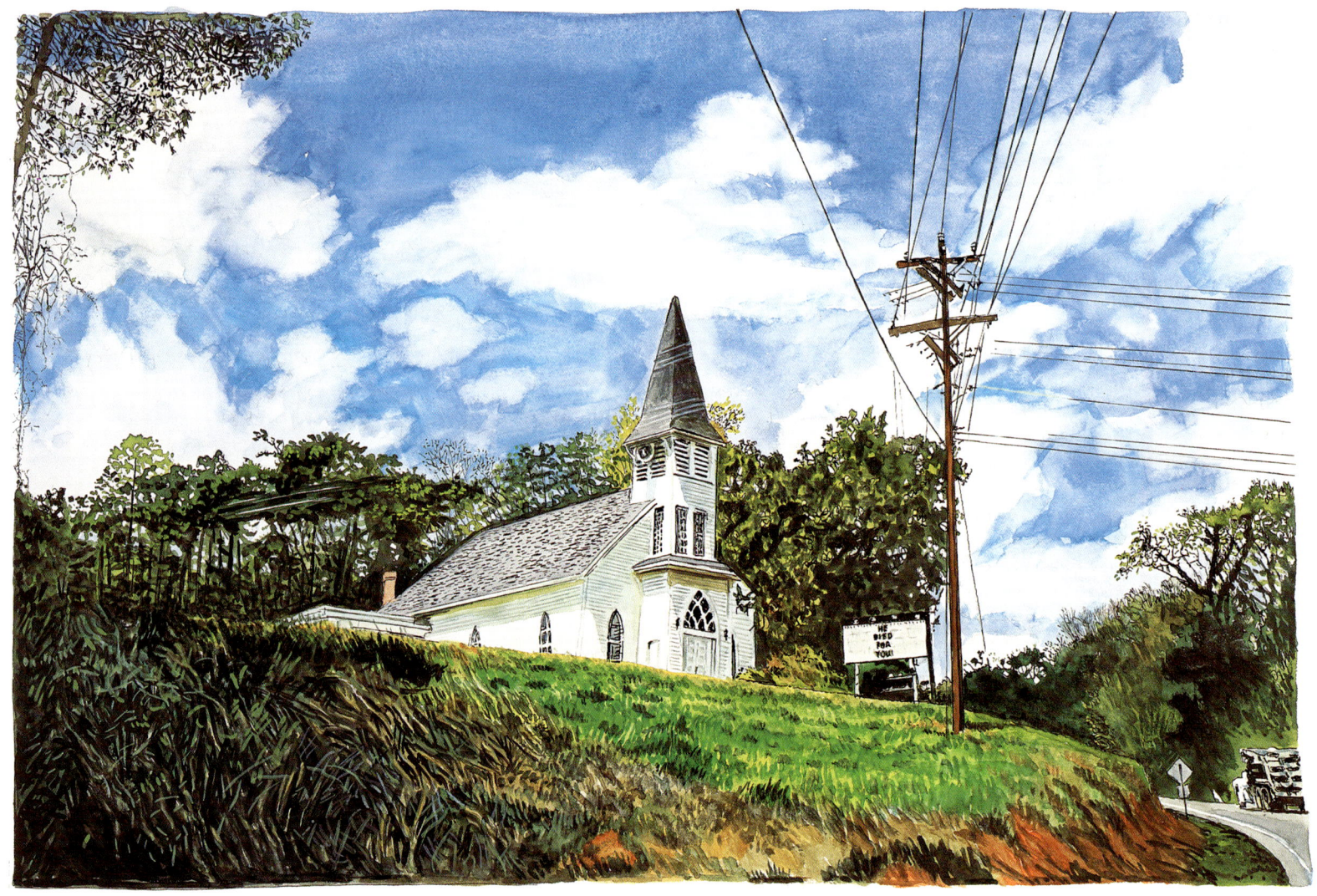

Tate

CHURCHES

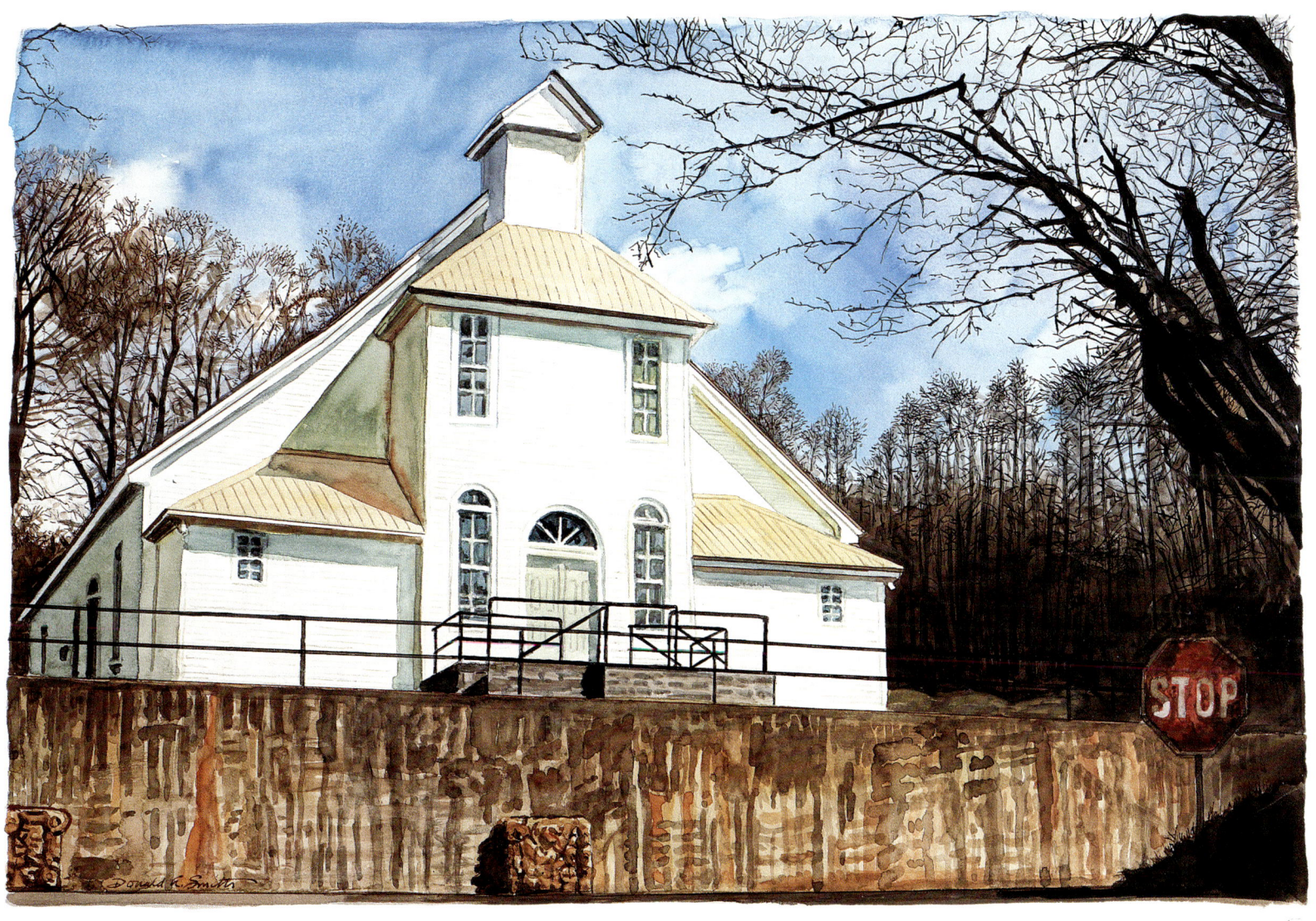

Graniteville

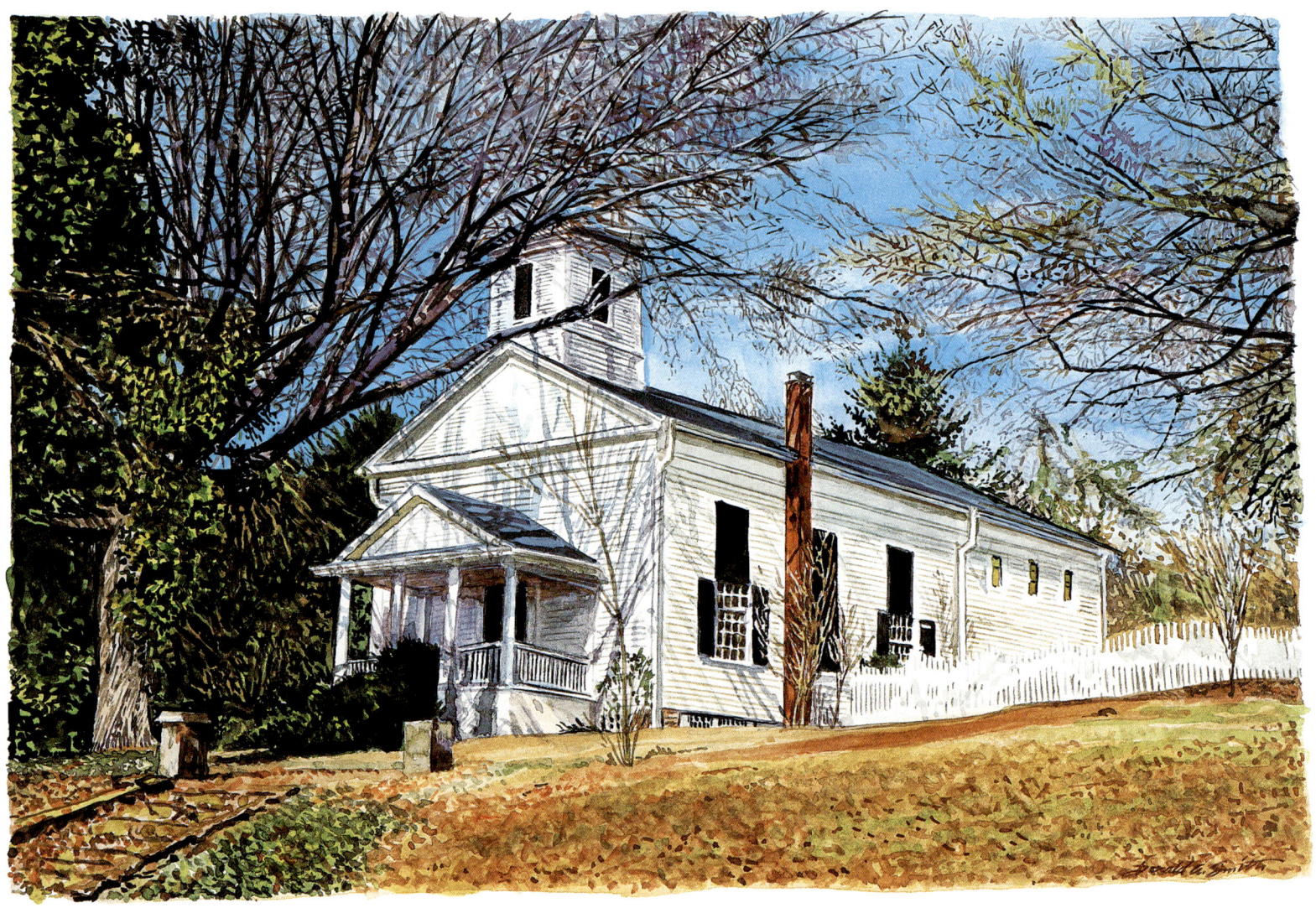

Clayton

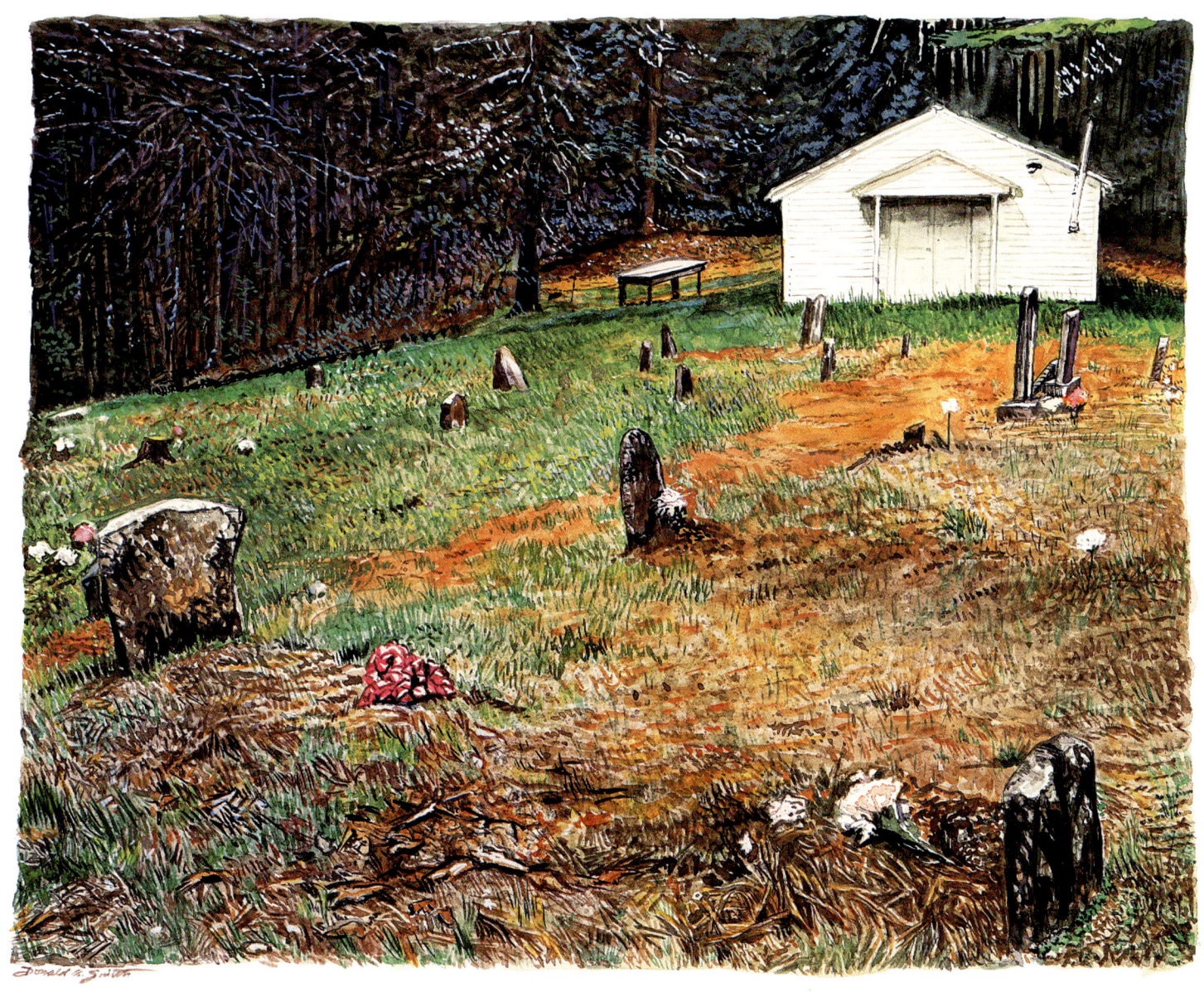

Union County

CHURCHES

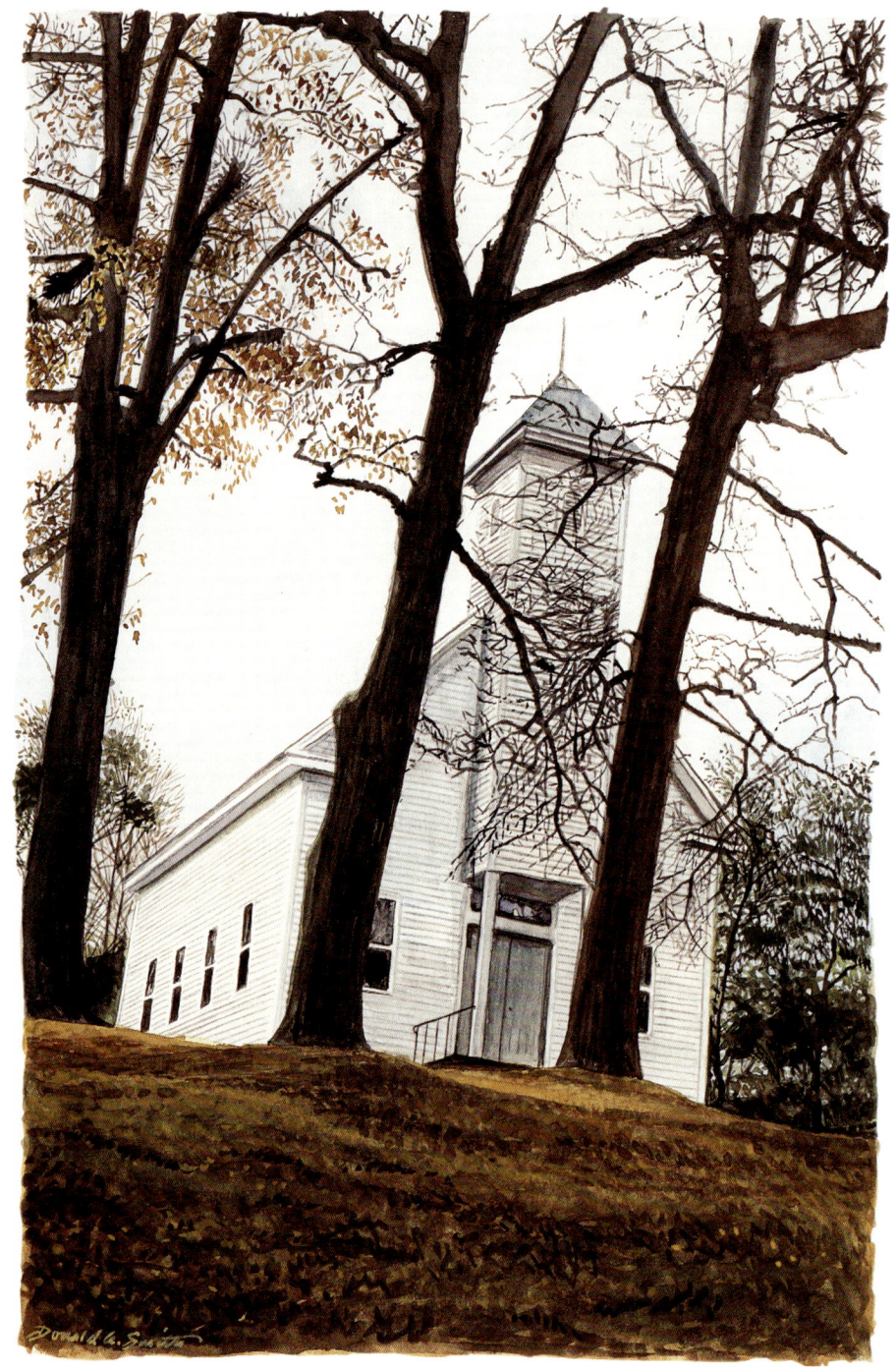

Blairsville

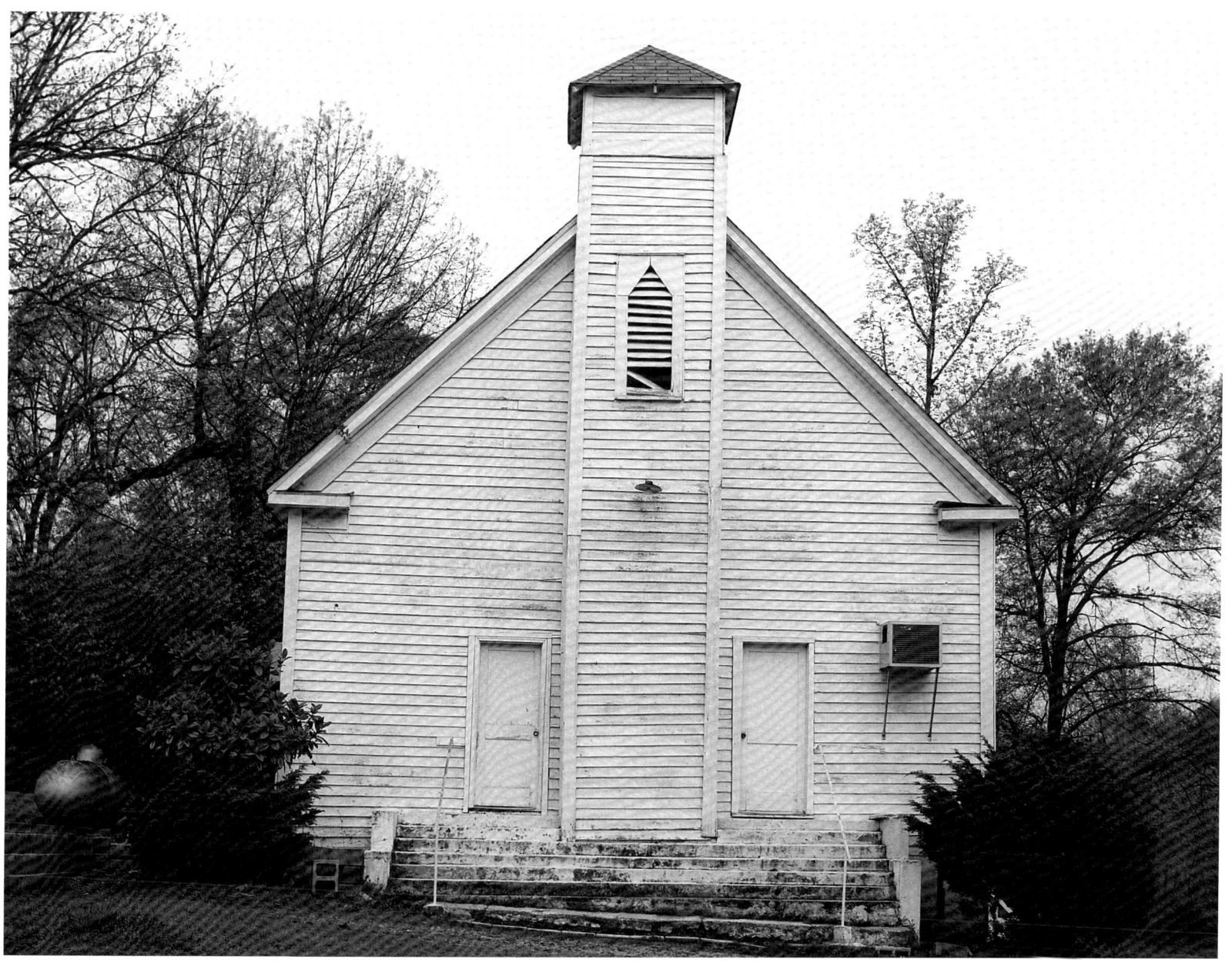

Wilsonville AL

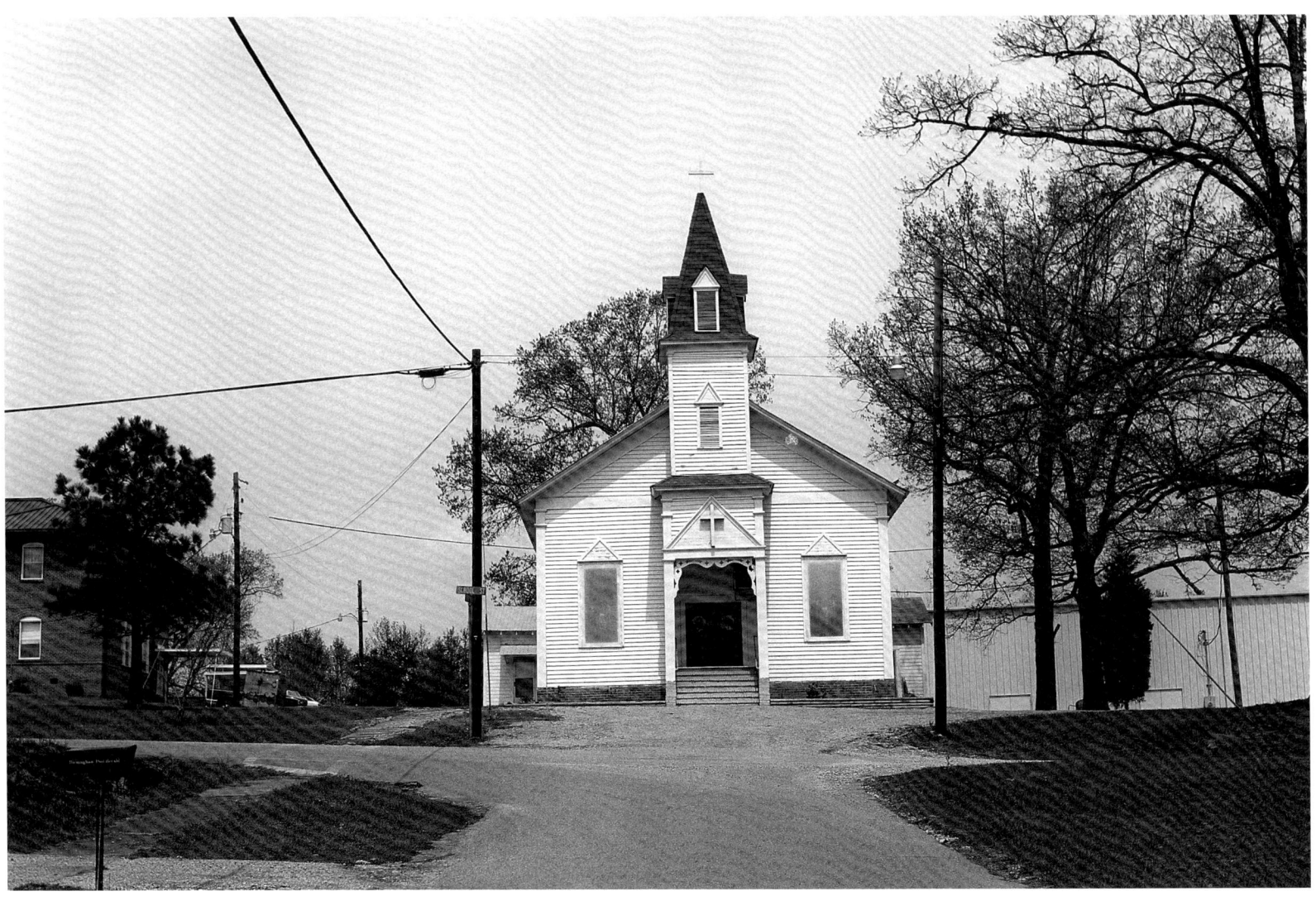

Wilsonville AL

CHURCHES

142

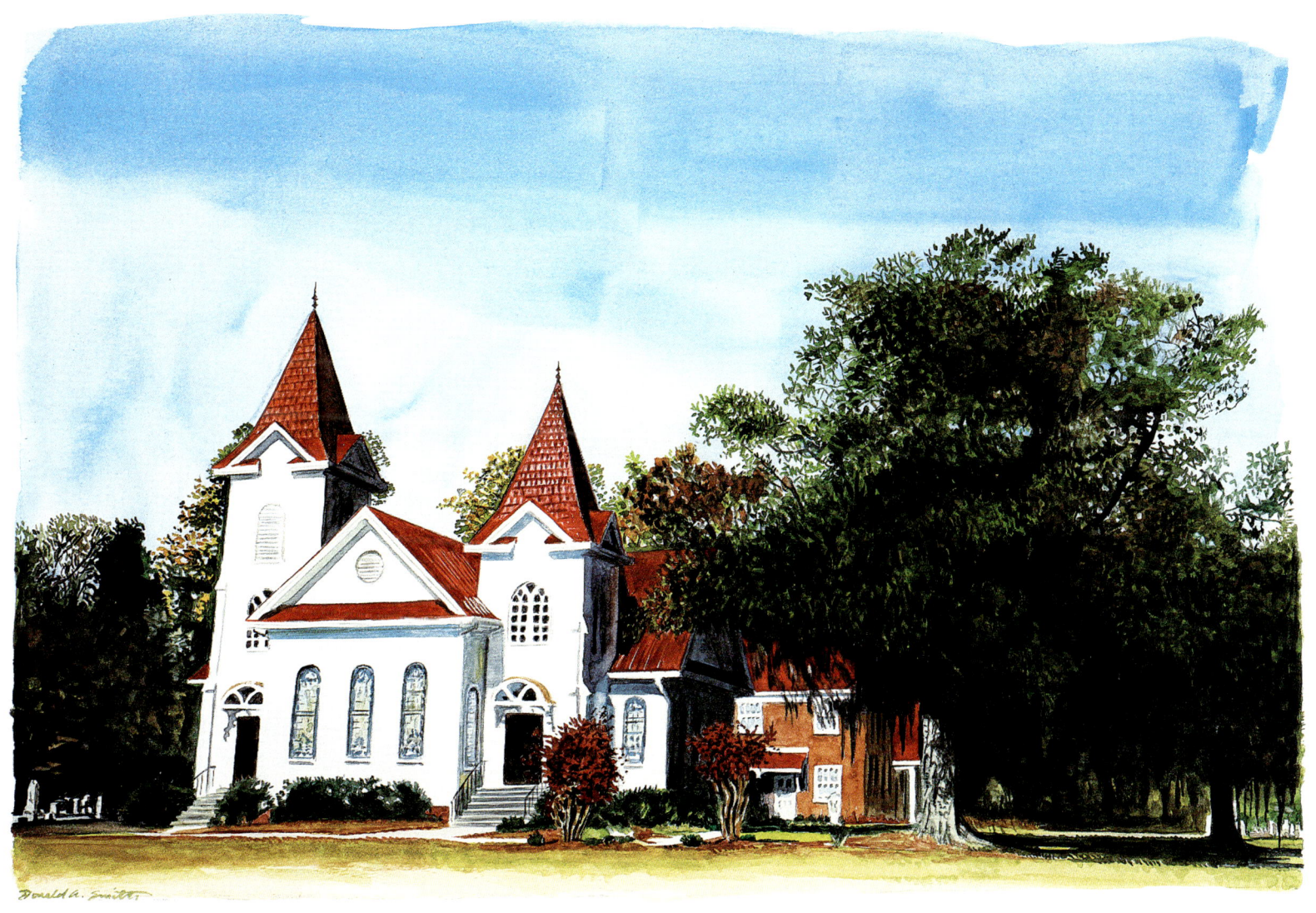

Florence SC

CHURCHES

143

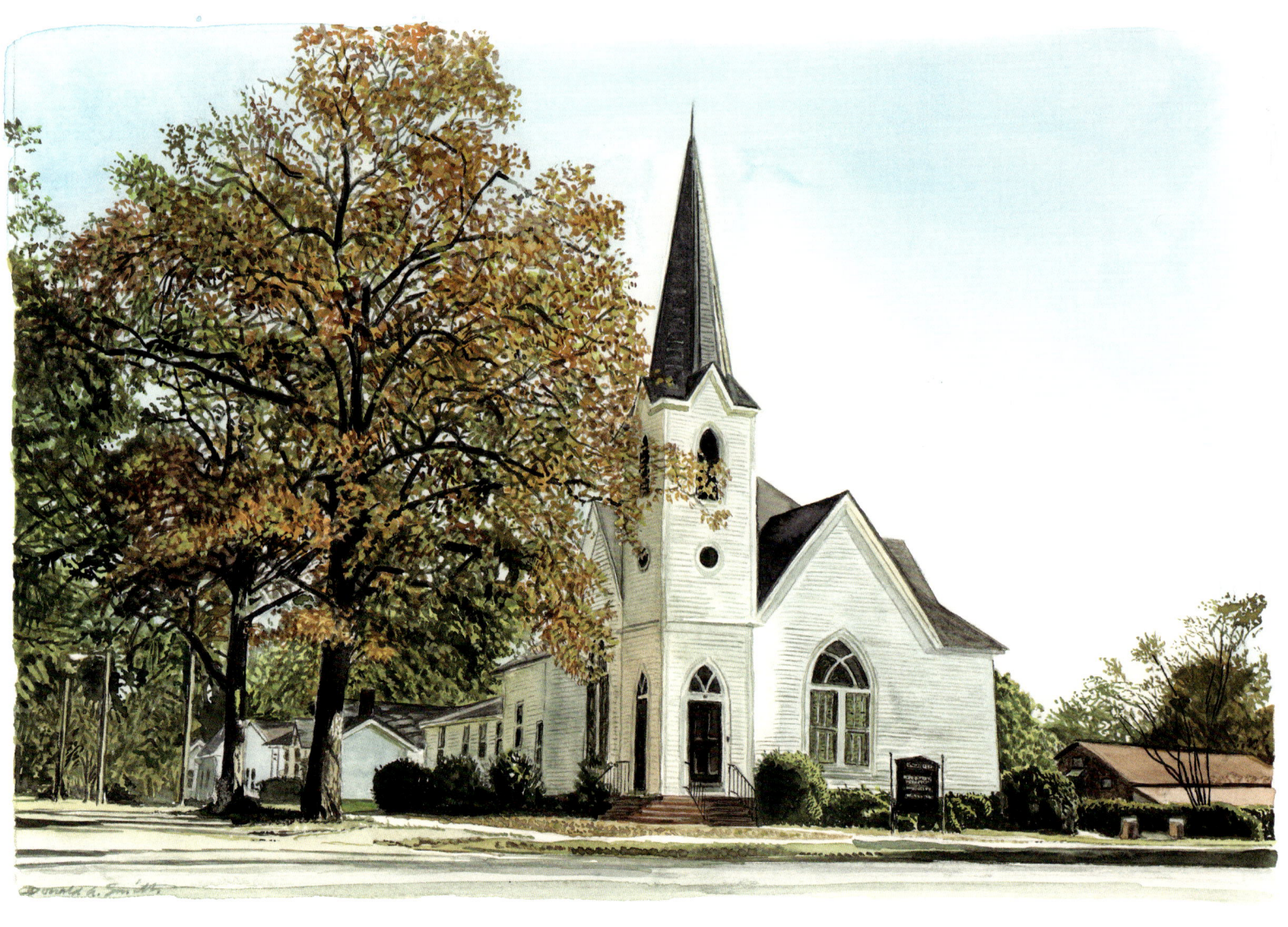

Latta SC